Haunted
Liverpool 31

Tom Slemen

The Tom Slemen Press

ISBN-10: 1092248471
ISBN-13: 978-1092248471

For
Merch the dog
&
Squidge the cat

CONTENTS

DARK WARNINGS

Actors are a superstitious lot; they'll avoid saying "Macbeth" by referring to it as "the Scottish play" because it's supposedly very unlucky to mention the Shakespearean tragedy by its proper title. No whistling is allowed in the theatre, and real money, flowers, mirrors and peacock feathers must stay off the stage if you want to ensure a successful performance. You should never wear blue onstage and you must never wish an actor "Good luck" before the play starts – but curse them instead by shouting "Break a leg!"

The theatre has always been a magical place, able to provide a window into another world, often a fantastic one, with its trap doors, two-dimensional backdrops and lighting effects, gunpowder genies, levitation by wire, cannonball-in-a-box thunder machines, sleight-of-hand illusions, retractable-blade daggers, transformative make-up and costumes – as well as some hell-raising performances bordering on demonic possession by the thespians who tread its boards. Furthermore, a lot of the subject matter of the theatre – Shakespeare's plays for example, feature ghosts, mischievous fairies, wizards and witches. A theatre crackles with energy when the actors and the audiences are in close symbiotic rapport, but after the final curtain has come down and every member of the audience has left, a strange unsettling silence crystallizes in the theatre. Within the walls of a playhouse, hundreds of strangers gathered in a darkened auditorium will roar with laughter at a farce, sing their heads off at a musical, or have their hearts collectively broken by some tragedy – and I believe the audience, in the release of its emotion, are not unlike cells in a vast battery, and the energy given off is somehow stored within the walls and very atmosphere of the building. This energy is in turn tapped by parasitic ghosts. Many a clowning actor has hid his or her tragic life behind the thin layer of greasepaint, and some have literally lived off the applause of the crowd to keep them going in the face of private personal problems. When such an actor exits the stage of life, he or she will find their spirit gravitating back to the limelight from the darkness of the grave, and our theatres are full of these resident undead understudies. Most theatres have a "ghost light" – a lamp that must be left on to appease the ghosts, because the darkness may remind the wanderers of the night of the stifling all-engulfing blackness of the coffin. All our houses of drama – in Liverpool and beyond - have their invisible companies of spirits, and I have hundreds of stories of supernatural goings-on onstage *and* offstage locally. In December 1973, actor Robin Nedwell came to Liverpool to star in the Beverley Cross play for children *Where's Winkle?* at the Playhouse. Robin had enjoyed enormous success playing skirt-chasing medical student Duncan Waring in the popular TV sitcom *Doctor At Large*, but had left the series to gain experience in the provincial theatres. After rehearsals one afternoon during the month's run of the play, Robin had a browse around the shops. Being a collector of Japanese swords and a formidable practitioner of the martial art of Kendo, he went to look at some old swords in an antique shop in the city centre before visiting Woollies on Church Street. Robin slowly became aware of a woman in a hooded plum-coloured coat and long black maxi skirt who seemed to be following him, and assumed she was a fan, as he was something of a TV heart-throb thanks to his television career. As he crossed Church Street, Robin heard the woman say his name in full, and he turned, thinking she'd want an autograph, but when she got nearer he saw the hood the woman wore was empty – just a dark space. Although in shock, Robin noticed a badge on the headless woman's coat featuring interlocking hearts; it looked like a National Blood Transfusion donor's award badge but he couldn't be sure of this. Robin turned and hurried away, spooked, and upon reaching Williamson Square, where the Liverpool Playhouse stands, he realised the creepy headless ghost was no longer following him. He went into the theatre and told no one what he'd seen, but some members of the cast did notice that he seemed distracted and a bit on edge. A few weeks later in early January, Robin was about to cross Hanover Street after a trip to a Bold Street café, but then he looked across the road and saw the hooded headless figure of that woman standing on the Church Street side, also waiting to cross, so he backed away from the kerb with a mounting sense of fear which turned his stomach – and as he stumbled backwards a bus that failed to brake in time because of black ice on the road, mounted the kerb – where Robin Nedwell had stood seconds ago. His reaction to a ghost – now nowhere to be seen – had saved his life. Who she was I do not know. Nor can I see the relevance of the blood donor badge the apparition wore on its coat. Perhaps the ghost was of a person who had helped others during its living years – giving blood etc – and she had perhaps known Robin would die on Hanover Street after being hit by a lorry skidding on ice but had decided to avert the tragedy by deliberately repelling him away from that kerb.

The hooded ghost reminds me of one of the most fascinating figures of the supernatural: the Grim Reaper – an entity most people would dismiss as a mere personification of the inevitable death that awaits us all, but for many years I have received reports of this eerie character from people of all walks of life, and if only a fraction of these reports are true, then in some instances, death really does pay a visit to those about to die, and some 'marked for death' even believe they have escaped him – for a while at least. What follows is just a small selection of these Grim Reaper reports. The first purported incident took place at Irby, Wirral on April 26 1954. That Monday morning, many people in Irby saw a strange abnormally tall figure resembling a hooded monk in a long black habit slowly walking along Thingwall Road and Mill Hill Road. A milkman on his predawn rounds approached the figure out of curiosity, and was shocked to see it vanish into the early ground mist, but the figure was later seen by a postman, a policeman as well as several residents from nearby Manor Road, but not one of these witnesses would approach the eerie wandering figure as they sensed it was something unearthly. Later that day, a strange double tragedy took place on the road where the black hooded entity had been prowling. Eileen McDonagh, aged 27, and her fiancé David Mitchell, both of whom had only recently moved to Irby from the remote village of Roundstone on the shores of Galway Bay to find work, were killed as they jumped off a moving bus. The bus was decelerating as it approached the stop at Irby and was travelling at less than 10 mph and yet Eileen and David were killed as they both fell over as their feet touched the floor. The couple were not even holding hands, so one did not pull the other down, and yet they both fell in a strange way, according to witnesses, and their heads smashed into the pavement. David was heard to cry out "Nellie! My God!" before he fell. Nellie was Eileen's affectionate nickname. They were taken to Birkenhead General Hospital but there was nothing that could be done to save the couple and they were officially pronounced dead. It was later claimed by those who knew Eileen that she had been having nightmares about a tall hooded figure in black following her onto buses, and she had told her friends she was being stalked by death.

In June 1974, a 45-year-old Birkenhead man named Ian Lloyd-Williams went to look after his ill sister Ann, a widowed woman living at her semi on Hillcrest Drive, Little Sutton. Ian was, by his own admission, a veritable nosy parker, and as he nursed Ann back to health as she recovered from a hysterectomy, he started looking over the hedges of the back garden to see what the neighbour's gardens were like, and he told his sister the old couple next door were almost naked as they sunbathed. Ann told him to stop this prying behaviour, but Ian couldn't stop snooping. Ann told her busybody brother to trim the top of the tall hedge in the back garden and when Ian did, he noticed something odd – the top of a black hood. Ian leaned forward to see more, and saw that the hood was being worn by someone in a long black robe, and this person had to be well over six feet in height. He went inside and told Ann what he'd seen. 'It can't be Mr Aspin,' Ann said, 'he's not *that* tall; and who'd be wearing a hood and a long coat on a scorching day like this?'

'Well I know what I saw, Ann,' Ian told her, 'and it gave me the creeps.'

That afternoon, an old neighbour named Mrs Sydney saw Ian looking over the fence and asked him if she could use his water to sprinkle the back garden as her water had been turned off because of a leak. Ian nodded and the old woman gave him the end of the hose with the tap connector, and Ian pushed the connector onto the cold water tap in the kitchen and then, as he was pushing back the excess length of hose, it looped around his neck – and tightened, choking him. The old woman had absent-mindedly put the other end of the hose down the bumper of her daughter's car (as she went to turn her roasties in the oven), and that car was being driven from the driveway.

As Ian realised he was being slowly strangled, he saw that hooded figure in black come through the fence towards him – as if it was a ghost. Inside the hood of the apparition was blackness, and what looked like two large greyish eyes. Ian almost lost consciousness as the tap connector in his kitchen came off, and he fell down and collapsed. His sister found him and called an ambulance. Ian had sustained injuries to his trachea but recovered. He recalled that sinister figure and wondered if it was the Grim Reaper, ready to take him, but a surgeon assured Ian it had been a hallucination brought on by oxygen starvation. Ann recalled that her brother had mentioned the figure before the accident, so she believed it had indeed been death calling to collect Ian.

Sometimes the reaper does not appear in his archetypal hooded form, but in something just as sinister: a dark warning in the form of a figure in a dream...

The warning dreams started when 35-year-old Fazakerley woman Molly read a newspaper article in 1984 which described how three attackers in their mid-20s broke into a flat above a middle-aged couple's newsagents' shop at two in the morning and subjected them to ninety minutes of sadistic torture which included hacking off the male shopkeeper's toe with a serrated carving knife and stuffing it in his mouth. The robbers had threatened to cut off the man's ear and genitals unless he showed them where the takings were kept but his wife had begged them not to harm her husband. Instead the woman was bound and gagged, then assaulted. The detective who led the search for the evil trio said that he had not seen anything as brutal in all of his twenty years on the force. This shocking crime might have triggered recurring nightmares in Molly's mind, for they started not long after she had read about it. These scary dreams always featured people breaking into her home who were out to rape, then murder her, and soon Molly realised there was a chilling pattern to them. The nightmares of the unknown intruders were bad enough, and she only saw them as shadowy figures or heard them moving about in her home in the dreams, but sometimes a shaven-headed man would appear in the nightmare. He had ice-blue eyes that were full of evil, and he wore white shirt, white trousers - which were tucked into a pair of "bovver" boots, and he also wore a pair of maroon braces. Whenever he appeared in the terrifying dreams, something very bad – and often life-threatening - would usually take place a day or so later. On the first occasion, Molly woke in a cold sweat after she'd had a dream that the intruders were breaking into her home via the bottom panel of her kitchen door (which led out onto the backyard). The 'skinhead' with the piercing blue eyes had appeared at the bottom of the stairs and smiled at her as Molly had tried to scream. She had run into the toilet in the dream in a bid to escape, but had been unable to climb out the narrow window – and then she had awakened with her heart pounding. And now she knew something bad would happen. Later that day, Molly's older brother Peter took her to see an air display of radio controlled model planes up at Southport. One of the planes – with a wingspan of six feet – spun out of control and swooped down to hit Molly in the chest, knocking her over and stopping her heart with the force of the impact. Fortunately, an experienced first aider was on the scene in a minute and somehow he managed to get Molly's heart beating again. Molly had another dream of the menacing shaven-headed stranger a month later, and this time she was knocked unconscious in her waking life when a plank protruding from the window of a builder's van slammed into the back of her head as she was walking along Longmoor Lane, close to the kerb. The injury left Molly with double vision for days. Eight weeks after this, she had another nightmare featuring the shaven-headed bogeyman, and this time Molly awoke and became convinced that she was going to be raped by two men who would gain entry to her home. She didn't know *how* she knew this but she had the overwhelming impression that it was going to happen and became so afraid, she considered moving home. She went into her back garden on the morning after the chilling dream and burst into tears as she was putting seeds and bread on a bird table, and her neighbour, a man in his fifties named Frank, overheard her and peeped over the fence. 'What's to do, love?' he asked, and Molly turned, startled, and said she was alright. 'You don't sound alright – what's the matter eh?' Frank queried with a concerned face.

'Just – just worries – silly worries, that's all,' said Molly, dabbing each eye in turn with her sleeve and trying to put on a smile.

'Come round and have a coffee, come on,' said Frank, beckoning Molly with a sideward tilt of his head.

'Nah, I'll be alright, honest.' Molly's smile looked so broken and unconvincing.

'A trouble shared is a trouble halved,' Frank told her, and then he paused, seemed so full of sympathy as he looked her up and down, then added: 'Come on, I'm not trying to cop off with you girl; I'm old enough to be your dad.'

Molly gave a sighing gasp of laughter and said, 'Okay.' She went into her house, left via the front door and went next door. Over the worst cup of coffee she'd ever tasted, she told him about the strange dreams and of her worrying impression she'd be attacked by two intruders. She really did expect Frank – who came across as a no-nonsense down-to-earth type of man – to think she was nuts, but he sat there in thought for a moment, and then he said, 'Sounds like you're psychic, and I have no reason to doubt what you have told me, so what are we going to do about the intruders?'

'It's great that you believe me,' said Molly, 'and she almost started crying again. She no longer felt alone now. She had told her brother about the dreams and he had advised her to go and see a psychiatrist.'

'You could move in here,' said Frank, 'but that means you'd be giving up your independence, and you must prize your independence to go through all what you've described as a single girl.'

Molly clasped her hands and looked at them as she nodded. 'I do love my independence. I was in a bad relationship for five years from the age of nineteen, and he was a control freak who used to dictate to me all the time.'

'You can't shoot them, unfortunately,' said Frank, with a faraway look in his eyes.

'Sorry?' Molly was taken aback by his random comment.

'The intruders,' replied Frank, 'not even in self-defence. You can't have a gun you see, British law. But I do have a few ideas.'

'Ideas?' Molly was intrigued and a little disconcerted. She hardly new this neighbour of hers, even though she'd lived next door to him for six years.

'Yes, I'm an engineer see, redundant like, but I'm very practical with my hands – you know, making stuff. Do you get the impression – or I mean, do you have visions or whatever, of where these fellahs will attack you? I mean where about in the house?'

'Yes,' said Molly, 'in the bedroom. I don't know how I know this – it might be a subconscious thing – '

Frank interrupted her. 'Then we need to build a trap.'

'Trap? What do you mean?' Now Molly really did suspect that Frank was a little 'out there'. But at least he was showing interest in her predicament and she no longer felt isolated.

'Reinforce the bedroom window – bars on the inside, hidden behind curtains, and put a sliding door of steel bars in that can be activated by a switch. Cage them.'

'But I'll be in that cage,' said Molly and gave a nervous imitation of a laugh.

'No, what you'd do is sleep somewhere else – you must have a spare room next door,' said Frank, his face becoming quite animated, 'and you could have a tape recording of your voice, and when you hear them break in, you switch on the tape, and the speakers of that tape recorder would be in the bedroom. They'd fall for it. You could call me – and I'd prefer it if you let me know before the police.'

'But is that legal?' Molly wondered. 'I think that's false imprisonment – even if you keep burglars or would-be rapists in your home - against their will.'

'Well now you're splitting hairs,' said Frank, and he looked as if he was disappointed by Molly's comments. 'The police are no help – you never see them round here. When I've finished with the intruders you won't require any help. I'd teach them a lesson.'

Molly suddenly didn't want anything to do with Frank; he was manically over-the-top and seemed to be hoping he'd catch the intruders to do God knows what to them. She made an excuse to leave, but over the coming weeks he was very forceful and kept coming round to Molly's home. Molly was a very submissive type and she went along with everything Frank did, and he duly installed windows in her bedroom made from very expensive unbreakable glass, and then he fitted bars on the inside of the windows. He took the bedroom door off its hinges and securely fitted steel runners at the top and bottom of the doorway. The sliding door of steel bars was fitted, and moved by two motorized gears embedded in a cavity which Frank had chiselled out of the wall. The door was opened and closed by an infrared remote control unit. Frank made numerous recordings of Molly saying phrases such as: 'Leave me alone or I'll call the police" and "Who is that?"

He drilled a hole through the wall of the room separating the bedroom and the spare bedroom – where Molly was now sleeping, and the wires from the tape recorder were fed from the spare room to the bedroom, where the large hi-fi loudspeakers were hidden. The bulb in the ceiling light had been removed so that the intruders would not see if the bed was empty. They'd hopefully wander into the trap and discover their prey was not there before the steel-barred door slid shut behind them.

Then came the waiting game. Molly said she could feel the approaching danger in her bones; the intruders *would* visit soon – she just *knew* it. Frank slept in an armchair in his bedroom, ready for a call from his neighbour. Molly just wanted to run away and regretted not moving out of the house. Three days went by, and then, at two in the morning, Molly awoke in her bed to the sound of splintering wood. She flew from the bed to the door of the spare bedroom and opened it an inch. She could see the silhouetted heads of two people in the small half-moon window of the front door. Time seemed to stand still at this point, and Molly tiptoed to the small table in the hall and her fumbling finger attempted to dial Frank's number, but in the darkened hallway, Molly misdialled and an unfamiliar voice said, 'Hello? Hello, who is that?'

The front door was levered open by the crowbar, and Molly put the phone down and fled into the spare room. She waited to the left of the door so she'd be behind it if they happened to venture into the spare room. She heard low muttering in the hallway, and then the sound of the telephone receiver being picked up and placed down. One of the intruders had cut the telephone's wires and had listened to the earpiece to see if the phone was dead before replacing the handset in its cradle. At this point, Molly was supposed to activate the tape recorder so the uninvited guests would hear the playback of her voice in the bedroom, giving the impression she was in there, but Molly was too scared to go and switch the tape machine on.

'She's not in here,' she heard a gruff voice say, and she opened the door of the spare bedroom about five inches or so and saw the hall was empty. She closed the door, went to the bedside cabinet and grabbed the remote control box and hoped to God it would work. The red button was pressed and she heard the door of bars slide shut with a mighty clang. She put the remote in her pocket and started to shake as a wave of nausea coursed through her.

'What the hell was that?' said a voice, and the way it echoed, it seemed to come from the kitchen, and Molly felt faint because she thought she hadn't trapped the intruders in the bedroom – but then she went into the hall, ready to make a run for it when she saw the black leather fingers of someone's gloves grip the bars of the installed door, and she heard a man's voice shout: 'The bitch has trapped us in here!'

Molly ran to the telephone to call Frank and discovered to her horror that the line was dead.

'Hey bitch, I've got a gun!' said a voice behind her with a slightly higher pitch than the other one.

Molly turned and saw the frightening ski masks the intruders were wearing as they peered at her through the bars. One of the trespassers started shaking the bars of the gate and the other had something in his hand, but Molly could see it was just a folded-up leather glove and not a gun. She ran to the front door, opened it, and ran to Frank's house next door. She hammered on the door, and seconds later, Molly heard the sound of a bolt being drawn back. Frank stood there in a dressing gown and slippers. His hair was a mess and his eyes were like two reddened navels.

'They – they're here – they're trapped!' said Molly, and she gulped the air and seemed unsteady on her feet.

'Good girl! Come in, I'll get changed!' said an excited Frank.

'They might escape – call the police!' cried Molly, and she looked over her shoulder, back towards the front gate, as if she expected the intruders to be there.

'They can't get out of there, calm down,' said Frank as he turned and rushed up the stairs to get dressed. He came back down within a few minutes in jeans and a wind cheater, holding a pair of Doc Martens boots. He wore an ear to ear grin, and Molly just felt sick with fear and couldn't understand why he was so pleased. He put on the boots and gritted his teeth as he tied the laces. He muttered the words, 'Bastards,' and 'cowards' and then he hurried next door. One of the intruders was shaking the bars on the windows, and the other one was looking through a dresser, perhaps hoping he'd find some key or some object to lever open that barred door.

'Well well well, what have we got here?' Frank said, standing a few feet away from the gate.

'We'll get you done for false imprisonment you old bastard!' said the criminal with the high-pitched voice.

'Now, how can you do that when you're dead, eh?' said Frank, and he reached into his jacket and said, 'Oh my, what's this here in my armpit? It looks like a Luger!'

Molly went to the telephone when she saw the gun, and she once again she listened but the line was still dead.

'You use that and you'll go to prison, old man,' said the intruder with the gruff low voice.

'I'm dying,' said Frank, and he wore a strange lopsided grin. 'Yeah, got less than a year to live, so it makes no odds to me, shitbag; I've already received my sentence – a death sentence. Now, I will count to five, and if you haven't taken off your masks by then, I'll shoot the two of you – got that?'

Frank then started humming a tune and he went into

the living room and came back with a large yellow throw cushion.

'What's your game, eh?' said one of the intruders and Frank pulled back the toggle of the Luger and pressed its 10cm barrel into the cushion, and that barrel was aimed at the trespasser who had asked Frank what his name was. There was an ear-splitting bang, and the 9mm slug winged one of the bars and buried itself in the bedroom wall. The gunplay caused Molly to scream and left the intruders with ringing in their ears. Frank's attempt to muffle the gunshot with the cushion had not really worked.

'One! Two! Three! Four!' Frank yelled, throwing the cushion down and nodding to each counted second as that old German pistol was aimed at the young interlopers. They quickly pulled their masks off.

One of the intruders was that shaven-headed man who had haunted Molly's dreams for so long, and she held her trembling hands to her mouth when she saw him.

'Very good, very good,' said Frank with a bright smile. 'Now, your names, or again, I'll shoot your bollocks off, and believe me, I am a crack shot with this!'

The men – who looked as if they were in their mid-twenties - gave full names – whether they were their real names could not be established – but their given first names were Tony and John. Tony was the blue-eyed skinhead of Molly's nightmares, and his friend John was an overweight man with a head of red curly hair.

'Why are you doing this, eh?' asked John, gazing in horror at the barrel of the vintage pistol.

'I was just about to ask you the same question you ginger beachball,' retorted Frank, 'why did you two come here? Was it to rape this girl? Robbery – or both?'

John advanced towards the door of steel bars. 'Hey, we're not rapists! We came here to turn the place over, that's all!'

'Stay where you are Pavarotti!' growled Frank, and he tapped the bar of the gate with the Luger's barrel. 'You're a big lad and easier to hit than a barn, so stay put. I don't believe you. I think you and that gormless bastard were after more than money.'

'How long are you planning on keeping us here?' Tony asked, and Molly watched him with a mixture of horror and fascination; how had she seen this man in her dreams?

'Till you beg for a drink,' said Frank in a very casual manner. 'I might throw some corned beef in there when you get hungry and then you'll get very thirsty, and after a week you'll be biting your arms and drinking your blood to quench your thirst.'

'You'll get done for keeping us here – and for using a gun – ' John said in a quivering voice, and Frank went ballistic. At the top of his voice he roared: 'You said all that before and I did tell you that I'm dying of cancer but I think you have a lot of fat in that brain of yours and the message didn't get through!'

The outburst left Molly shaking. She hoped the shouting and that gunshot would wake the neighbours and spur them to call the police. Then she recalled the night before last when an absent neighbour's alarm had gone off all hours in the morning and no one had bothered to call the police.

'He's insane,' Tony said to John, 'so just shut up.'

'Insane am I?' Frank asked Tony, and then he beckoned him with a curling index finger. 'Come here arsehole, I want you to do something. Come on.'

Tony remained still, his eyes fixed on the Luger pointing at him between the bars.

In the tense silence, John broke wind.

'Come here now or I'll drop you where you are, right through that baldy head of yours,' said Frank, sounding as if he was making a very sincere promise.

Tony walked to the bars and Frank stepped back and aimed the pistol at the intruder's head.

Molly could see droplets of sweat oozing from Tony's forehead.

'Come closer love,' Frank said in a put-on effeminate voice. 'Get your face right up to those bars – between those bars. Come on!'

Tony did as he said. He pushed his face into the bars and Frank said, 'Now, open your mouth, Tony dear.'

Tony seemed puzzled at the request.

'Open your mouth!' Frank's voice boomed.

Tony opened his mouth, and Frank gently pushed the barrel of the Luger in, its end touched the back of Tony's throat and made him retch, so the barrel was pulled back just an inch.

Frank smiled and nodded. 'Very good, very good. Now, let me tell you a little story before I blow your brains out the back of your head – and I *am* going to do that, and if you even think about pulling your mouth away I'll blast you into the life to come. I've killed before and I am not afraid to kill again – especially animals like you. These slugs can go through concrete walls – did you know that?'

Tony remained as still as possible, and his eyes looked resigned to a certain death.

Behind Tony, John started to sob.

'Save your tears for St Peter, John!' Frank shouted to him.

'Shall I just call the police?' Molly asked, and she was in tears, but Frank didn't notice the state she was in.

'I'll give evidence against him if you let me go,' John pleaded, 'I'll tell you everything – I didn't even want to come here.'

'You'd better say a few prayers John,' said Frank, 'make your peace with the Creator and that, because you'll be going out of here feet first with a couple of holes in your head.'

'Don't Frank,' Molly said in a choked voice, hardly able to see because her eyes were flooded with tears.

'My wife was raped by scum like this many years ago,' said Frank, looking intensely at Tony's face. 'They got away with it. Three of them there was. Broke in and had turns with her, and she never recovered. And she became depressed, and she ended her life. They said it was an accidental overdose, but it wasn't – she'd had enough. Let it go, they all said – yeah – let it go Frank, because I wanted to walk the streets until I found them. I wanted to destroy vermin like those three. I'm ex British Army see, and I don't let things go – not me!'

Molly reached into the pocket of her dressing gown for a tissue to wipe her eyes and her searching hand touched something in her pocket that felt rubbery – and suddenly the door of bars started to move as electric motors whirred. Molly had accidently pressed the soft button of the remote control box in her pocket. The moving door distracted Frank for a moment and Tony withdrew his head from the bars and the Luger was fired. The two young men flew out of the bedroom and Tony yanked open the front door, but by then, Frank had the Luger trained on the back of John, ready to empty the pistol into him. Molly pushed at Frank's arm and the Luger blasted a hole in the half moon window of the front door.

'I'll kill them!' Frank shouted, 'Get out my way!'

'No, Frank, you'll go to jail! Don't kill anyone!' Molly screamed, holding on to his arm.

He threw her to the hallway floor and ran to the front door. He could hear the two men running somewhere in the darkness, but he couldn't see them. He was furious when he went back into the hall and he roared at Molly and blamed her for letting the intruders go, but she just stood there sobbing, her face buried in her hands. Eventually he apologised and hugged her. He promised he'd get rid of the gun and she went along with it all until a few days later, when she moved all of her belongings out her house and went to live with a relative. Molly eventually managed to sell the house, and was so afraid of meeting Frank again, she moved to a flat on Liscard Road, Wallasey, and for company she bought a beagle and named him Theo. She had also decided to look a little more glamorous and had her long hair chopped off, styled into a bob and dyed blonde. She also stopped wearing her usual dowdy clothes and treated herself to some trendy outfits. She also felt as if it was time to ditch her old introverted personality and she intended to start going out with a cousin to look for someone. One day, when Theo was just a year old, Molly took him for a walk along the promenade, and at one point the beagle somehow slipped out of his collar and ran off. Molly's heart somersaulted when she saw the young dog run down a set of stone steps leading to the river. She went down the steps and slowly tried to grab hold of Theo, when he suddenly turned and ran back up the steps, but Molly slipped on the bottom stone step's coating of slimy green moss, and her legs plunged into the water. She tried to get up onto the steps but to her horror she discovered that her fingers were slipping on the moss. She started to yell for help, and kept on shouting until her throat was raw, when she heard a man's voice above. 'Alright love, keep still!' he yelled. She then felt a hand grab the shoulder of her coat and she was pulled out of the water.

She looked up – and saw that her rescuer was that man – Tony – the man who had appeared in all of those horrendous nightmares and the intruder Frank had tried to kill. She saw his eyes widen with shock when he recognised her. Last time he had seen her, she'd had long black hair – now she had short blonde hair. He backed away, then ran up the stone steps and she could hear him running away along the promenade. Seconds later, Theo came down the stairs and started to lick Molly's face, unaware of the almost fatal incident he'd caused.

Molly went home in a terrible state. All of the terrible memories of those terrifying memories and the constant dread of being visited by intruders came flooding back, and she sat in all day with the door bolted. Fortunately, Molly met someone a few months later and her nerves settled down again. She ended up marrying a Cumbrian man and later went to live with him in the Lake District, and she never saw the ominous Tony in dreams or in her waking life again.

And finally, the last story of a dark warning concerns a young lady of Knotty Ash.

It was teatime on Sunday 25 June 1967, and the 2-year-old twins Lucy and Luke were sitting in their high chairs at the table of Nanny Joan and Grandpa Sid watching ventriloquist Ray Alan and his puppets Tich and Quackers on the telly. The mother of the twins, 25-year-old Gail Rowntree, sat facing them at the table between her brothers and everyone was talking about the live broadcast the Beatles would be making later in the evening on a TV show called *Our World* - the first global telecast in history, going out live to over 700 million people, and it was due to run from 7.55pm till 10pm on BBC1. The Beatles would close the historic broadcast with a performance of *All You Need is Love*. Gail had a good gab with her mum Joan after the tea, but after 9.30pm, her mother, a woman who claimed to be psychic, kept telling her daughter to get home before it got too dark as she had a 'funny feeling' something was going to happen tonight. Joan had experienced these eerie warnings before and they always seemed to foretell something ominous.

'I'll walk you home,' said Gordon, Gail's 18-year-old brother. Gail smiled and shook her head and said: 'Nah, me Mam's round the bend with her premonitions. I'll take Bob to ours – he can guard me.' Bob was the family's little mongrel dog.

'Your husband should be walking you home instead of working late at that factory,' Sid told his daughter Gail, but she just raised her eyebrows and said, 'Dad, I'll be alright, and George [Gail's husband] and I need the extra few bob so I'm grateful he's working.'

And so, Gail left the Knotty Ash house of her parents pushing the twins along in their pram, and Bob the little dog trotted along after her. Gail only had to go half a mile to her house on Finch Lane. Two hundred yards later, Bob was suddenly nowhere to be seen. Gail looked about then continued on her way. There wasn't a soul around, probably because everyone was indoors watching the Beatles live on that TV special, and twilight was falling. Gail pushed the pram around a hole workmen had left in the pavement next to a small red warning lantern. As she sang to the twins, Gail felt Bob touch her ankle with his wet nose, and she turned, saying, 'Back, are you?' when she saw it was a gigantic rat, bigger than her dog! Another, even bigger rodent came out of the hole in the pavement. As Gail lost all movement in her legs with fear, the overgrown rodent came over to her, stood up on its hind legs with perfect balance, and looked into the pram at the twins. Gail screamed profanities at the thing as its twitching whiskers swept across the faces of the twins. On its hind legs, the head of the 'super-rat' reached her waist, and it looked at her with bloodshot eyes and bared its long front teeth. Gail Rowntree let out a scream and ran, pushing the pram. She covered about fifty yards, then looked back and saw one of the king-sized rats slithering back into that hole left by the workmen. Those abnormally large rats – the result of a rare chromosome condition called polyploidy – were later seen in the area and never caught. Gail recalled her mum's dark warning - and shuddered.

THE GHOST SAID "I LOVE YOU"

This chapter is concerned with an entity which became fixated with a certain Liverpool woman. Being stalked by the living is bad enough, but imposing a restraining order on something immaterial and ethereal is almost impossible, unless an exorcist is called in, and even then, after the Rite of Exorcism has been carried out, the being from beyond may still manage to return and haunt the object of its strange affection. In my own experience, person-centred hauntings are much more terrifying than hauntings where the ghost is attached to a specific abode or place, for no matter where the victim goes, the supernatural stalker will follow and there's no escape.

One sunny Saturday afternoon in May 1973, 60-year-old Terry Martin was having a shave in the bathroom of his home on Wavertree's Thingwall Road when he heard a loud knocking at the front door. 'Alright, alright!' he yelled, descending the stairs. Whoever this caller was, he or she had no patience whatsoever and the knocking became louder as Terry sprang down the steps. 'I said alright!' he cried and swore under his breath with his face lathered in shaving foam.

He opened the door, ready to give the caller a piece of his mind for bringing the knocker down so heavily, when a bizarrely-dressed man lunged at him with what looked like a dagger and stabbed him repeatedly. Terry fell backwards in the attack, winding himself as he hit the tiled floor of the hallway. He felt the stinging sensation of the dagger blade going into him, but when he looked up there was no one there. Terry felt his abdomen and chest and to his utter relief he saw he had not sustained any wounds at all. In shock, Terry walked outside his house and first he looked up and down Thingwall Road, and then he peeped behind the low wall of his garden, and even looked behind the bushes, but it was plainly evident that the attacker was not there; he'd really gone to ground awfully fast. Terry wondered if some idiot dressed up in a fancy dress costume had played a prank on him – but why would anyone pull a stunt like that? It didn't make sense, and the weird attack left Terry feeling very uneasy. He went back to the bathroom to swill the dried foam from his face and after applying some new foam from the soap stick, he started to shave again. He was getting ready for a trip to town to meet up with his ex-wife Anita at a pub on Paradise Street. He'd been divorced from her for nearly ten years but in recent weeks he had been drinking with her after a chance meeting at a christening and now it looked as if he and Anita were falling in love again. When Terry arrived at the pub he bought her a gin and tonic and sat her in a quiet corner to tell her about the weird attack.

When Anita heard Terry's account of the oddly-dressed assailant the colour was seen to drain from her face and she gasped, 'Oh no,' as if the story struck some grave chord with her. She then told Terry something he couldn't take in at first.

'Terry, you know me – I've never been one for

believing in ghosts and all that supernatural malarkey, but well – you're going to think I've gone a bit tappy.'

Terry opened a box of Woodbines and offered them to her, and she took one and he lit it. 'Go on, I won't think that at all,' Terry assured her, 'is this something to do with that divvy who attacked me this savvy?'

Anita puffed on the Woodbine, grimaced, because she was accustomed to filtered cigarettes, then nodded, and her wide eyes seemed full of fear. Terry noticed her hand tremble as she held the Woodbine. She told him: 'Terry, as I said, I don't go in for all that spooky stuff, but there's a ghost following me everywhere.'

There was a pause between the couple, and the sounds of the all the drinkers in the place seemed to fade away for a moment as Terry processed the words Anita had spoken. 'How do you mean?' he asked, and already he was having ominous feelings about the course of the conversation.

'I swear on our kids' lives Terry – ' Anita began.

'You don't have to say that,' Terry interjected, as if he thought Anita was tempting fate, 'I believe you; I've never known you to tell a lie, even a white one.'

Anita's hand grasped Terry's large rough weathered fist. 'Terry, if you told me what I'm going to tell you I'd have you sent to Rainhill hospital, but I know it's true because it's actually happening to me and other people have seen him as well.'

'Calm down love, your shaking like a leaf,' Terry told her, and squeezed her trembling hand.

'My nerves are gone with it all,' said Anita, and her left eyebrow went into a spasm.

'Gotcha!' The face of an old friend of Terry named Stuart Briggs came round a pillar to the left of the corner table, and as Anita let out a shriek in fright, Stuart laughed and in a silly voice he shouted: 'Caught in the act – the blue nose and the redneck in flagrante delicto!'

'Piss off you idiot!' Terry roared at his joking mate, and then he looked at Anita and asked, 'You alright love?'

'God, you can't take a joke can you?' shouted a deflated Stuart. Most of the drinkers looked at him as he stormed out of the pub in a huff, and as he went, Terry gave him the two-fingered salute. 'Always arsing about he is,' seethed Terry, 'and he's older than me – acting like a big kid.'

With her hand on her chest, Anita let out a sigh and shook her head. When she calmed down she continued from where she had left off before the rude interruption. 'It all started last Christmas after I stayed in Betty O'Hare's house in Wavertree,' Anita recalled, 'you remember Betty don't you?'

Terry nodded. 'Yeah, the one who worked in Littlewoods; her husband passed away.'

'Yes,' said Anita, 'well she gets lonely in her house – and you should see how big her place is; her garden's like the ponderosa as well. Gardening keeps her going. All her kids have left the nest, so I went out with her on this night; Christmas Eve it was. To cut a long story short I got a bit tipsy and decided to stay at her place rather than try and get a taxi home at one in the morning, and I slept in a spare room. Anyway, I woke up around 3am and there was a man standing by the side of the bed.'

'Oh aye, who was he like?' asked Terry pretending he was joking but Anita could see he was concerned at the mention of a man. He needlessly flicked his cigarette over the ashtray.

'No, not a man – not a living man anyway – a ghost,' said Anita, lowering her voice at the mention of the G word. 'He had on one of those wigs like the ones you see in the films about the French Revolution, and all of his clothes were old fashioned – even though it was dark, he had a sort of glow around him. I thought I was dreaming at first. I felt for the bedside lamp, turned it on, and my eyesight's terrible nowadays, so he was just a blur, so I got my glasses out my handbag, which I'd left on the bed, and put them on.'

'And?' Terry asked, intrigued.

Anita took a sharp intake of breath, as if she was reliving the shock of seeing the ghost. 'I was sorry I put the glasses on. Terry, he looked ghastly. He had a round face, and it looked as if he had thick – and I mean *thick* make-up on, and red rouge around his cheeks – but what scared me most was his eyes – they were not bloodshot, but deep red, and the coloured part of his eye looked black, maybe dark brown. He had this weird sort of crooked smile on his face, and he had this creepy deep voice.'

'What? He spoke to you?' asked Terry.

Anita nodded. 'Yes, he said, "I love you". And then I started screaming for Betty, and he put his finger to his lips and said, "No, be quiet my love". And the next thing I got out the bed. He was on the left side, and I nearly threw myself out the right side and outside on the landing I bumped into Betty; she'd heard me screaming and had come to see what was up. I told her what had happened; I said, "Betty, there's an effing ghost in there!" And she said, "What?" and I barged

31

past her and went down to the kitchen. She said she had never seen or heard anything supernatural in all the years she'd lived at the house and she said I'd had a nightmare, but when she went into the spare bedroom she found a rose on the bed.'

'A rose?' Terry asked, and he kept thinking about the weird man who had attacked him earlier in the day. He was startling to feel more than a little unnerved.

Anita nodded and sipped her drink. 'As true as God's in Heaven – yes – a rose.'

'And this was when? At Christmas?' Terry enquired.

'Yeah' Anita replied.

'Mind you I think roses bloom all year now in special industrial greenhouses,' he said, expressing his thoughts regarding the availability of the flower.

'Oh, and listen to this,' Anita continued, 'it was a big red rose, and I said "Keep it away from me" and Betty put it in a little vase, thinking it was a joke, and later on when she was making us breakfast we heard a smash, and the vase was shattered, water everywhere, and we looked high and low but we never found that rose.'

Terry knew there was more to the story, and he nodded and said, 'Go on.'

'A few weeks after this, all that stuff about the ghost had been forgotten, although I wouldn't stay over at Betty's after that, but anyway, I went with Betty to the pictures to see *Carry On Abroad* - she needed cheering up – and after the film as me and Betty were walking through the foyer, this old man came up to me and grabbed my arm, and he said, "Listen love, you'll probably think I'm a nut, but I'm not, I'm a medium from the spiritualist church round the corner," he said, and he looked around, then said, "There was a ghost sitting behind you when you were watching the film. He goes way back – the eighteen-hundreds I'd say, and I couldn't get his name, but he was touching your hair. I don't know if you know about him, and if you don't I'm not trying to scare you, but he sat behind you for the whole length of the film". Well, you should have seen my face. Betty went white as well. There were three empty seats behind me, and I don't know if it was just my imagination but I thought I felt a draught down my neck a few times, and later on I thought *was that his breath?* I was supposed to go to the spiritualist church this fellah was from; his name's Stanley – but I didn't go.'

'So he followed you to the pictures,' said Terry, and he nodded to Anita's glass and said, 'drink that love, it'll calm you down. I'll go and get another one.'

'Look at that,' Anita drew back her sleeve, and Terry could see the goosepimples on her forearm. 'I've had enough, I have,' she said, and drank the gin and tonic. 'I'll tell you the rest in a minute,' she said, and she took her purse from her handbag but Terry said, 'Behave.' He went to get two more drinks, and as he waited for the barmaid to notice him, he happened to look in the mirror behind the bar – and there was that man again: the bewigged one who had attacked him and undoubtedly the ghost that was stalking Anita. He was standing behind and to the left of Terry, and he had an intense angry look upon his face, but when Terry turned, the outdated figure of fear was nowhere to be seen, and Anita was looking through her handbag, seemingly unaware of the ghost's latest appearance. Terry decided to say nothing to her, but he began to rack his brains for a way to tackle this unearthly problem.

Anita told him the rest. She had awakened a few times in the night and seen him standing in the bedroom, and she had even felt him kiss her face when she was half asleep.

'Why has he taken a shine to you?' Terry pondered. 'Maybe you remind him of someone he had a thing for years ago when he was alive.'

Anita held Terry's hand again. With a tearful look she said: 'If I went to a doctor and told him about this, he'd have me committed. I was going to see Betty's Catholic priest because they do exorcisms but I lost my nerve.'

'Look, love, maybe you should move in with me,' suggested Terry, 'just to feel a bit safer. You don't have to give up your house or change your way of life; it's just that I'd feel better looking after you. I don't know how to fight *him* but I don't like the idea of you being alone with him. And that's not some devious way of getting you back – you know I still have feelings for you.'

'Or you could move in with me,' said Rita, and she leaned forward and kissed Terry.

'I don't mind, as long as I can look after you,' he said, and he embraced her and suggested going to a cosier pub. The place was filling up and so the couple went to a pub on Cases Street, where Anita decided she would stay with Terry three nights a week for a few weeks, and then – who knows? She wondered if she'd end up remarrying him. At 11pm, Terry and Anita went to the chippy on Cases Street, then they got a taxi to Terry's home on Thingwall Road. A few days later, as Anita was packing up some of her clothes at her house, her nephew Kevin called in to see her. He'd been to Kensington Library to get some books for his history homework, and on the cover of one of Kevin's books there was a man who was dressed identically to the ghost who was smitten by her. According to the history book, the man belonged to the Rgency Era (1811-1820). Anita suddenly felt as if the ghost was present, but not showing itself, and to keep Kevin there till she'd finished packing she asked him to help her stuff the suitcases and carry them into the hallway till "Uncle Terry" arrived in his car. She then gave Kevin 50p and he went straight to the nearest sweetshop.

In the car, Anita told Terry: 'I think he knows we're having a go at a reconciliation, and doesn't like it. I can just sense his anger somehow. I think he might try and do something horrible. Ghosts can't kill you can they?'

'I think they can give you a heart attack if you're scared of them,' said Terry, stopping at traffic lights, 'but I'm not scared of him – just angry at him.'

The lights changed and the car stalled. Anita knew her ex-husband was a very able driver and it was not like him to stall any vehicle, but unknown to her, Terry had glanced in his rear view mirror and seen the accursed ghost sitting in the back seat for a moment. Like the last occasion, the apparition wore an expression of severe hatred as he glared at Terry. However, for the next two weeks, the ghost was noticeably absent, and Terry thought that he had scared the thing off, but then it returned with a vengeance one afternoon. It was a Saturday, and around 4pm, Terry and Anita were strolling through the sunshine on Bold Street, intending to do a bit of shopping before going to a restaurant when Anita stopped dead and squeezed Terry's hand. She dragged him into a doorway and said, 'It's him!'

Terry didn't know who she was referring to at first, then he recalled that look of fear in Anita's eyes. 'Oh you mean *him*?' he said, realising who she was talking about. 'I'm not afraid of him,' he said, and he stepped out of hiding, gently pulling Anita with him off the doorstep of a shop.

In broad daylight, under a bright sun, that ghost in the powdered white wig, heavy make-up and a long embroidered coat was striding towards the couple up the street – and in its hand it held a dagger. The blade of the weapon glinted in the sun, and Terry and Anita heard the visitor from beyond make some guttural sound as it advanced. It said something which neither of the couple could understand, and Anita let out a scream. Terry stepped in front of her, and she yelled, 'Run! He'll kill you!' but Terry stood his ground and he adopted a stance from the boxing days of his youth, and he raised his fists, ready to do his best to lay this freak from the spirit world. Terry was not a particularly religious man, but he found himself shouting to the ghost: 'In the name of Our Lord, get yourself back to the pit from whence you came! Go in the name of Jesus Christ!' And Terry meant every word that came from his lips.

The ghost grimaced as if it was in great pain, and then it turned around, put the dagger away, then staggered a few feet, and slowly faded away. Anita thought she heard it scream. The unidentified ghost was never seen again. Why it was so intensely attracted to Anita remains a mystery. Terry and Anita remarried in the following year after that bizarre ad hoc exorcism, and every now and then Anita would have a nightmare about the ghost. Perhaps it returned to some existence in the world beyond the living, or perhaps it is still roaming this earth, looking for a new love – it really is hard to say.

THINGS WE'RE NOT
SUPPOSED TO SEE

The late, great American astronomer, freethinker and popularizer of science, Carl Sagan, once remarked, 'There is a lurking fear that some things are not meant to be known; that some inquiries are too dangerous for human beings to make.' I see where Carl is coming from. In the many years I've spent investigating the world of the supernatural, I have gradually come to the unsettling conclusion that there are certain things which we are not supposed to see – things that are strictly out of bounds to the people on this level of existence, and they are normally well-hidden by someone or something to prevent us from delving into them – but it would seem that every now and then there is some metaphysical mishap and we get glimpses of a hidden reality. Take for example, the case of the "fairy funeral procession" witnessed by dozens of people on Smithdown Road in November 1973. I received a letter about this alleged incident from a woman named Rita Rowlands and after reading part of it it out on a local radio programme I'd been invited onto to discuss supernatural incidents, the station's switchboard went haywire. Most of the accounts given by the listeners claimed that upon the dull overcast Saturday afternoon of 17 November 1973 at around 3pm, people gasped out of amazement and fear and traffic came to a standstill as a procession of about thirty people – none of them more than 2 feet in height – crossed Smithdown Road, following four similarly-sized pallbearers who were carrying a miniature purple coffin. One of the best descriptions of this unearthly funeral cortege came from a policeman on his beat named Ken. He thought the train of little people was children at first as they crossed the road from a housing estate, but as they drew nearer, he could see they were tiny adults – and one child – and they were dressed in black pointed caps and suits made of velvety black and green material with hammer tails. Their faces were very pale except for one girl who was dressed in strange pink clothes with red hair. She had rosy cheeks and appeared to be crying. In front of the pallbearers walked a woman in a green dress with a cone-shaped hat, and with her was a boy with a green trefoil on the front of his tunic which resembled the symbol for clubs on a playing card. Ken was relieved when an old an woman made the sign of the cross and said to him, 'That's a fairy funeral. I saw one when I was a child down Princes Park. It's very unlucky to witness their funerals; I'll have to go to church tomorrow.'

'Thank God you can see them as well,' said Ken, and the worried-looking woman turned and hurried away. A cacophony of car horns then filled the air as impatient drivers, unaware of just what had stopped and slowed the cars on Smithdown Road, lost their patience in the traffic jam. Rita Rowlands, who first wrote to me about this uncanny procession, had been walking up Smithdown Road with her 5-year-old daughter when the little girl had tugged her hand hard before pointing to the long file of elf-like folk and remarking: 'Mummy, look at those funny people.'

Rita and a handful of people of all ages standing by a nearby bus stop gingerly made their way to the corner of Yanwath Street to get a better look at the weird spectacle. The eerie retinue of little people snaked into Yanwath Street, presumably headed for some ethereal fairy burial ground. Those brave enough to follow the diminutive mourners said they all vanished upon reaching Lodge Lane. Wanting to keep his job, Ken said nothing about the strange incident back at the police station, but ironically, a colleague came into the station later that day and said traffic had come to a standstill on Smithdown Lane as he drove to work because "a large group of children dressed up as gnomes" had walked across Smithdown Road and caused a jam. Ken wanted to tell his associate that the 'children' had been beings of some sort, but he had to bite his lip. Ken heard other accounts of the "fairy procession" and most said it had all been down to mass hysteria – the same explanation that was trotted out when hundreds of people claimed to have seen leprechauns across Liverpool (but mostly in Kensington) nine years earlier in 1964. Ken lived in mortal fear of being struck down by the alleged bad luck promised to him by the old woman in her ominous remarks about the preternatural procession, but nothing misfortunate happened in the months following the weird incident. Henry Jones was another witness who saw the faeries' funeral cortège that November afternoon, and he was fifteen at the time. He went home and told his mum what he'd seen and his Scottish grandmother – a font of esoteric information concerning the supernatural – told Henry:

"The Little Folk are around us all the time but we are not meant to see them. They are protected from humans because of our horrible cruelty towards things smaller than us, but sometimes the thing protecting the wee folk forgets to cloak them in invisibility and we see them.'

'Oh, don't start filling his head with all this daft talk, Mam!' Henry's mum told her mother. 'It's been a school outing to the baths on Lodge Lane, or kids going to a pantomime dressed up, that's all.'

'A pantomine in the middle of November?' queried Henry, with a crooked smile and a quizzical scrunch of his eyebrows.

'Yeah, it starts round now, the panto season,' replied Henry's mum.

'It's the Little Folk I'm telling you,' insisted Henry's grandmother, 'I saw them waiting at the traffic lights a few years ago on Smithdown Road. Waiting for the lights to change they were, all holding hands, and no one else could see them and I had to pretend I couldn't see them or they might have blinded me.'

The notion that there might be an invisible society of faeries all around us is obviously not a new one; our folklore locally and nationally tells us how the Little People are mainly invisible as they do not like to be watched, although they can choose to present themselves to anyone and sometimes they seem to be caught unawares, as described in the previous paragraphs about the strange funeral procession. The Gaelic scholar and minister, the Reverend Robert Kirk (1644-1692) aptly described this unseen society of faeries in the title of his authoritative treatise on witchcraft, ghosts and faery-lore: *The Secret*

Commonwealth. There was another case of humans seeing something they shouldn't have, again involving the Little Folk. This weird and frightening incident took place on a blistering summer's day in less complicated times, specifically Saturday 29 July 1967 at 5.40pm. The Irving family of Ashford Road, Meols, were returning home in their trusty 11-year-old Morris Minor 1000 Traveller after a day out in Chester, shopping, sightseeing and enjoying a lot of sandwiches, ice cream and sarsaparilla. It should have been a forty-minute trip at tops, but Mr Dennis Irving, a down-to-earth man who had moved to Wirral from Norris Green when he was seven, had an annoying habit of pulling over at certain points along the 25-mile return journey to either point out historical sites of interest (to him, anyway) or places where he had worked or lived, and his wife Jill and the couple's two daughters, Juliet and Suzanne, just wanted to get back home because the heat was unbearable. As the car travelled down Heron Road, Dennis Irving said, 'Ah, see this farm here on the right? That's where Tommy Briggs and I were chased by a bull. We'd just moved over here from Liverpool, and we'd never seen a live farm animal before.'

Jill had had enough of her husband's nostalgic rambling. She turned to him and groaned: 'Oh Dennis, never mind all our yesterdays.'

'I know, I know, but just let me show the girls where the bull chased their old dad,' said Dennis, pulling over near a hedge.

Jill shook her head. 'No, Dennis, the girls are dying from heatstroke and I want to get home and put my feet in a bowl of ice cold water and watch *Jukebox Jury*

– which started five minutes ago, by the way.'

'You're so selfish sometimes Jill,' retorted Dennis, and he turned and looked at his listless daughters in the backseat and asked, 'you *do* want to see where the bull ran after me and Tommy Briggs don't you?'

'I want to go home,' moaned 6-year-old Juliet, 'and Suzanne wants to have a wee!'

'Right! Home it is then!' said Dennis gazing straight ahead through the windscreen at the sun-scorched road. He sulked as he drove off, and the atmosphere was now tense in the sweltering car. Jill made small talk to alleviate this tension. 'Look, there's a mirage down the road with the heat; looks as if there's a big puddle of sky-blue water down there.'

The girls in the back didn't even bother to look at the mirage. Then, about fifty yards further along the road, Jill Irving said, 'Hey, look at that!' and pointed to something colourful through a gap in the hedgerow on the right. In the brief glimpse she'd had of something through that gap, she had thought she had seen a miniature model of a village. Dennis slowed the car and halted, after they had passed the gap. He reversed the car and saw it was indeed a breathtaking replica of a village of thatched cottages, and each quaint dwelling was painted in bright vibrant colours of orange, pink, yellow, green and blue. The Irvings got out the car and walked along a gravel path which led to a 4-foot-tall dry-stack wall of the type usually seen around cemeteries or on farms to demarcate boundaries. The top of this wall was level with what seemed to be the neatly manicured grass of a village green in this hamlet of doll-sized houses. There was some wooden platform in the middle of the green with a vertical beam in the centre. Mr Irving thought it resembled a gallows. He went back to the car to fetch his camera, and when he came back inside of a minute, his wife grabbed his hand and said, 'Dennis, how do they do that?' She nodded to the little figures of people in old-fashioned clothes forming a crowd on the green. 'They look too realistic to be dolls,' said Dennis, taking the camera out of its case, 'I've got to get a few pictures of this.'

'Mummy, can we take some of them home?' Juliet asked, and she crawled forward on all fours, intending to go and visit the little people, who looked as if they were about six inches tall.

'No you can't! Come here Juliet!' Jill Irving grabbed her daughter's ankle and pulled hard, almost removing her white ankle sock and Mary Jane shoe. Jill had a very bad feeling about this strange spectacle. 'Are they fairies?' asked a beaming Suzanne, and suddenly, before anyone could answer, a faint cheer went up from the crowd of tiny folk. Dennis Irving tried to take a picture of the weird scene at this point but his camera's lever jammed.

'Oh!' Mrs Irving threw her hands to her face and gazed in horror at the development on the centre of the green. The little people were positioning one of their kind on the wooden platform. A little man in a black hood then grabbed the rope dangling from the wooden arm jutting out from that upright beam, and he took the noose at the end of that rope and looped it around the head of the man in front of him.

'What in God's name – ' Mr Irving gasped as his wife, anticipating what was going to take place, pulled the children off the village green.

'I want to see them!' moaned Juliet, trying to climb back up the wall.

There was a cheer as the little people hanged someone.

Dennis Irving and his wife saw the little hanged body with its hands tied behind its back kick its legs about as it dangled. The parents, being much taller than their children, could clearly see this macabre spectacle, but Juliet and Suzanne were below the level of the wall and could only see the horrified expressions on the faces of mum and dad.

The couple saw the gaggle of little people quickly form a circle around the gallows. They all chanted something and kicked their legs in the air reminiscent of the Can-can dancers, and the hooded executioner standing on the platform pulled down his trousers, presented his bare bottom towards the hanging victim, and slapped his buttocks in a strange indecent gesture to the dying man.

In a daze, Jill Irving started pulling the bewildered children to the car, but her husband kept trying to get his camera to work, and seeing the ghastly behaviour of the little mob he swore at them – and they all stopped dancing and noticed him looking on. A cry went up from the miniature lynch mob and they charged towards the human onlooker across the green. Dennis noticed that some of the diminutive beings brandished what looked like sticks, swords and pitchforks. He turned and ran, and as soon as he got in the car, he ignored the questions about the little people from his children, started the engine and the vehicle tore off up Heron Road. It didn't get far because the engine inexplicably conked out. As Mr Irving tried desperately to start the car, his wife screamed as she looked in the wing mirror of the vehicle. Those little people were pouring down the road. The car engine suddenly started and Mr Irving drove off. He kept looking in his mirrors and was very relieved when he saw the tiny pursuers give up the chase and fade into the distance. When Dennis told his mother what had happened, she said he'd had a run-in with the Poldies, an ancient faery race that inhabited Wirral, Cheshire and parts of Lancashire. She had heard some hair-raising stories about this branch of the Little Folk tree, but never knew they had their own form of capital punishment. From that day, Dennis Irving refused to go anywhere near Heron Road, where the phantom faery village is still occasionally seen if the reports I've received over the years are anything to go by.

A similar instance of something being seen that is not normally taken in by our eyes concerns a 12-year-old Waltonian boy named Barry Flynn in the 1960s. One thundery Saturday afternoon in August 1966, Barry left his home off Rice Lane in Walton and went gallivanting aimlessly. Concealed upon his person were a catapult and a penknife he had received off his grandfather. Barry's mother had called her father irresponsible when she had caught him teaching Barry how to throw the penknife so its blade would stick in the garden fence. Barry walked up Rice Lane and called at the home of his new friend Davey on Yew Tree Road, but Davey's mum came to the door and said her son had left to play football about a quarter of an hour ago. Barry walked away feeling bored, and decided he'd fire his catapult from the railway bridge on Lynwood Road, but when he got there, he accidentally dropped the catapult off the bridge while trying to fire it at a hare that was running across the railway tracks. He stayed on the bridge, took out his penknife and decided to scrape out his initials in the stonework – when he heard a strange noise to his left. It sounded like a crackle of electricity, and Barry wasn't sure if it was some discharge from the electric railway line down below or whether it was the weather with the recent thunderstorms that had just passed over Liverpool. He saw nothing to account for the crackling noise at first, and he was the only person on that bridge, but when he happened to move a few feet he saw a very bizarre sight; he saw seven little people, all about the size of his youngest sister Ada's doll, and they were dressed from head to toe in black tight-fitting one-piece uniforms with some sort of black balaclavas on their heads. The faces were pale green, and their eyes were huge and staring – and all of the eyes were upon him. They seemed shocked at Barry noticing them, and they walked slowly in his direction. 'Can you see us?' said one of the little figures, and his voice sounded like that of a child.

Barry stood there rock-firm, unable to move for a moment out of sheer fear. Then he moved sideways a few inches, ready to run, and saw the images of the advancing dwarfish entities change to a greenish-yellow colour and fade somewhat, but when he moved back to where he had stood, Barry saw the little manikins appear solid again. The one of the seven who was nearest to Barry suddenly charged at him, and in one reflexive movement, the boy threw the penknife he had been holding at him – and it stuck in his chest. The impaled uncanny-looking pygmy fell on his back and gasped the word, 'Bastard!' as his comrades ran towards him. Barry turned and ran as fast as his legs could carry him up Lynwood Road and he never looked back and arrived at his Auntie Rita's home on Orrel Lane half a mile away about fifteen minutes later. Rita opened the door to see her nephew in tears, and at first she couldn't make head or tail of what he was talking about; she thought he said he'd thrown a knife into a little man, and she imagined he meant a man of small stature, but eventually Barry explained that the man he'd probably killed had been as big as a doll, and Rita warned him about telling lies to get attention. She treated Barry to a slice of sandwich cake and a glass of orange juice, but he said he couldn't eat the cake because he felt sick with worry, and when he insisted he really had thrown his penknife into some type of elf, Aunt Rita lost her patience and told Barry he should go and tell his mother and father what had happened. Barry left the house in tears and went to his terraced home off Rice Lane. Barry's father was out drinking but his mother listened to his strange story, and she yelled at Barry: 'I *told* you to throw that penknife away! Wait till I see my dad over this! He's to blame for all this, giving you the knife in the first place!'

'Mum, will I go to jail?' asked an extremely distraught Barry.

'Barry, tell me again,' said his mother starting to cry, 'did you throw that knife into a kid?'

Barry's hand felt his neck because his throat was drying up with worry. 'No, it was a little man with a balaclava on, Mum! I swear on our Ada's life it was a little funny-looking man, and there were seven of them!'

'Oh my God, they'll be witnesses then,' said Mrs Flynn, and she fell back into the armchair by the fire and held her face with her hands on each cheek.

'Will they pin my ears back in jail?' Barry asked, and there was a roll of heavy thunder which shook the foundations of the house, followed by a torrential downpour of hammering rain.

A tapping at the front door startled mother and son.

'That'll probably be the police!' Mrs Flynn shot up from the armchair and Barry held onto the table with his legs about to collapse from under him.

Mrs Flynn couldn't see anyone's head through the window in the top half of the front door, so perhaps it was one of Barry's friends calling. She opened the door – and recoiled in horror. Standing there in the heavy rain was four tiny men with ghastly pale green faces, and each wore a black balaclava and a black one-piece suit.

'Ooh! What are you?' Mrs Flynn backed into Barry, who smiled and yelled: 'They're them! They're them Mum! You didn't believe me!'

'You threw a knife into our chief,' said one of these little men who only came up to Mrs Flynn's knee. Rainwater dripped from his nose and he wore an expression of intense hatred as he looked at Barry.

'I – I'm sorry, he scared me!' Barry replied, and tried to get behind his mother but she swung him round towards the unearthly visitors so he was in front of her.

'Only you can remove that knife,' said the menacing visitant as the other three walked towards him from behind. 'If you remove it before the sun goes down the chief will live but if you don't, he'll die and you and your family will be cursed for twenty-one years.'

'What are yous?' Barry asked, then gazed up to see his mother looking at the four little people with an expression of horror.

'Never you mind,' replied the weird black-clad entity, 'you come with us now or you'll be cursed and eventually all your family will die.'

'Mum?' Barry looked up at his mother, unsure what to do, and expecting her to protect him, but she pushed him towards the visitors and said, 'Go on, do as he says Barry, this family has had enough bad luck!'

'Are you coming with me?' Barry asked his mother but the little spokesperson of the four visitors interjected, saying, 'No, she cannot come! Only you must come!'

Barry walked in a daze out the door with two of the little people behind him and two in front of him, and throughout the journey to the railway bridge, the boy saw no one. Thunder rolled and lightning flashed, and Barry arrived soaked to the bone at the railway bridge. He saw no one but the eerie foursome accompanying him, but when he was just past the half-way point of the bridge, a group of other dwarves in black appeared, and they were standing around the one he had thrown the knife into. The impaled chief was sitting up, his face twisted in agony, and when he saw Barry he shouted words that the boy could not understand. The little man who had told Barry to come to the bridge said to the nervous boy, 'Carefully withdraw that knife from our chief, then turn around and don't look back or we will kill you.'

Barry knelt at the side of the chief and took hold of

the metal handle of the penknife with his finger and thumb. He gently pulled it out the diminutive being's chest, and a little purplish-red blood was evident on the blade.

'Now stand up, and turn around!' shouted the chief, and then he groaned.

'Keep walking!' someone else cried, and Barry walked unsteadily with his soaked fringe stuck to his forehead and rainwater trickling down the back of his neck. He reached the end of Lynwood Road and turned into Rice Lane, then ran off, his shoes squelching because the rain had infiltrated them via the tiny holes in the soles. When Barry got home he hammered on the door and grimaced from the agony of that stitch in his side. His mother opened the door and he said, 'I took it out! He's alright!'

Mrs Flynn resented her palm to her son and asked, 'Where's that friggin' knife?'

Barry took the penknife out his trouser pocket and his mother dashed outside and bent down near the gutter. She carefully posted the penknife between the gaps in the grid. She ran back into the house, then burst into tears and hugged her soaked son. Mrs Flynn told her husband what had happened when he came home and he laughed, thinking she was pulling his leg. Barry told his mates at school, which turned out to be a big mistake as from then on, for well over a year, they would mockingly ask him if he'd seen any goblins. About a week after the strange encounter with the weird little men, a 10-year-old girl named Teresa who was very shy and normally never talked to anyone, stopped Barry one day on his way home from school and told him that she too had seen those little people in black on the bridge. Barry was fascinated by this claim and listened to the girl's account. Teresa said she and a friend had seen them on the railway bridge, but only when they stood at a certain spot, and the weird little men had chased her on several occasions as far as her home on Eskdale Road, so she now steered clear of the railway bridge. Barry started hanging round with Teresa and she eventually became his girlfriend. Over the years I have heard of strange goings on in the vicinity of the Lynwood Road bridge, including reports of people experiencing lost time and even incidences of amnesia. It's possible that the location is some sort of portal or window area to some other realm, but the elves – or whatever they are – are good examples of things we're not supposed to see. And here's another thought-provoking paradigm of something secret – and very sinister – that exists among us right under our noses.

In October 1978, a 25-year-old Birkenhead printer named Duncan Nevis inherited a small fortune from his oldest aunt when she passed away in a West Kirby nursing home. Duncan was strongly advised by his father to invest the inheritance money for a rainy day but the sound advice was not taken and Duncan blew most of the legacy by purchasing a Datsun 280Z import. He drove the sleek orange 3-door coupé to Hoylake where he cruised in a circuit, passing up and down Avondale Road, hoping to see an old flame named Laura. He had met her in the summer of 1970 when he was eighteen and she had just turned seventeen, and as Laura was a tennis buff, Duncan had proposed to her that July day after taking her to the Hoylake Tennis Championship to see Patti Hogan beat

Virginia Wade and Karen Krantzcke in straight sets. The wedding was to have been held at St Andrew's, Bebington, followed by a reception at Poulton Hall, and the illustrious owner of that stately pile – Roger Lancelyn Green – would hopefully write a wedding masque to music composed by Laura, just as soon as she could buy the music manuscript paper from Rushworths. These romantic castles in the air came crashing down when Laura started her job in Liverpool's Lewis's store, where she met a co-worker named Jimmy who looked like her crush of the year – Paul Newman. He swept Laura off her feet, and after six months he callously dumped her for someone else. Laura went crawling back to Duncan, but he didn't want to know; he felt as if he'd had his fingers burned and had no intention of loving and losing Laura again. Now, in 1978, he had realised Laura was the one. He must have performed about twenty laps, orbiting Avondale Road in his new flash car, when he finally saw Laura trudging along through a thin drizzle near the corner of Hoyle and Dovedale Roads, and he beeped his horn and melodramatically pulled up by her with a screech of tyres.

'What are you doing round here?' she asked, eyeing the showy car.

'Do you fancy going for a spin? It's my car, like.' He said.

'You must have come into some money if you're telling the truth,' she said, and crouched to look into the plush interior. 'All legal is it?'

'As legal as eating – get in!' Duncan leaned over and opened the door and she deliberately took her time getting in, not wishing to appear easy. He advised her to belt up and she told him she couldn't stay out long as her mum wanted her to go and collect catalogue money from customers. The Datsun took off, and Duncan said, 'Hey, do you fancy going down to Heswall? You used to like that place – Hugh Foulerton – they sell like cutlery and decanters.'

'Er, no thanks, and I've got to get back soon,' Laura reminded him, but she did enjoy the drive. He asked if she was with anyone, and in a roundabout way she said she was single but had no shortage of men asking her out.

Duncan took Laura over to Liverpool, and then in the late afternoon he headed back to his home off Grange Mount when Laura asked him if she could 'have a drive' of the Datsun. Duncan said he'd only just got the vehicle insured and said he was worried she'd crash it and that it was a left-hand drive set up, but she reassured him she'd been having driving lessons from her brother, and so Duncan reluctantly drove the car to Park Road East and pulled over. It was surprisingly quiet there, and the couple swapped seats.

'Look Laura, this car cost me a fortune; you can drive it about two-hundred yards and then that's it,' stipulated a worried Duncan. She gave him a peck on the cheek and said, 'I'll surprise you; our Tony said I'm a fast learner.'

She started the car and took off smoothly, and then she turned to Duncan and said, 'See?'

'Keep your eyes on the road Laura!' said a very anxious Duncan. Laura got cocky and bombed along at sixty - then she turned to Duncan and said, 'James Hunt eat your heart –'

'Laura!' Duncan cried out, his wide terror-stricken eyes fixed on something beyond the windscreen, and he tried to seize the wheel.

There was an almighty bang and the car shuddered. The windscreen was spattered with something green and slimy. Laura braked, and in shock, she gasped, 'What did we hit?'

Duncan got out the vehicle and saw the body of a man lying crumpled about twenty feet behind the Datsun. He ran to him, noticing the green trail of sludge, and an old woman and a young man of about twenty came over. What they all saw was very strange indeed. The 'man' lying on his back had a face that was yellowish-green with scales, and the half-closed eyes were reddish. *He did not look human.* Hanging in threads from this ghastly reptilian head were fragments of a flesh-coloured mask of some sort and a wig. Laura came over sobbing and several cars passing by halted and their drivers got out and came over to look upon the bizarre scene. Within minutes the law turned up and an ambulance. A detective (who never identified himself) later took Duncan and Laura into custody and warned them to say nothing about the strange accident victim or they could be imprisoned.

'Imprisoned for what?' Duncan wanted to know.

'Just keep that mouth of yours shut and you'll be fine,' said the unknown 'detective', 'but if you tell a soul what happened I guarantee you'll end up in a padded cell for a long, long time.'

The Datsun was thoroughly hosed down by someone and returned to Duncan after almost a fortnight. Duncan and Laura received phonecalls for months after the strange incident from persons unknown, reminding them to say nothing about the bizarre accident. What was that thing which seems to have been masquerading as a human? Was it an alien or a mutation of a human? We can only speculate. There has been a lot of talk in the conspiracy-theory community over the years about a supposed inter-dimensional reptilian race that has infiltrated our society disguised as humans – and usually humans who hold positions of power in the world. Why, some conspiracy theorists have even claimed that certain members of the British Royal Family and some American Presidents are actually reptilian invaders. These seemingly outrageous claims have been made with great seriousness by people like the controversial writer and lecturer David Icke. Strangely enough, the human brain is thought by some neuroanatomists to consist of three brains: the neomammalian (the new brain), the paleomammalian (the old brain), and the *reptilian* brain. The new brain is concerned with planning, abstract thoughts, reasoning and language, and the old brain is the seat of motivation, memory, emotions and skills like parenting. The reptile brain in humans is ruthlessly concerned only with basic drives such as the search for food, drink, shelter and sex, and this brain is responsible for carrying out habitual unconscious routines (such as parking your car or putting your house keys in a certain place without thinking). Does this mean humans – warm-blooded mammals – are somehow related to reptiles? Well, humans evolved from mammal-like reptiles called synapsids which roamed the Earth during the Permian period (299 to 251 million years ago), so it's possible we *are*, in partly reptile, but this still doesn't explain what the thing was that got knocked down (and killed?) on a street in Birkenhead. All we can glean from the weird incident is that other races from other worlds or other times might be among us disguised as humans, and perhaps they have been here for centuries.

From the Birkenhead of 1978 we now move forward in time seven years to the West Derby district of Liverpool in 1985, and to a semi-detached house on Glentrees Road. In January of that year, a 50-year-old woman named Mary Owen lived at a semi-detached house on this road, and one Sunday afternoon that month her youngest sister, Deborah came to visit with her 7-year-old son Dominic, a very disobedient boy. Not long after his arrival at his Aunt Mary's house, Dominic said he wanted to go to the toilet, and his mother warned him: 'If you're just saying that so you can go mooching round Auntie Mary's rooms you're going straight home and I'll also tell your grandfather as well.'

The boy sulkily went upstairs, messed about with the shower in the bathroom, then sneaked out the bathroom and crept into the spare room at the end of the landing. Dominic had been in this room before and liked to play on the old guitar in there. The room was full of junk, but the boy loved rooting about in there. He heard footsteps coming up the stairs. It sounded like his mum. Dominic switched off the light, hid behind the dresser in the corner and waited. The footsteps never came to the spare room. It was his Aunt Mary apparently going to get something for Dominic's mum. He heard her faint voice behind the door shout: 'I've never worn these two pairs Deborah, so you may as well have them. I don't like heels.'

As Dominic hid, he heard music somewhere close by in the room. It sounded like something being played on a xylophone – an instrument he played in school. The boy was just going to crawl out from under the dresser when he saw a light shining out of the fireplace in the corner. It was a steady blue light which became brighter and brighter, and a silhouette of a man appeared in it – and this man had four horns sticking out of his head. Then Dominic recognised the shape – it was a jester; something he'd seen in a history book at school. The figure was walking towards him, and he could hear a jingling sound. Dominic didn't know whether to run out of the room or stay put on all fours under the dresser. The silhouette of the weird man crouched and started to come out of the fireplace so Dominic turned on the floor and hid behind the dresser. He heard someone walking about in the room making muttering sounds but the frightened boy could not make out what was being said. The person seemed to be pacing up and down, and Dominic wished his mum and auntie would come up and get him. He then heard his mother shouting him downstairs. Dominic gingerly peeped out from behind the mirror of the dresser and saw the jester standing with his back to him. He was quite tall, much taller than Dominic's father (who was a six-footer). The child could see a yellow or orange tunic on the stranger, a thick black leather belt, a type of 'skirt' with weird pleats in it, and pale yellow tights. He could not see what the jester was wearing on his feet from his vantage point, but he could see the foolscap the entity wore with silver bells as the end of its four horns.

'Dominic! What did I tell you?' shouted the boy's mother, Debbie, just outside the door of the spare room.

The jester casually sneaked over to a dark corner and positioned himself between a wardrobe and the wall. Deborah came into the room calling her son's name and switched on the light.

Dominic quickly crawled from under the dresser and went straight between his mother's legs as he headed for the open door. 'What the hell are you playing at?' Deborah asked and went after her son. He ran along the landing and down the stairs, and to his Aunt Mary he said, 'There's a ghost in that spare room!' He pointed at the ceiling, unable to get his words out for a moment, then told a bewildered Aunt Mary: 'It's a jester! I'm not lying auntie! I want to go home!'

Dominic's mother stormed into the living room and was about to tell her son off for messing about in Mary's spare room when there was an almighty thump upstairs. Mary looked at Deborah, then their eyes turned up to the ceiling, and Dominic grabbed hold of his mother's skirt and pleaded, 'Let's go mum, it's that jester!'

Mary and Deborah and Dominic went next door to the house of neighbour Mr Rix, a big stocky man in his fifties, and told him about the possible intruder. Rix hurried next door and went up to the spare room, and found that someone had overturned the wardrobe – but whoever it had been, that person had gone. Rix looked behind the dresser and even looked inside the toppled wardrobe but there was no one about. Dominic insisted that it had been a man dressed as a jester who had come out of the fireplace and Mr Rix smiled and told the lad's mother, 'He's got a real vivid imagination, hasn't he?'

'Well what knocked over the wardrobe then?' Deborah asked Mr Rix.

He replied, 'Well, what it's probably been is a warped floorboard under the wardrobe, knocked it off balance like.'

'I've heard music playing in here all hours of a night,' Mary Owen suddenly told her sister and Mr Rix. Little Dominic looked up at his aunt with his mouth open, feeling a bit more scared now. He looked to the dark corner where he'd seen that uncanny man hiding.

'Probably been someone with a radio on, Mary,' said Mr Rix, 'you're letting your imagination get the better of you now.'

A week later, a hysterical Mary Owen was on the phone to her sister Deborah.

'I saw him,' Mary gasped, and then she sounded as if she was crying. 'I saw the man Dominic saw! The child was not imagining things! I want to move out of this place!'

'Mary calm down,' said a startled Deborah, 'now what did you see?'

'That ghost upstairs Deborah,' Mary replied. 'I was tidying up the spare room and I saw him come out of the fireplace! I ran out the room. He'll still be up there!'

Deborah and her husband Frank came over to Mary's West Derby home and Frank had a look in the spare room and he searched the other rooms too, but there was no sign of an intruder. However, Frank, Deborah and Mary all heard strange music coming from the fireplace. It was not music from a neighbour's radio – it was actually coming from the fireplace somehow and after it eventually stopped, Mary asked Frank - a man who was a builder by trade - if he could remove the old fireplace, as she believed it was haunted. Frank said he could remove it, and he did this as Mary stayed over in her sister's house. He had to remove several old rusted lugs which fixed the cast iron surround to the chimney breast, and then he used plasterboard to seal the rectangular hole left behind. He then told Mary she should sell the fire surround as cast iron ones were in great demand. Mary told him to keep the fire surround; she wanted nothing to do with it. There were no more strange goings-on in the spare room of Mary's home in Glentrees Road, but that is not the end of this strange matter. Frank advertised the Victorian fire surround in the *Liverpool Echo* for £30 and it was bought by someone named George Hunt in South Liverpool, but a week later Mr Hunt returned the fireplace and demanded a refund because it was haunted. Hunt was a huge man and Frank gave him his money back. Frank advertised it in the Items for Sale column of the *Echo*, and this time he listed the asking price as just £15. Frank would also make a point of telling anyone who bought the cast iron fire surround that it was a case of "sold as seen" and that once the money had changed hands there was to be no refund.

Around this time over the water, Raymond and Melissa Earle moved from their cramped home in Birkenhead to a five-bedroom Victorian semi-detached house on Bebington's Woodhey Road. The Earles and their two children, Hollie, aged 9, and Jon, aged 7, soon settled into their new home, which was much bigger than their old house in Birkenhead. Raymond Earle had once pledged that he'd give his wife a "country room" – a special rustically themed sanctum where she could escape from the stresses accrued from the toils of housewifery, and now he was about to fulfil that promise. Raymond and his brother Mike worked tirelessly on turning a spare room on the second floor into the country room, and they removed the skirting and architraves and laid down a beautiful wooden floor. Melissa picked the wallpaper and the pink gingham curtains, and she had a rocking chair put in the room, a spinning wheel, as well as a hammock where she could relax and read. Something was missing though, and Mike said an old-fashioned fire surround would complete the country room. Melissa agreed, and Raymond scanned the items-for-sale columns of the newspapers and ended up fetching a Victorian cast-iron fireplace from a house in Liverpool's West Derby district; yes, he'd bought the accursed fireplace Frank had put in the *Echo*. Raymond Earle told his wife it had only cost £15 – an absolute bargain, or so Raymond thought, because he had no idea it was haunted by a very sinister figure. The installation of this fireplace was the finishing touch. On the first day in the country room after the beds had been made and the staircase and landings had been vacuumed, Melissa lit a patchouli joss stick and sat in the rocking chair reading a book of short stories by Guy de Maupassant with a mug of coffee on the little walnut side table. After about twenty minutes of reading, Melissa heard what sounded like a jangling ice cream van somewhere in the distance, but what the glockenspiel melody was she could not tell; it sounded vaguely familiar but she couldn't identify it. The tune slowly faded away, and Melissa bookmarked the page in her ghost stories book and rose from her comfy chair. She looked out the window, wondering if the chiming tune had originated from an ice cream van, but there was no such van in the street, and so Melissa sat down to continue reading when she heard the eerie melody again – and when she angled her head to try and ascertain where the music was coming from, she realised that the tune seemed to be coming from the fireplace. Melissa thought the composition was being played on a harp, but where was it coming from? She refused to believe it was coming from the fireplace and tried to rationalise what she was hearing by imagining it was the strains of a neighbour's radio. All the same, Melissa felt a bit unnerved by the ghostly music, so she switched on the little transistor radio on the bookshelf and listened to Schubert on BBC Radio 3. She could still hear that ghostly music playing in the background though, so she went down to the lounge, and her friend Thelma paid a visit minutes later. When Melissa told her friend about the weird tune, curiosity got the better of Thelma and she went up to the country room and she too heard it. Thelma had studied music at college and she identified the untraceable melody immediately; it was *Sumer is Icumen In* – medieval for "Summer has Come In" – a piece of music which dates back to the 13th century. The music faded away, and Thelma smiled and said, 'Melissa, you have a haunted fireplace. Oh I'd love that in my home.'

'Don't say that, Thelma,' said Melissa, feeling a chill inside at the mention of the word *haunted*. 'If one thing scares me it's the supernatural.'

Melissa stopped going to the country room for a few days and she never told her husband about the weird music she and Thelma had heard.

Days later Raymond bought an antique Edwardian fire screen for his wife, and she noticed that when this screen was in place, there was no music from the fireplace. A few days before Hollie and Jon were due back at school after the summer holidays, the children sneaked into their mother's country room. Melissa was in the garden and Raymond was at work. The children played I spy, and then Jon removed the fire screen and suggested burning something in the fireplace, but Hollie's eyes widened and she gazed at the fireplace with a face lit up by blue light. 'Jon, look!' the girl said excitedly, and took a step back.

In the fireplace there was now a bright vivid scene; it was as if the children were looking at a TV screen. Beneath a crystal-clear blue sky they could see a castle in the distance, perched on a mountain, surrounded by acres of snow. Jon and Hollie crept nearer to the vision in the fireplace and felt the cold draught coming from it – it really was an opening to some wintry wasteland with that castle of a dozen towers dominating the scene. Hollie gingerly reached out into the fireplace and felt a stinging coldness in her fingers.

'Let's tell mum!' suggested Jon. He seemed afraid of the 'vision'.

'What's that?' Hollie noticed a tiny dot leave the castle's arched opening. It was moving rather fast, and it had some colour to it which contrasted to the bright white snowfields. Was it an animal? Hollie realised it was coming towards her and Jon, and this frightened her. 'What is it?' Jon kept asking.

Then the superior eyesight of the children discerned that it was not an animal hurtling towards them, but a person, running on all fours as fast as a greyhound. 'Jon, let's go, quick!' Hollie grabbed her brother by the arm and began to gently pull him towards the door. They could now see that the thing was dressed like a jester in pied clothing of orange and yellow, and his cap had four horns of scarlet, purple, blue and green with jingly bells close enough to hear!

The children rushed out of the room with Jon crying, and they almost fell over one another rushing down the first flight of steps. They heard the door of the country room burst open behind them and that jingling jester came running towards the terrified brother and sister on all fours. 'I'm Mr Kipper! Hello! Hello!' he cried in a very sinister-sounding high-pitched voice that echoed down to the hallway.

At that moment, Mike, the uncle of the children, let himself into the house, and "Mr Kipper" instantly turned like a snake and ran back up the stairs and into the country room. The children threw themselves at Uncle Mike and told him about Mr Kipper, but when he went upstairs he found no one about in any of the rooms. Raymond Earle said his children had got the name "Mr Kipper" from the news reports regarding the recent disappearance of estate agent Suzy Lamplugh, who had been showing a flat to a Mr Kipper when she mysteriously vanished, but Mrs Earle then told her husband about the music she heard in the fireplace.

'So, you're trying to tell me that the fireplace upstairs is haunted?' Raymond asked with a wry smile on his lips.

Melissa nodded, and her eyes were full of fear. 'Ray, I heard it, Thelma heard it, and now the children have told us they were chased by this – this thing! I know it took an awful lot of bother to put that fire surround in, but please – can you take it out?'

Raymond paused, and wanted to argue against his wife's suggestion, but he felt that something sinister really was connected to that fire surround, and he nodded, and said, 'Okay love. I know you – you're not one for believing in ghosts and all that, and I can tell just looking at you that something – well, something strange – happened up there, and the kids haven't got the imagination to make something up like that – so I'll get Mike to take it out. Do you want me to just cover the wall up or put another fireplace in?'

Without even considering the question Melissa said, 'Just cover it up, please.'

Out of curiosity, Raymond Earle drove over to Liverpool and called upon Frank in West Derby and the latter seemed to be expecting him. Raymond asked him about the fire surround and if he'd heard anything strange about its history. Frank brought Raymond into the kitchen and over a cup of tea he told him about the weird ghost of a jester that had been seen coming out of the fireplace and how something had pushed over the wardrobe in the room where the fireplace had been installed. 'I'm sorry I sold you a ghost,' said Frank apologetically, 'the first person I sold it to – A Mr Hunt - also returned it. He said it was haunted but didn't tell me any more than that and I refunded him.'

'Why would a jester be haunting a fireplace?' Raymond mused, 'doesn't make sense.'

'Maybe the iron the fireplace was made from was

some medieval item that was melted down,' speculated Frank, 'or maybe it's to do with our local history here. West Derby is ancient. I remember reading that an old Saxon fort literally stood round the corner from here, and then some Norman castle was built there too. All the houses round there have the word "castle" in them.'

Frank was referring to a small Norman motte-and-bailey fort built just 200 yards from his home around the year 1100 by Count Roger de Poitu, the First Lord of Lancashire who ruled all of the lands from the banks of the Mersey to the Ribble and parts of Yorkshire – which took in 398 manors. This vast area had been given to Count Roger by William the Conqueror, just after the Norman Conquest of 1066. However, the motte-and-bailey castle built by Count Roger was no vast castle with a dozen towers, as seen in the vision in the fireplace; it was a simple mound of earth with a moat around it and a wooden fort on the top. I personally believe the ethereal castle seen by the children, the uncanny jester, and the medieval music point to some other castle, but how we connect the strange phenomenon to a cast-iron fireplace is anyone's guess. I mentioned a short version of the strange story on a radio programme many years ago and one woman who gave her name as Joan called me but would not give her surname or any other details about herself. Joan knew the address of the house on Glentrees Road and claimed her mother had lived there in the 1940s. She said that when she was aged ten, she heard someone singing 'Three Blind Mice' in the room where the fireplace was installed, and on the following morning three dead mice were found on the hearth rug of the fire with their eyes gouged out. Their severed tails lay nearby. The woman also said her sleep would be disturbed at the house all hours in the morning by someone with a strange high-pitched voice singing terrifying songs about throwing babies into fires and hanging someone called "Sweetheart Green". These disturbing songs sounded as if they were accompanied by a lute. Joan said her mother seemed to know something about the haunted room but when she was asked whose ghost was haunting the room, her mother would always say, 'That's not for you to know. Just say your prayers at night and *he* won't bother you.'

Just who *he* was remains a mystery.

The strange history of the cast iron fireplace - like its present whereabouts - is unknown...

And finally, let us conclude this chapter on the subject of things we are not supposed to see with an excellent case which indicates that there is much more to commonplace reality than meets the eye. Let us briefly dwell on the philosophical background to this odd story first to put it in perspective. If you compressed the age of the universe into 365 days, then the life of a person aged 75 would be the equivalent of one-seventeenth of a second. Furthermore, compared to the size of the universe, our bodies aren't even atom-sized; they are almost non-existent, yet we think the Cosmos revolves around us. We see and know little because we *are* so little, and there are things going on right under your nose – astounding things – but most of the time you are completely unaware of them because of your mundane cares and robotic thought processes. Andy Drake was a classic example of this type of person. The 69-year-old widower rarely stopped to look at the stars and wonder about his place in the grand scheme of things, and one unusually mild afternoon in December 1975, Andy came to Church Street and sat on the benches, just to be among people. Since the recent death of Kathy his beloved wife of fifty years, he had been plagued by loneliness. He sat on a bench facing C&A watching the never-ending traffic of people as he puffed on his pipe. The man sitting besides Andy was in his eighties by the look of it, and he was rambling to himself in incomprehensible mutterings. Compared to the crystal heartbreaking silence of Andy's home, it was soothing to be among the hubbub of passing voices, the laughter of children, the cries of the market stall folk, and the groaning foghorns of the river. This ocean of ambient sound engulfing the gregarious Mr Drake was so soothing, he dozed off but was awakened sometime later by his pipe falling out of his relaxed mouth and into his lap. 'Oh!' he said, jolting his head back as he rejoined the world of the waking.

And then Andy saw him – and thought he was dreaming. The bizarre spectacle lay just twenty feet away.

Picture Andy's view from the centre of Church Street looking west towards Lord Street, and imagine the scene projected onto some giant screen ten storeys high; now, imagine a vertical tear in that screen, about fifty feet in height and a few feet wide. This is what Andy saw, and through that tear in this grand but impossible 'scenery curtain' the dumbfounded widower saw a misty forest with strange, monstrous animals moving about within it; they reminded Andy of dinosaurs. A man in black tight-fitting clothes and a type of balaclava came out of the opening in the curtain and seemed to be trying to pull the edges of the torn fabric together, and another identically-dressed man stood 'behind the scenes' – visible through the gap in the great torn curtain. The people walking by did not seem to notice the immense vertical tear or the strange duo, and as the nearest man in black yanked at the screen as if he was losing his temper, the images of people and buildings became distorted and out of kilter the way images would if you ripped down the projection scene while a film was playing on the cinema. The language the two unearthly men spoke sounded like some cross between Polish and Russian, and they began to shout at one another in the strange tongue. Andy watched these surreal goings-on for about three minutes, and then the two weird men managed to repair the tear, but before they did, they suddenly noticed Andy, and seemed shocked at him being able to see them. They withdrew into the mind-boggling screen and vanished, but after about fifteen seconds the two balaclava clad heads peeped out the curtain at Andy, and this really unnerved him. He tugged on the sleeve of the old man sitting next to him and said, 'Can you see them?' And he pointed at the heads of the sinister men (which were apparently suspended in mid-air) but the old man just smiled before he started talking to himself again, and he got up off the bench and walked away. Andy turned to look back at the heads of the men but they were gone and everything had returned to normal. These entities – I call them "the Fixers" – have been seen before, as far back as the 1950s and 1960s, and they have also been seen on Back Lime Street. I do not think they are ghosts, but perhaps some maintenance officers who repair the very fabric of space-time. Andy Drake thought he glimpsed prehistoric monsters lurking in that forest that was visible through the 'tear'; imagine the carnage on Church Street if some of the carnivorous dinosaurs had ventured through what seems to have been a rip in time and space. The Fixers are occasionally captured by the cameras of mobile phones and CCTV security cameras and usually interpreted as ghosts, and sometimes they are seen with the naked eye, and when they are spotted they always seem startled. Who employs these Fixers? Some organisation in the future which rectifies faults and weaknesses in the spacetime continuum? I simply do not know, and the strange hybrid Polish-Russian language the Fixers are said to speak only deepens the mystery.

QUANCASS

In the 1970s there was a curious, little-known case of a teenaged arsonist named Terry who was caught with a box of matches and a bottle of paraffin in his possession near an industrial warehouse in Birkenhead. Detectives who were investigating a recent spate of arson attacks across Wirral had watched the youth leave a hardware shop where he had purchased a can of paraffin, and they had also observed him throwing jars filled with petrol (siphoned from cars) the night before on wasteland near the docks. The arsonist had used an ingenious detonator (which I will not describe) which ignited the jars of petrol on impact. The youth was confronted by the police near the warehouse and broke down almost immediately, but he said he didn't want to start any fires – it was Quancass who was making him do it. The police took Terry in and a consultant psychiatrist examined the pyromaniac. The medical man had heard about this "Quancass" before from other arsonists over the years, all in the North West area, and the firebugs all said the same thing: Quancass was some demon in a weird leather mask and glowing eyes who appeared in their dreams and tortured them with fire. He always tied them down on some rack then burned their toes and fingers with something resembling a blowtorch, and sometimes he would train the jet of flame from the tool of torture on the nipples of his victims and they would suffer the most agonizing pain imaginable, often losing consciousness (which seems paradoxical as the victims are already asleep). Whilst inflicting this intense torment, Quancass would make a weird stipulation. 'If you do not burn down a building when you wake, I will burn you alive in your dreams and you shall never wake.'

And sure enough, the terrifying masked torturer would appear in the dreams of his victims on successive nights, subjecting them to all sorts of agonising treatment until the dreamer awoke in agony – and quickly decided to do what the sinister demon in the dream had ordered them to do. There were reports of people who had suffered from these highly lucid nightmares dying in their sleep from heart attacks after crying out for the sadistic demon to stop its savage torture. If one person had experienced these weird dreams, it would be explained away as some mental disorder, but this was the fifth time the psychiatrist had heard about Quancass. The teenaged arsonist Terry was allowed to live at home with his parents under a two-year supervision order, but he subsequently died in his sleep just under a month later after experiencing continual nightmares about the demonic Quancass. The mystery of Quancass ran much deeper than the psychiatrist of that time knew. In the 1990s, a certain Wirral pub was being renovated when a small scroll of parchment was found in a hole in a wooden beam, and written upon this scroll in faded brown ink were the chilling words, 'When you read this you shall be sorry you did because you read the name of Kuancass with the skin of shadow and you shall never be rid of him haha'.

Christine, the wife of the pub landlord, began to have terrible nightmares about a weird figure in a black leather mask with mad-looking eyes. This figure of fear would always tie Christine by rope to a frame made of wrought iron, and then he would burn her toes and fingers with a large red candle. The nightmares were so realistic, Christine would awake screaming in agony, and she ended up staying in the house of a Catholic priest and attended Mass each day in a bid to make the agonizing nightmares end. Meanwhile, back at the pub, the figure from Christine's dreams would appear and terrify the drinkers. The apparition was well over six feet in height, wore a long dark coat and a black leather mask fastened with studs and straps and a 'snout' so it resembled the head of a dog. One report said that this menacing figure wielded an enormous knife. I mentioned the "bogeyman" on a local radio show where I was a guest talking about matters of the supernatural, and the station received many calls from listeners who had allegedly encountered a towering entity in a bizarre leather mask of the type I had described. Over and over I heard of the *modus operandi* of the terrifying figure from listeners. He would invariably appear after dark in places ranging from New Ferry Park to secluded locations in Birkenhead, Bebington, and parts of Liverpool, sometimes sporting a silver pentangle on his chest, and in a whispering voice he would always ask, 'Who is your saviour? The one above or the Lord below?' And if the person the question was addressed to failed to supply an answer or had the composure to say "Above" the tall masked menacing inquisitor would scream and strike the victim with a large machete, but at that precise instant he would vanish, so the blade of the weapon would only inflict psychological damage. The target of the strange attack would also experience a string of nightmares commencing that same night which involved being tortured by fire. The description of the tall attacker matches that of the "Quancass" mentioned by the arsonists – but who or what is Quancass? It is probable that he is a demon, given his mention of the "Lord below" in his strange query – but demons are usually conjured up by someone, perhaps an occultist or Satanist, although it is possible for these beings to take leave of Hell of their own volition sometimes. Quancass seems to have been at large in the North West for centuries, and as recently as 2016, I received a report of a weird exceptionally tall figure in a leather mask who stalked a woman walking her dog in New Ferry Park. She sensed he was evil and made the sign of the cross, and the unearthly figure vanished. The woman described the leather mask of the entity as resembling bondage fetish masks she had seen in films, but the eyes behind the mask looked as if they were luminous and she had the feeling that the thing was not human at all. The woman's dog was ill for days after the incident and would not eat. In response to my brief description of Quancass on the radio programme, a retired policeman named Paul contacted me and said that in March 1981, he and a colleague were on patrol in the city centre of Liverpool at around midnight when they pulled over by the Albert Dock, which was then in a dilapidated state. As Paul had a smoke, his vigilant colleague Darren drew his attention to a figure walking amongst rubble along the quayside of the Albert Dock, and the officers left their vehicle and trained their torches on the figure, which turned out to be a woman in her thirties. She wore a fur coat and a very short skirt, and she was stumbling in high heels as she tried to negotiate the debris and thick weeds on the tumbledown quayside. 'She's on the game – I've seen her before,' said Darren.

'Oh aye,' said Paul in a jokey manner, 'is she cheap?'

The woman came towards the policemen with her arms outstretched, whimpering, and seemingly unable to get her words out because she was in shock.

'Alright love, calm down,' said Darren, grasping her hand, 'what's up?'

'I think I've just seen the Devil!' the prostitute gasped, then started that whimpering again.

'You been drinking or are you high or something?' Paul asked the sex worker and he grabbed her other hand and the policemen led her to their car in an area that was much better lit. Now they could see the tears on the woman's face.

'I – I was with this arl fellah – his car's parked over there,' the woman pointed into the darkness towards the silhouetted hulk of a warehouse, 'and we went over there, where I just came from, and he said he wanted a quickie and we were against one of those thingies – a column – and this thing turned up all in black, with a mask on – a black mask, and we could see his red eyes staring through the holes in the mask and – ' the prostitute started crying.

'Here, do you smoke, girl?' Paul offered her a cigarette from his pack and she nodded as she sniffled and said, 'Oh, thanks!'

Paul lit the cigarette and said, 'Alright, now this

fellah in the mask – is he still there?'

The prostitute shook her head. 'No, he disappeared – like a ghost, just disappeared. He asked the fellah I was with if he believed in God or the Devil, and the fellah said, "Piss off, I'm busy here," and then he struck him – I think it was a knife or a stick, and then he wasn't there!'

'And is the fellah you were with still here?' Darren asked.

The prostitute coughed on the cigarette and nodded. 'He's lying over there – and I swear to god I didn't do it. No one's gonna believe me are they?'

'Come on, show us where he is,' said Paul, grabbing the lady's hand, 'no one's going to accuse you of anything, love. You look as if you couldn't punch a hole in a wet *Echo*.'

The policemen went to the spot the woman directed them to, and there was a white-haired man, perhaps in his late sixties or early seventies, lying unconscious on his side with his penis protruding from his flies. Paul radioed for an ambulance and Darren asked the prostitute where the attacker in the mask came from.

'He just came out of nowhere,' she said, 'from up that way I think,' and she pointed to the Colonnades. Darren stepped over thickets of weeds and fallen masonry and now the moon came out from behind the inky clouds and cast long shadows from the columns lining the quayside. His torchbeam picked out a gaping black doorway in one of the many deserted warehouses, and the policeman went to this doorway and raked the darkness with the beam of the high-powered flashlight – and there on the walls were pentagrams drawn with silver aerosol paint and the words Satan Lives in huge letters. The policeman also saw the stubs of melted candles which had been arranged in a circle, and he had the feeling he was being watched. There was no one about, so Darren returned to his colleague and the traumatised prostitute, and now the old client was sitting up against a large black rusted mooring bollard. His account agreed perfectly with the prostitute's version of events. He had been having intercourse when a man – well over six feet in height – with a black leather mask and a long type of dark trench coat – appeared and said, 'Are you for God or the Devil?'

'I thought it was someone acting the goat, and told them to piss off, I said, "Can't you see I'm busy here you stupid divvy?" and he raised this thing – it looked like a machete – and he brought it down hard, but as the blade touched my right shoulder he vanished, but I thought I felt it go into me, and I fainted, and hit my head on the wall going down. I heard the lady screaming and then I was out of it.'

'There's no sign of anyone up there,' Darren told his colleague, 'not a soul.'

'Look, have I got to be charged for being with her?' the client asked Paul, 'only my wife's disabled and if she knew about all this she's probably have a fit. I've got a heart condition as well.'

'I don't know,' sighed Paul, 'there's a lunatic round here with a machete, so we'll have to report it.'

'Can't you just say I was having a Jimmy riddle here and he attacked me?' the client asked, getting to his feet. The woman of the night helped him up.

'No one is going to take this serious – a man in mask vanishing,' Darren said to Paul. 'We'd be a laughing stock back at the nick.'

Paul thought about the situation and turned to the elderly punter. 'Look, I don't want to ever see you round here or anywhere else. I know you have your needs but keep that thing in your pants, okay?'

'Ah, thanks lad,' said the client, and he held out his hand but Paul gave him a weak handshake and reiterated, 'I mean it; if I see you kerb-crawling I'll take you in.'

'Scouts honour lad, night,' said the unsatisfied customer.

Paul and Darren could not believe their eyes as the man was helped to his car by the prostitute – and then she got in the car with him and he drove away.

The figure who had struck the man at the dock did not give his name as Quancass but he everything else about his behaviour matches that of the demonic being, and this theory is strengthened by Darren's description of the Satanic graffiti and symbols in the deserted dockside warehouse. I have an uneasy feeling I will be hearing more of the enigmatic Quancass in the not-so-distant future...

BACK TO THE CAVERN

Regular readers of my books and newspaper columns will know I've been investigating urban time slips for many years, and although most of them are confined to what I term the "Bold Street Time Fault" there are other parts of the city where there is a noticeable concentration of time slippages, and one such locus is a timeslip I term the Mathew Street Manifold. Instead of going into higher mathematics and the possible relevance of the Friedmann Equations (which would take up many pages and undoubtedly bore most readers), I will relate the following story as an example of the intriguing time-flow deviancy in the Mathew Street area. In 2011, a 54-year-old woman named Mandy visited me after I'd been on a radio station talking about the paranormal in a short fifteen-minute slot. Mandy lived in London and was paying a visit to her home town, and had heard me on her car radio talking about the nature of time slips. Mandy had a very strange story to tell concerning Mathew Street, a place most people associate with the Beatles because they played at the Cavern Club on that street in the early 1960s. One afternoon in October 1979, Mandy – who was then 22 years of age - and her friend Erica were having lunch at the Armadillo Tea Rooms on Mathew Street (where Flanagan's Apple now stands), when a friend of the girls named Chris came in and said he could hear 'ghostly' music outside. Mandy and Erica thought Chris was joking at first, but he insisted that there was a busker strumming a guitar and singing outside in the street but he was not visible. 'He's a bloody ghost, honest,' Chris asserted. Mandy and Erica went outside and they too heard this busker singing as he played an acoustic guitar, but just as Chris had said, this street musician was nowhere to be seen. Mandy identified the song as the old 1966 Chris Farlowe hit, *Out of Time* - written by Mick Jagger and Keith Richards. Chris stepped out the Tea Rooms and said, 'See? Weird isn't it? You'll never find him.'

The three young people walked along Mathew Street and could not locate the busker. A man up a ladder painting a sign overheard the trio and said: 'I heard him yesterday; he was singing that song by what's his name; *Mr Tambourine Man* and it sounded as if he was at the bottom of my ladder, but when I went down he stopped singing. Really odd it was.'

Mandy raised her eyebrows and then she and Erica and Chris returned to the tea rooms. At this time in her life, Mandy was a biker, and she wore a black leather jacket, leather trousers and boots, and with her tall slim figure, long mane of glossy black hair and strikingly beautiful face, she certainly turned heads, but she could be a bit stand offish, and was single, and looking for work. She'd lost her job at a factory in Speke a month back after she had knocked out her boss after he'd criticised her tomboy image and taste for punk rock. Mandy was currently sleeping on the sofa of Erica's flat on Falkner Street, and often disturbed the peace there playing her Sex Pistols records at full blast. The girl had a tough exterior but underneath, Mandy was quite sensitive and held a long-term interest in the occult and the Tarot in particular. Upon this afternoon Mandy and her friend Erica heard the "phantom busker" again and, determined to get to the bottom of the mystery, Mandy went outside to try and find the elusive street performer again. Erica and Chris, meanwhile, were involved in a heated discussion about Ian Dury and the Blockheads with a mutual friend, and none of them noticed Mandy's absence.

On Mathew Street, Mandy let her ears lead her to the source of the unseen busker, who was now singing the old traditional folk song *Greensleeves* in a very soulful voice which echoed down the long grey street. Mandy walked in a laser-straight line to the apparent origin of the singing and strumming, and a curious thing took place; the girl felt as if the music had some hypnotic hold on her mind, and all of the things in her peripheral field of vision faded away so Mandy saw only a fuzzy disc of greyish light before her, as if she was looking down a tubular tunnel filled with swirling fog. One part of the girl's mind told her to snap out of this spell, but the adventurous part of her psyche urged her to go on and pursue this unusual experience. She walked on, and her boots now felt as if they were no longer walking on a solid floor; they were walking on something which felt spongy. She saw the busker now as a silhouette in the strange vapours. He was bit smaller than her by the looks of it – about 5 feet and five inches in height, slim and the shape of his head suggested he had a Beatles cut. A loud beep made the girl jump and she saw the headlamps of an old van to her right.

'Come on dozy drawers!' shouted the young driver, and as Mandy stood there, trying to get her bearings, he popped his head out the driver's window and shouted, 'What are you waiting for? The duration? Move out the way!'

Mandy noticed that it was now almost getting dark. She had walked sixty yards down this narrow street of seven storey warehouses and gone from a chilly grey autumnal lunchtime to a warm evening. The clammy air smelt of petrol fumes and the traceries of smoke. Two young women brushed past Mandy, one with her honey blonde hair piled up into bun whereas the other sported an enormous head of back-combed flaming ginger hair, and both girls wore miniskirts – nine inches above their knees. The impatient van driver tore past Mandy, and she felt the edge of the vehicle's wing mirror scrape the back of her leather jacket. She swore at him, more out of nerves than anger, and the two girls passing by looked her up and down in a condescending manner.

Around this point in time the singing and strumming of the busker faded away, and Mandy could plainly see that she had somehow gone back in time. The vehicles parked in the street looked new, and yet they were vintage, and those girls and the attire of other people in the vicinity screamed the Sixties. Mandy refused to believe she had gone back in time at first; she tried to rationalise what she was seeing; maybe there was a film about the Sixties being shot in the street, or perhaps there was some Beatles convention, but gradually Mandy faced the astounding truth when she left Mathew Street and walked up Whitechapel and then Church Street, and saw that it was the same everywhere; the shops, the people, the vehicles – this was the 1960s, and then with the soaking in of the realisation, Mandy started to panic. How could she get back to 1979? She walked back to Mathew Street, and hoped she would find herself back where she belonged, but nothing happened. She asked two separate people she met on the street what the date was, and they all said the "the twenty-seventh" without specifying the month or year, until Mandy asked the third person, a girl of about eighteen, what year it was, and the teenager seemed puzzled. 'What year is it? I'm not joking, honest,' said Mandy, and the girl replied, '1966, obviously. Strange question.'

'Oh my God,' replied Mandy, and she went to ask the girl what month it was but the teen hurried away, probably thinking Mandy was mentally unhinged.

People do strange things when they are in shock, and for some reason, unbeknownst even to herself Mandy walked into a pub near Mathew Street and a smartly-dressed man around her age immediately noticed her. He saw that Mandy looked confused and worried by something and asked her if he could get her a drink. She nodded, and he said, 'Well, what are you having?'

'Lager, please,' she said, and then she added, 'oh thanks by the way.'

'Where are you from?' the young man asked as he waited for the drink to be pulled, and he looked Mandy up and down.

She told him what had happened – how she'd somehow walked from 1979 to 1966, and the man, who subsequently introduced himself as Roy Connor, seemed to think Mandy was pulling his leg. 'I'm from Garston originally but I've just moved to a flat at the back of Hope Street,' he said, and he passed over the half-pint glass of lager to her and a crowd of rowdy men came into the pub on this Saturday evening of August 27, 1966, so Roy asked Mandy to join him in a quiet corner. There she told him once again what had happened, and she read the look of disbelief in his eyes. 'Look, Roy, I give you my word, I've come from the year 1979; I'm telling the truth; why would I make such a ridiculous story up? And I want to go back, this is scaring me.'

Roy eventually took the mind-boggling claims of Mandy seriously, and he took her to a coffee bar because the Saturday night crowds were pouring into the pub and it was hard to hear the girl speak. Roy asked her what life was like in 1979 and Mandy told him it wasn't all that different from life in 1966. Despite being from different eras, Roy and Mandy got on quite well, and she discovered that he was a Mod who drove a Vespa scooter. Mandy said that she rode a CB400T Honda Dream – a motorbike Roy had never heard of because it would not be produced until 1977. Roy asked Mandy if she'd come to his home on Egypt Street, less than a mile away off Oxford Street. The girl wanted to go back to Mathew Street, hoping she'd somehow return to the sane world of 1979. Roy went with her but nothing happened, and she really started to worry. 'Do you fancy going the Cavern?' Roy asked, sensing the mounting panic in this beautiful girl who had come into his life in such a bizarre way.

'I don't want to go anywhere, I just want to go home,' Mandy replied, and she seemed to be hyperventilating now. She leaned against a wall and gasped for air, and Roy tried his best to reassure her everything would be alright.

He made a serious suggestion. 'The best thing you can have when you're all aeriated like this is ale – or better still, whiskey. Come on Mand, let's go and have a few in the nearest pub. It'll calm you down and I swear everything will turn out fine.'

Mandy smiled at the way he had called her "Mand" – the way her late mum did, all those years away in the future. Paradoxically, she thought she'd better stop thinking of the future and start living in the past. After all, the future was a dark place where she had no job and no roof over her head, and there were one-and-a-half million people out of work. This was the Swinging Sixties and The Beatles were still going. At the pub, Roy asked Mandy what music she was into, and when she mentioned Blondie and the Sex Pistols he was naturally puzzled. He was also taken aback at Mandy's requests for pints of ale instead of the usual half-pint glass measures girls had in those days. After almost an hour, Roy took Mandy to the Cavern, and by then she was quite tipsy. On stage that night at the Cavern Club were Jimmy Paige, founder member of Led Zeppelin, renowned guitarist Vic Flick (probably most famous for twanging the well known *James Bond* guitar riff), and legendary guitarist Albert Lee, and these musicians of note were all backing pop-singer/songwriter Crispian St. Peters, but unfortunately, Mandy does not remember much about this incredible night at the basement venue. All she recalls is asking for a drink and being told by Roy that the Cavern did not have a licence to sell alcohol, so she had to make do with soft drinks. She then recalled being taken up a flight of steps and out onto Mathew Street by Roy and two men before she threw up. Somewhere in the city centre as she walked with Roy, she felt strange, and he kissed her, then gently pushed her against a wall and asked her to come back to his place. And then everything became fuzzy and insubstantial to Mandy, and the times literally changed and she found herself on the School Lane of 1979. Roy was nowhere to be found. She walked in a dizzy state to a telephone call box with her mind trying to take in everything that had happened. Finding she had no money upon her to make a call, Mandy dialled 100 and asked the operator to reverse the charges. She was put through to Erica's flat on Falkner Street, and when Erica accepted the call, she was so relieved to hear Mandy's voice because she had been missing nine hours and Erica, imagining the worst, had even reported her friend's disappearance to the police. Mandy tried to explain what had happened over the phone but Erica told her to wait till she came home, and she went and drove to School Lane to pick Mandy up. Mandy gave her account of what had happened, and Erica was convinced someone had slipped her a "Mickey Finn" – slang for a drink laced with an incapacitating drug – but Mandy was adamant that what she had experienced really had happened. Mandy's other close friend Chris was of the opinion that someone had hypnotised Mandy. 'It is not possible to go back in time,' Chris had told Mandy, 'the past has gone and it's just not possible to go back to something that no longer exists.'

Mandy became really irritated at the sceptical attitudes of her two friends and reminded them how they had both heard that ghostly busker. Mandy was certain that the busker, whoever he was, had somehow caused that timeslip, but Erica and Chris still refused to believe that Mandy had gone back in time thirteen years and had even visited the old Cavern Club which had been long demolished. In the end, Mandy refused to talk about her experience and she wondered where Roy Connor was nowadays; he'd be thirteen years older, unless he had died. I mentioned the name on the Billy Butler Show on BBC Radio Merseyside and a few people recalled several individuals of that name, but they seemed to be different people. One person did recall something intriguing about a Roy "Conner" he knew – his surname spelt differently than what had sounded like "Connor"; this Roy Conner had been a busker from Garston (and the Roy that Mandy had met had said he was from that area of Liverpool), and Roy had been a dabbler in the Occult. What happened to him is unknown, and one person thought he'd emigrated to Canada. Had this Roy somehow opened up a portal in time with his dabbling? I personally don't think so; I have heard of so many timeslip incidents around Mathew Street and I believe the phenomenon is caused by some weakness in the very fabric of the space-time continuum in that area. The busker might simply be some occasional dimensional 'replay' of a street performer from years back. I am told, incidentally that the eerie busker playing *Out of Time* and *Greensleeves* is still occasionally heard...

CHERRIES JUBILEE

It was the evening of Friday 25 January 2013 – a major date in the Caledonian calendar - Burns Night – the Scottish celebration of the life and poetry of the famous bard Robert "Rabbie" Burns – and the MacDonald family was throwing a Burns Night party at their cottage in Raby Mere. There was the usual visceral dish of haggis on the menu of course and the Johnnie Walker and Ballantines Finest Blended whiskies were in full flow. There was dancing and singing (accompanied by bagpipes), but 18-year-old Dickey Riley, who had driven fourteen miles from Kirkdale to the Wirral cottage, had only come to see his beloved 17-year-old girlfriend Rowena - a girl he had met on the Snapchat messaging app. The plan was for the young couple to escape into the January night unnoticed and spend the night together at Dickey's house (while his parents were away) once the whiskey took hold of everyone, which wouldn't be long from now by the looks of things. The MacDonalds and their in-laws numbered forty-five, and at 8.40pm, in the middle of a mild altercation, Dickey and Rowena slipped away from the madding crowd of rowdies and got into Dickey's old Vauxhall Corsa. 'You didn't have a drink did you?' Rowena asked her boyfriend, and she leaned towards him and sniffed the left side of his face.

He smiled and said, 'No, I'm not daft. I've only just passed me driving test – don't want to get pulled for drink-driving do I?'

A thick fog invaded the locality as the car turned into Willaston Road, and Rowena told Dickey to slow down. He wasn't that familiar with the area – having only visited Rowena once before – and that was in daylight. 'So we go straight on and through the roundabout up there don't we?' said Dickey.

'Don't ask me,' Rowena told him, 'haven't you got a SatNav thingy?'

'I've been meaning to get one,' replied her boyfriend, 'but I think I know the way so we'll be okay.'

Somehow, Dickey took the wrong exit on the roundabout and the fog was so thick he almost ran into the back of a van. Rowena screamed for him to slow down. 'Are we lost?' she asked. Dickey didn't reply. 'Dickey, I think you've taken a wrong turn somewhere,' laughed Rowena, looking out the side window, 'because we've just gone over that bridge – the one that goes over the M53. You've sort of gone like that,' she said, thrusting the back of her hand in front of his face, 'instead of that way.'

'A minute, Rowena,' said an annoyed Dickey, and he tried to read a roadsign through the jade fog. 'I think that said Thornton Common Road,' he murmured, 'that looks familiar.'

'Oh God, we're miles off course,' Rowena groaned, and the Corsa crawled along through the fog for a few minutes – then hit someone. It was an old white-haired man, and Rowena screamed as he rolled across the bonnet and fell into the roadside ditch. She and Dickey got out, and the man assured them he was alright, and got up in a sprightly manner, but he limped away, so the young couple went after him and said they'd help him home. He pointed to the hulking silhouette of a large detached house about fifty yards away. The diffused disk of a moon that was almost full glowed above the roof through the thick night mist.

'Are you sure you're alright?' Rowena asked the elderly man, 'Only I've heard of people dying from shock hours after they were knocked down.'

'Rowena! Will you put a sock in it?' Dickey glared, and his eyebrows squirmed about as anxiety coursed through his nervous system.

'I'm fine, really I am,' the old man told Rowena in a reassuring voice, and he took hold of her hand, lifted it to his mouth, and kissed her knuckles.

The three of them walked up seven broad stone steps and the old man slammed down the knocker on the door three times. Within seconds the door was answered by a middle-aged spectacled lady in a dark blue cardigan, black knee-length skirt baggy-looking tights and a pair of shiny Mary Jane shoes. 'Oh, Alfred, what have you done this time?' she asked in a well-spoken but rather loud voice.

'We accidentally knocked him down,' said a timid Rowena, and a worried Dickey added, 'because he just walked in front of the car. In the fog. I was only doing about fifteen miles an hour.'

'Oh dear, come in all of you,' said the woman, smiling as she beckoned Alfred and the young couple indoors. 'He's a bloody nuisance. I only realised he'd sneaked out a few minutes ago.'

'We really must be going,' said Rowena but the woman just bolted the door, then introduced herself as

Mrs Bestelle, spelling out her surname. She ushered the reluctant guests through the vestibule area, across the chequerboard-tiled hall, and down a green-carpeted oak-panelled corridor to a high-ceilinged room, where Alfred ran to a long dining table that had been set for seven. He seized a dessert spoon. 'Cherries Jubilee!' Alfred cried. His eyes narrowed as he grinned and he licked his lips.

'We really can't stay,' said Rowena, but Mrs Bestelle started humming a tune and almost pushed the couple to the table and dragged out two chairs for them. She left the room, closing the door behind her, and a chandelier lit up above the table. Rowena whispered to Dickey: 'I think she's got a screw loose; let's just leave.'

Rowena then screamed as Alfred's head appeared between her legs under the table. He smiled and with his hands gripping her thighs he hauled himself up with the fall of the tablecloth over his head, and rested his face on Rowena's bosom. He pursed his lips and made a sucking sound as if he was imitating a suckling baby.

'Hey! Get off her!' Dickey protested, and he tried to drag the brazen old man off his girlfriend.

Mrs Bestelle barged into the room, dragged Alfred off the guest and slapped his face, before marching him back to his seat. She apologised to Rowena, and said, 'They're all – well – not right in the head in here. I look after them. The others are in bed. It's been a long day I can tell you.'

She then left the room, and a minute later a hatch opened at the far end of the dining room and Alfred rushed to it and came back to the table with a silver serving dome. He placed it in the centre of the table, and then Mrs Bestelle came in and lifted the cover, grabbed a ladle, and gleefully announced, 'Cherries Jubilee!' It looked like a mound of ice cream covered in red sauce. As Bestelle served Rowena and Dickey she explained how the dessert of cherries and a liqueur had been a favourite of Queen Victoria. The guests were very wary of the 'treat' and gingerly tasted the ice cream dessert. Rowena thought there was a salty undertaste to it. Alfred ate his serving quickly, and Mrs Bestelle came in, picked up the serving dome and headed for the door, tutting. Alfred cried like a baby and chased after her.

'Let's just go,' Dickey said to Rowena, and she nodded, and replied, 'What a creepy place this is.'

As the couple stood, Mrs Bestelle's head appeared at the hatchway at the end of the room and she shouted, 'More cherries jubilee?'

'Ah, no thanks, we've really got to go!' Rowena yelled back, but the idiosyncratic host beckoned her, so Rowena and Dickey went to the hatchway.

'Cherries Jubilee?' Bestelle asked again, and she held a bloody carving knife. On the silver tray, resting on the dessert, was the severed head of Alfred, and his eyes were rolled back, and blood was still oozing out of the newly-sliced arteries of his neck stump, mingling with the ice cream and sauce.

The couple do not remember leaving the dining room, just the utter panic at trying to undo the bolts of the front door as they heard Mrs Bestelle screeching with maniacal laughter as she hurried down the corridor – with that knife in her hand.

The door was opened just in time and Rowena and Dickey ran down the seven steps to the car, and

Rowena felt a weakness in her knees as she gasped for breath. The young couple got into the car, unaware if they were still being chased, and then the car wouldn't start. Dickey swore and tried the ignition again, and the Corsa's engine thrummed. Without belting up, he drove off blindly in a screech. Dickey kept asking his girlfriend, 'Are you alright?' as she cried. Some five minutes elapsed and the couple were startled by the frantic beeping of a car horn behind the Corsa. The woman in the vehicle had glasses on – but as this impatient motorist overtook Dickey and Rowena, they saw that she had blonde hair and was *not* the murderess Mrs Bestelle.

Rowena reported the terrifying incident to the police in Liverpool – but no such house could be found anyway near the spot the couple specified – on a long lane close to Thornton Common Road. In the summer of 2014, Dickey and Rowena went in search of the mysterious house of murder, but could not find it. Then something took place that sent cold shivers down the spine of the couple on that blazing hot day. Dickey was turning a corner on Poluton Hall Road, when that same old man - Alfred – came out of nowhere. The Corsa hit him and he was thrown by the impact into a roadside hedge. It was definitely him because he quickly got to his feet and looked in at Rowena with a lopsided grin. He made a sucking gesture with his lips – the way he had when he had mimicked suckling her that night at that house – but the young lady screamed, and Dickey tore off in the car, leaving the figure standing. So, it was obvious that he was some ghost; he simply could not have survived that decapitation. Was Mrs Bestelle also a ghost, along with the people she 'looked after' – and even the house itself? Rowena and Dicky are now married and live up in Southport, and they have vowed to never again go anywhere near the site of that baffling and gruesome haunting.

WHISTON'S GHOSTLY
PINK BRIDE

On the chilly Monday night of 13 February 2006 a 30-year-old Hackney driver named Lewis Missenden was flagged down in his vehicle on Berry Street by a young lady who was dressed in what looked like a pink wedding gown. The time was fast approaching midnight when Missenden pulled up and remotely unlocked the passenger door. The brunette got in smiling and slammed the door rather hard before almost falling onto the seat. 'Wait a moment while I get my bearings – I'm a bit tipsy,' she said in a well-spoken voice, and she giggled, then seemed to recall the destination as her eyebrows rose. She said, 'Windy Arbor Road please. Do you know where that is?'

'Yeah, I used to live up near Whiston,' said Lewis Missenden, turning on the meter, 'had a nice night?'

'Oh yes,' said the passenger, and she gripped an eyelash between her finger and thumb and grumbled something unintelligible as she gently tugged on it. As the cab moved off the inertia pushed the girl back into the seat with a jerk and she gave up trying to extract the troublesome eyelash.

'Where've you been – if you don't mind me asking,' said Missenden, trying to make pleasant conversation.

'Flintlocks – it's a cracker club, real friendly people,' said the young lady.

'Flintlocks? Never heard of it, but there are so many clubs sprouting up nowadays, it's hard to keep track of them,' said the driver. 'Is that a wedding gown you've got on?'

The girl suddenly looked at the floor of the hackney and stopped smiling. She said nothing. Lewis Missenden realised he'd somehow upset the girl with his query so he changed the subject quickly. 'Been following the Winter Olympics?' he asked.

The woman continued to look down with a sad expression. Lewis got the message – the passenger didn't want to talk, so he put the radio on, and not a word was spoken between the driver and the passenger during the twenty-five minutes of that nine-mile journey. As the Hackney cab reached Windy Arbor Road, Lewis turned on his intercom and asked, 'Where about, love?'

'Just a bit further along by St Nick's Church up there,' said the girl, and a minute later she shouted: 'Just here will do!'

The girl got out the cab, and Lewis leaned over to the kerbside window, ready to tell her how much the fare was – when the lady ran the couple of feet towards the low wall surrounding the cemetery of St Nicholas – and jumped over it. The moon was full that night, and Lewis clearly saw the girl literally vanish as she landed on the other side of the wall. He got out of his taxi, walked in a state of shock to the two-foot-tall wall, and surveyed the moonlit cemetery. The girl was nowhere to be seen. At first he desperately tried to rationalise the incident by imagining that she had been some very agile fare-dodger, but he slowly admitted to himself that he had given a lift to a ghost in his hackney, and he felt as if that ghost was watching him. He quickly got back into the cab and went to an all-night café in south Liverpool that was frequented by other cabbies, and here over a black coffee and a microwaved pork pie, he told his story of the 'pink bride' to an older taxi driver named Ian.

'Tony Mack had her in his cab about two or three years ago,' Ian casually told Lewis, who returned a suspicious glance.

'You winding me up?' the younger cabby asked.

Ian slowly shook his head as he read the tabloid spread out before him on the formica table top. 'I twigged when you mentioned Flintlocks; that place closed years ago. Used to be on Wood Street. And if my memory serves me I think it was Valentine's Day when she got in Tony Mack's cab. I've got his number here.'

Ian called Tony on his mobile and handed it to Lewis, and the latter told Tony what had happened, and Tony said the passenger had been brunette, hair styled in a bun, and had worn a type of pink wedding dress with a small train. She had run into St Nick's cemetery. All these facts matched the lady who had sprung from Lewis's cab and vanished.

The news of Lewis Missenden's encounter with the ghost spread quickly through the local community of taxi drivers, and a retired cabby named Hughie Dennis got in touch with Lewis through a mutual friend. Hughie said that in February 1978 he had picked up a girl in town near Bold Street one night, around midnight, and she had worn a long pink diaphanous dress, and the apparel reminded Hughie of a wedding dress. The girl was of slim build, about 5 feet 3 inches in height, and had dark hair done up in a bun. Hughie even recalled that this girl's eyes were of a pale blue. She had asked to be taken to Windy Arbor Road, and she had said something about having had a great night out, but as the cab went along Upper Duke Street, the girl leaned sideways and became silent, and Hughie initially thought she had dozed off because of drink, but when he took a good look at her in the rear view mirror he saw that her eyes were wide open. He also detected a very sweet scent of something akin to lavender in the cab at this point, but naturally assumed it was some perfume the girl was wearing. Hughie asked her if she was okay and she said nothing until reaching Windy Arbor Road, where she suddenly shouted: 'Just here will do!'

Hughie pulled over in front of a large detached house next door to St Nicholas, and presumed this was where the girl lived, and when she got out the car she slammed the door, turned right and Hughie Dennis wound down the nearside window, expecting the passenger to pay the fare, but she suddenly started running north, parallel to the road, and so the cabby drove after her, and after she had covered around fifty yards, the young lady jumped over the low wall of the church cemetery – and vanished. The moon was not full that night – it was in its first quarter and had just set, so the cemetery was cloaked in darkness. Hughie hurried back to his cab, grabbed his torch, and went back to the wall of the cemetery and swept the beam of the flashlight across the rows of marble and granite headstones. The luminous eyes of a cat reflected back the light, but beyond that feline there was no other living soul about. Hughie wondered if the girl was hiding behind one of the gravestones, and although this was not an impossibility, the possibility that there was something *supernatural* about the fare-dodger suddenly arose in his mind, and he returned to his hackney cab and went back to Liverpool.

I mentioned the case on a local radio programme and received lots of feedback on the ghostly girl in the pink dress. Many of those who contacted me claimed the solid-looking carnate phantom has been hailing cabs since around 1977, but so far, I have not been able to identify her. I assume she's buried in the hallowed ground of St Nicholas' Church. I have a feeling someone out there probably knows the sad story behind the pink bride of Whiston.

OVER AND OVER

The ghost featured in the previous chapter is an excellent example of a re-enactment ghost – an entity that does the same thing over and over. These types of ghost seem to be stuck in a kind of behavioural groove with very little variation to their haunting routine; they perform in a rigid clockwork manner, going through the same motions at the same time, sometimes once a month or upon a certain date, year in year out. On some occasions a medium might confront the ghost and try to break its obsessive-compulsive disorder by telling the entity that it no longer has to carry out its habitual ritual. This chapter is concerned with five of these ghosts that do the same thing over and over.

In October 1973, a 59-year-old Halewood window cleaner named Sid Parker was reading through a local newspaper when he noticed a very interesting offer in the Businesses for Sale section. The advert read: Laundrette for Sale in Huyton; superbly built and well-equipped, established 1960. Good clientele, promising catchment area. Quick sale due to owner's business interests elsewhere. £5000 o.n.o.

A phone number was given in the ad – which Sid circled with a red-ink biro. He discussed it with his wife, Betty, and she thought it could be a risky venture as more and more people were buying washing machines, but Sid eventually persuaded her to give the business a try. He was good at haggling and he managed to get the laundrette for £3500. Sid had recently been diagnosed with an inner ear condition that was giving him vertigo so he was only too glad to pack in his window cleaning job. Betty gave up her part-time job as a cleaner and Sid's brother – a professional decorator – did the laundrette up with a new lick of paint. Betty's cousin Frank was a qualified time-served mechanical engineer and he had a look at the washers and dryers and said they were all in good working order. On the first day of business only three customers used the place, so Sid made plans to advertise the Huyton laundrette in the local newspapers. Just before the laundrette was about to close, at 11pm that night, Sid glanced out the window at the full moon, when a tall and very pretty blonde girl who looked about twenty years of age dashed into the laundrette and started to cry. She had her hair done up in a high ponytail and Sid and Betty thought her short sleeveless dress and calf-length boots harked back to the fashion of the Sixties.

'I've been in a car crash!' the girl told the couple in an excited state, and then she began to sob.

'I'll phone for an ambulance,' said Sid, 'just sit her down love,' he told his wife, but the young lady wouldn't sit down and could not be consoled. Then something very strange took place: bloodstains started to blossom in the girl's dress, and as the distressed youth noticed the spreading stains, she screamed and then she began to take her clothes off. Betty watched in shock as she saw that even the girl's underwear was soaked in blood, and the apparently injured lady opened the door of a washing machine and threw the clothes in, saying, 'I'll be alright! I'll wash it all out! It's just on the clothes!'

And then she literally vanished into thin air. In a state of shock, Sid looked in the washer, expecting to see the bloodied dress – but it was empty. He and Betty realised that a ghost had paid a visit, and when the ambulance turned up at the laundrette, Sid found he had some explaining to do – and his account of the vanishing blood-soaked girl was not received well by the fuming ambulance men. Sid was asked if he had been drinking.

That same girl appeared at the Laundrette a month later on November 10 – again during the night of a full moon, but upon this occasion Sid closed the door on the ghost, and she stood there looking through the window with her mascara running down her face as she cried, and then she vanished. Sid went to see his reverend, and he seemed to think the whole affair was some hoax staged by someone with a macabre sense of humour, so Betty, who was a Catholic, went to see her priest, and he said, 'It sounds like an earthbound ghost. She needs prayers.' He said he'd dedicate a Mass to the troubled ghost, and he also promised he'd pay a visit to bless the laundrette, and this he did. However, on 10 December that year, there was another full moon, and this time the girl called in much earlier – around 8.30pm, and in front of seven customers, she burst into tears and said she'd been in a car crash – and blood trickled down her nose and from her ears, and then bloodstains began to spread out from the injuries under her dress. Blood which spurted from the girl's nose dripped onto the floor.

'No! In the name of God, you will go to your Maker!' Betty yelled at the ghost, which reacted by looking up at the full moon outside with a blank expression. The startled customers then looked on as Betty continued her spur-of-the-moment exorcism. 'You died a long time ago and have no business to trouble the living! Depart spirit – and stay away!'

The ghost closed its eyes, smiled, whispered what sounded like, 'Thanks - Amen,' and vanished. Two customers ran out the laundrette, never to return. Sid was later told by a local Huytonian that the ghost was that of a girl from Bakers Green Road, Huyton, who had suffered horrific injuries in a car driven by her boyfriend when it had collided with a tree. The girl crawled out the wreckage and staggered into the laundrette in shock after the crash, bleeding to death, and tried to take her clothes off, thinking she'd be okay if she washed them. And then she had dropped dead from severe internal bleeding. The crash had occurred on the night of a full moon in the early 1960s, and every few years the ghost of the tragic girl would go through the motions of that terrible night and visit the laundrette. In the end the owner put the laundrette up for sale as people kept away because of the ghost. We next move forward in time eleven years from Huyton to Liverpool city centre to chronicle another repetitive ghost.

In 1984, a 16-year-old Tuebrook school-leaver named Tracey Cartwright was given a placement - via the Youth Training Scheme – at a well-known shoe store in Liverpool's Church Street where – according to Tracey's Careers Officer - she would undergo twelve months of on-the-job training and - in addition to receiving £27.50 a week – she'd acquire practical work experience; in this case, selling shoes. On the first day at the shoe shop, Tracey was put in the stockroom to sort out hundreds of boxes – many of which had gathered dust for ten years. The teenager started at 9am and an older member of staff named Sandra came in at eleven with a soft drink, a Kit Kat and the latest copy of *My Guy* magazine. 'Have a little break for twenty minutes love,' said Sandra, and she stooped down and picked up a dusty shoebox with a peculiar look on her face. Tracey thought the woman looked very edgy all of a sudden. Sandra opened the shoebox, which had a yellowed label upon it which read: 'H. & M. Rayne – size 6 black suede court shoes'. 'I didn't know we still had these,' Sandra was heard to mutter, and she gingerly removed the elegant court shoes from the box. Tracey noticed that the shoes had the Royal Warrant sign of approval in gold on their soles – a sure sign of quality. A cold draught from nowhere suddenly chilled the two females, and Tracey shuddered as she felt an icy jolt up her spine. 'Ooh!' she said, 'What was that?'

'Someone just walk over your grave?' joked the observant mullet-headed manager, standing in the doorway, startling the two ladies. 'Can I talk to you a mo, Sandra?' he asked his top employee and Sandra left, closing the door behind her.

Tracey was now alone in the stock room.

Five minutes passed, and Tracey saw someone's shadow to her left. She turned to see a tall beautiful woman with a huge helmet of black glossy hair in a long pink dress – and she was barefooted. In a well-spoken voice the woman – who looked about 25 – said: 'They're *my* shoes.'

'Oh,' was all that Tracey could utter. She initially wondered how the woman had come into the stockroom because the door was closed, but then Tracey had a sneaking suspicion that the visitor was a ghost. The lady put on the old suede court shoes, smiled, and sighed. She turned and walked to a badly-lit corner of the room – and vanished, along with the shoes.

Tracey ran out the room and told Sandra what had happened. She learned from Sandra that in 1974, a woman who was due to collect the shoes before she went to a party, had been knocked down and killed. Her barefooted ghost then started to turn up at the shop almost every week – sometimes in full of view of customers but also in the stock room - and it always asked for the Miss Rayne shoes. The manager tried to send the shoes back but they were mislaid – until today, when Tracey had found them. Tracey immediately left the shop and got a placement with TJ Hughes on London Road.

And now for a very strange tale about a persecuting ghost that did the same thing over and over, but before I tell you about it, I must digress for a moment to say I'm intrigued how some people die and are heard from no more. They do not give the slightest indication from beyond the grave or crematorium incinerator that they are still there, surviving in spirit form – even to the closest loved ones who have been left behind with shattered lives. And then there are cases I have investigated where the apparent spirits of the departed have haunted complete strangers, and these person-centred hauntings can be the most frightening. There was a case many years ago in Victorian Neston where a well-dressed but unusually small boy of about five approached a policeman in tears, saying he couldn't find his mama. The hysterical child calmed down a little as the policeman asked him his name. 'My name is Johnnie Jinty,' the boy replied in a well spoken voice.

The policeman smiled and stooped to look at the tearful lad. 'Well Johnnie, you have an unusual surname, so we'll soon find your mother.' The constable offered his hand to the boy and said, 'Let's go to the station.'

'May I have a piggyback?' the tiny boy asked, then sucked his thumb.

The policeman crouched and said, 'Ha! Come on then, laddie!' The boy climbed up his back and sat on the lawman's shoulders with his little hands gripping the helmet. When the policeman reached the station, he realised the boy was some sort of ghost, because he was now invisible and yet he could feel his slight weight on his shoulders and could hear him giggling. Try as he may, the police officer could not remove the clinging boy from his shoulders. No one at the police station could see or hear the child and the policeman ended up being seen by a Dr Russell, who diagnosed the 'phantom piggyback boy' as a symptom of *Dementia praecox* – a long-defunct term for what we now know as schizophrenia. The policeman was dismissed from the force and only 'regained his sanity' two years later when the boy climbed down and left him. Many of the older folk of Neston claimed Johnnie Jinty was some sort of demon or ghost who'd been encountered in the area for years, but whatever the entity was, it is typical of a person-centred haunting. In the last case, the being was unknown to the persecuted victim, but in the following account, the supernatural entity was well-known to the person it continually harassed – it was a former best friend. In 1960, two best friends Danny and John – both aged eighteen – were passengers in a car driven by Danny's father when it crashed, not far from Birkenhead Park. The driver almost escaped without a scratch but the teenagers were badly injured, and Danny later died from his injuries. About a week after Danny's funeral, his grotesque-looking ghost started visiting John in his bedroom. On the first visitation, Danny appeared as John was listening to his pop records, and the apparition wore the same black blazer, polo neck sweater and drainpipe trousers Danny had worn on the day of the crash, and his raven hair sported the same Brylcreem quiff – but his face, which had been so handsome, was almost the face of a skull, and his blue eyes stood out starkly in their black sockets. The ghost said: 'John, I've come back because of our blood brother oath – remember?'

Danny was referring to the day when both friends were 14. Danny first cut John's palm with a penknife then cut his own palm and they shook hands so their blood would mingle and by that ritual they would become bonded brothers forever.

'Danny – you're – you're dead,' gasped John, trembling as he backed into the record player. The needle got stuck in the groove of the single which was appropriately *Shakin' All Over* by Johnny Kidd and the Pirates. John fled from the bedroom and when he told his parents about Danny's ghost they thought he had imagined it because he was still upset over the loss of his best friend. But Danny visited night and day and followed John everywhere he went, and no one but John could see him. Danny didn't want his friend to have a girlfriend so whenever John would start seeing a girl, Danny would always appear and stroke the girl's neck and she'd scream after she experienced an icy sensation. Danny also claimed he could cause serious diseases in these girls just by touching them. By December 1963, things reached a head with this unearthly situation. John met a beautiful girl of eighteen named Rose, and John just knew she was *the* one. He warned "Dead Danny" as he mockingly called his deceased and obsessed friend that he'd tell a priest about him if he came anywhere near Rose – but on the first proper date with Rose at a Birkenhead pub, John was shocked to see Danny appear. The persecuting ghost sat behind Rose and put his hand on her shoulder and the girl said, 'Ooh! Just felt a cold shiver – like someone walked over my grave.'

'Let's go over by the fireplace, love,' said John, and he led rose away from his jealous dead 'friend'. On the following day John visited the priest of his church – a man who had known Danny – and he told him everything. The priest dedicated several Masses to 'moving Danny on' and the ghost paid a final visit to John in tears, apologised for wanting to stay with him, then vanished, never to return.

And now we turn to ghost of habit who seems to have been doing the same thing for quite some time, but unlike Dead Danny, this ghost is exceedingly benevolent and considerate.

In November 1961, a struggling 32-year-old poet named Stanley received another rejection letter from a London publisher, along with his returned manuscript. 'Philistines!' he seethed, then decided to end it all. He climbed out the skylight of his attic flat on Mount Street, and being terrified of heights, Stanley felt dizzy when he looked towards the Liver Birds in the distance, silvered under a full moon. He crawled on all fours across the roof, when the skylight of his neighbour opened, and an old man with a smiling face said, 'Beautiful night, isn't it? Look at those stars and that moon.'

'*I'll* never see them again, I'm going to jump,' Stanley replied, and he stood up and clung to a chimney stack. He told the old man how he had given up his job in the post office a year ago so he could write poetry full time, but no one would publish his work and now his savings were running out – so he'd decided it wasn't worth going on, and then a tearful Stanley added, 'I'm a failure – I was born to lose; everything I do ends in disaster!'

'They that fall today may rise tomorrow,' said the old man, 'and I foresee great things for you.'

'You're just saying that so I won't jump,' sulked Stanley.

The man shook his head and said: 'No, I've got second sight, and I can see you writing with a golden-haired lady. You'll make a fortune with her.'

'I write alone, so you're wrong,' Stanley replied, 'and now it's goodbye from me!'

Stanley let go of the chimney, and suffered a severe spell of dizziness. He swayed back and forth, cried out, 'Oh!' then fell backwards through the open skylight, landed on the bed in his attic and burst into tears – and then one of the legs of the bed broke and the budding suicide fell out the bed and rolled into the bottom of an over-stacked bookshelf – which then toppled on top of him. Stanley lay there, buried under volumes of Shakespeare, Keats, Larkin and Wordsworth, and he sobbed his heart out. There was a loud click from the electricity meter. The electricity had run out. The feeble light bulb and the one-bar electric fire died, leaving the room lit by the moon. 'I hate you, life! Piss off reality!' Stanley screamed. He threw a thick tome of modern poetry through the open skylight above, and a moment later he heard a thud, followed by an agonized cry and a distant female voice saying, 'Are you alright love?'

Three days later on a Saturday night, Stanley half-heartedly decided he'd jump in the Mersey, and headed for the Pier Head. Surely nothing could go wrong this time? He wondered. It was just a simple case of jumping into freezing waters, the shock making you incapable of breathing, and then going to sleep under the waves. He left his flat on Mount Street, patted the head of a stray cat he often fed, saying, 'Goodbye little friend, you won't see me again.'

The cat purred, rubbed its face against his shin, and followed him as far as Bold Street, where a teary-eyed Stanley had to shout, 'Go on! Beat it! You can't go where I'm going!'

The cat ran off into the night. The night life of the city centre went on as usual; young couples passed Stanley laughing and some held hands with eyes full of contentment. Swaggering beer-fuelled young men deliberately bumped into Stanley as he shuffled along, head bowed. With each step along Bold Street on his way to the appointment with death, Stanley thought of the rejection letters. 'They'll soon publish me when I'm dead though,' he whispered to himself, all choked up, 'posthumous fame, like Van Gogh and Emily Dickinson! They don't deserve creative people like us!'

At the bottom of Bold Street Stanley saw a car with two girls pull up, and one of the girls – a very pretty blonde – wound down the passenger window and shouted, 'Can you direct me to Mount Street?'

An old man with a familiar voice said to her, 'I'm sure that gentleman there can direct you.' It was the old man who had talked to Stanley from the skylight on the night he had tried to jump off the roof, and he was dressed in a very smart pinstriped suit. Stanley gave directions to the girl – Jenny – and she explained she was a student looking for a flat on Mount Street that had been advertised in the *Liverpool Echo*.

'I live there – Mount Street – small world,' said Stanley.

'So we just continue up that road over there and turn – did you say left?' Jenny asked.

Her friend Gail, who was at the wheel of the car, corrected her. 'Right,' she said.

'Do you want me to show you exactly how to get there?' asked Stanley with a smile, tentatively reaching for the handle of the car's rear door.

'Oh could you?' said Jenny.

Stanley got into the car and directed them to Mount Street, and on the way, Jenny explained that, although she was an art and fashion student, she was also into writing poetry, and hoped to be published one day.

'Me too!' said Stanley, his eyes aglow with glee.

It turned out that the flat Jenny and Gail were after was under the one Stanley lived in. Stanley really hit it off with Jenny. They loved the same poets, wrote similar verses, and had even been rejected by the same publishing houses. They often went to the local pub Ye Cracke and penned poems together over a drink, and within two years Stanley and Jenny made a fortune writing above-average verses for greetings cards and even lyrics for a few songs. That old man's prophecy came true – but when Stanley went to thank him, he found his flat empty and discovered from an old neighbour that it had been unoccupied for seven years. Furthermore, the elderly neighbour said the man – a Mr Johnson is all she knew him as – had been seen by various people at large in the city after his death as a very solid-looking ghost. I mentioned this mysterious old helper on a local radio programme dedicated to Liverpool mysteries of a paranormal nature, and quite a few people called in and said they had either encountered his ghost or heard about his post-death activities – and all of the accounts were in agreement about him being a very helpful ghost. He's said to have comforted a man who was trapped in a crashed car on Hardman Street in the early hours of a bitter winter morning and even called for an ambulance, and in the 1970s a woman who was not familiar with Liverpool left her train at Lime Street one night and became lost in a fog as she searched for her brother's flat on Huskisson Street. Two men approached the woman demanding money when the ghost of old Mr Johnson appeared and told the woman he'd just called the police. The ghost then led the woman to her brother's address on Huskisson Street and was seen to vanish.

One of the later stories concerning Mr Johnson happened in broad daylight one summer afternoon in 1982. A couple in their thirties – a Mr and Mrs Wilcox - were out for the day in the city centre with their three children. Mr Wilcox had lost his job the year before and was still looking for work (such was the crushing effects of the recession), and his wife had just been made redundant. With a mortgage and the usual various bills to pay, the couple had very little money, and on this day as the Wilcoxes headed for the bus stop on Leece Street, they walked along Bold Street when the youngest of the family, a boy of five, saw a certain toy in a shop window. He went into the shop and his brothers followed him, and the couple rushed into the shop to tell the children they must never sneak away like that. The boys were enthralled by the latest toys in the shop, and they begged their parents to get them these toys. Mr Wilcox felt his heart break, as he and his wife had barely enough for the bus fares home to Netherley.

'Put that back!' Mrs Wilcox told her youngest son. He had hold of a huge box containing a two-foot-tall robot.

'Dad, can't we even have a Frisbee please?' asked another son, aged nine.

'Oi! Could you be careful with those, please?' said the man behind the counter, eyeing the Lego Train Set box the oldest son of the Wilcoxes had picked up. The boy was spellbound by the pictures on the box and never heard the shop owner.

An old man suddenly entered the shop. He was dressed in a smart dark blue blazer, grey trousers and polished black shoes. He smiled at Mr and Mrs

Wilcox, and patted the youngest boy on the head before walking to the counter. The reaction of the shopkeeper was very strange. Mr and Mrs Wilcox saw that he seemed to be in complete shock at the sight of the old man as he approached the counter. The old man said to the shop owner: 'You've got a very short memory haven't you? Remember when you were like these lovely people here? You were very poor and you had many children. Remember?'

'Yes Mr Johnson,' gasped the shopkeeper, as if he was retrieving some traumatic memory.

Mr Wilcox was a proud man who did not care for someone referring to him and his family as poor, and as he told the children to leave the store, his wife let out a yelp.

The old man had vanished before her eyes. He had looked at her, smiled, then he quickly faded away whilst still maintaining eye contact.

The shop keeper lifted a hinged section of the counter and rushed to the Wilcoxes, saying, 'Wait! Take this bike for him!' And he pointed at the oldest son. 'And take the Lego Train set, and this robot as well – and this!' he went on, picking up boxes and giving them to the bewildered children.

'I can't pay for any of this,' said a confused Mr Wilcox, 'I haven't got a light!'

'No sir, it's all free, just let the kids take them, please!' the shopkeeper told Mr Wilcox.

How had the ghost motivated the shopkeeper to give these toys, some of them fairly expensive, to the children of the Wilcoxes? I don't know, but it's as if Mr Johnson had somehow pricked the conscience of the retailer by perhaps reminding him of some emotional memory from his younger days.

I wonder if Mr Johnson is still doing his good turns from beyond the grave in these days of inhumane austerity.

When a doctor tells you about something inexplicable that happened to him, you tend – perhaps unfairly - to give him more credence than you normally would to an 'average' person, as doctors are – on the whole – level-headed people who are not predisposed to flights of fancy. I've had to change a few details in the following strange account, which seems to fly in the face of reason. On the Wednesday evening of February 9, 1966 at half-past seven, 35-year-old Dr Harvey Richards was at his Queen's Drive home in Childwall, helping his 10-year-old son Gareth with his maths homework when there was a frantic hammering at the front door. Dr Richards answered and saw a man of about thirty with red hair. His face was streaked with blood coming from gashes in his forehead. He seemed confused and dazed, and panted out something. To the doctor's ears it sounded as if he was referring to a person named Hugh. The man gasped out the words, as if he had been running. He said: 'It's Hugh! It's Hugh! Hugh – died!'

The man then said something barely intelligible about a crash and turned before hurrying away. Dr Richards ran after him, assuming the man was in shock after being involved in a car crash. The doctor followed the injured man over two-hundred yards to Childwall Priory Road, near to the Fiveways pub – and here, the red-headed man seemed to vanish into thin air. He was there one moment - when Dr Richards apologised to a young lady he'd run into, but when he looked back to the direction where the distressed man had been – there was no one there. Harvey Richards searched for the ginger-haired man in vain, then trotted home, baffled by the incident. The physician told his wife Moira what had happened and she said it could have been someone who was either carrying out some prank – or perhaps a con-trick to draw him from the house so an accomplice could burgle it. Harvey said he felt as if there was more to it than those explanations – but when his wife asked him what he meant, the doctor just shook his head and said, 'I'm not sure myself.'

Exactly a week later, again at 7.30pm, the doctor was chatting to his wife (who was preparing dinner) in the kitchen about the plans for his mother's forthcoming birthday party when there was a succession of heavy knocks at the front door.

'Who's calling at this hour?' Dr Harvey sighed as he left the kitchen and crossed the hall. He answered – and was exceedingly surprised to see the same red-headed man he'd seen last Wednesday. Again his face was dripping with blood.

'You again?' the doctor gasped in surprise. He suspected those crimson streaks on the caller's face of being Kensington Gore – theatrical blood! What *was* this clown's game? The doctor wondered, and he gritted his teeth and closed his hand, making a fist that he was ready to launch into the face of this joker.

'It's Hugh! Hugh died!' he said, and this time Mrs Richards saw the red-haired man as she came hurrying across the hallway to the sound of the raised voices. As the man ran off, Dr Richards turned to his wife and said, 'Close the door after me in case this is a con-trick!' and then he raced after the oddball caller, and this time he saw him fade away by the Fiveways pub, which shocked him. He turned around and slowly walked to his house, unable to diagnose the cause of this phenomenon. The doctor dealt with things in the real world – literally flesh and blood problems and materialistic matters pertaining to the living – but this reoccurrence of last Wednesday's events simply confounded the medical man. If his wife had not seen the caller he would have doubted his own sanity and booked himself an appointment with a psychiatrist. As the doctor neared his home, he saw his wife and son at the gate, watching him. 'He vanished again – into thin air,' Dr Richards told an anxious-looking Moira, and his son, puzzled at his father's words, asked, 'You mean disappeared like a magician?'

Dr Richards said nothing. He didn't want to give his son nightmares. Moira told her son to go to his room to do the rest of his homework, just to get him out of the way.

Mr Richards told his wife how he saw the red-headed man fade away before his eyes and she said, 'He must be a ghost – but why is he calling here? Why is he haunting us? And I wonder who this Hugh is? I don't even know anyone named Hugh – oh, except my Uncle Hugh in Cornwall.'

On the following Wednesday at 7.30pm, Mr and Mrs Richards waited tensely for the ghost to call, and Moira even had a camera with a flash bulb at the ready, so she could obtain evidence of this solid-looking ghost – but the red-haired phantom did not call. However, on the following Wednesday evening, which fell upon 2 March, there was a ran-tan at the door of the doctor's home – and this time it was around 7.20pm. Moira Richards was having a bath and her son was in his room gluing a model aeroplane together. Dr Richards had been watching *University Challenge* on television when he heard the knocking. Before he even answered the door he could see the tell-tale silhouette of the man's head, and now he felt more curious than afraid; he really did want to get to the bottom of this bizarre mystery. He opened the door. The man who had called twice before said the same things, then turned and ran off. The doctor ran after him, but this time the red-headed man led him to a red sports car that had crashed into a lamp post on Childwall Priory Road. The red-haired man pointed to the driver. The steering wheel was embedded in his chest with the impact and the unfortunate man sat there with his mouth slightly open, and blood was coming out of it as he made a gurgling sound. That driver was Dr Richards. The redheaded man pointed to the doctor and said, 'It's you! You died!'

He hadn't been saying the name "Hugh" on those previous occasions – but "you". Dr Richards staggered away in shock, truly afraid as he shook his head. 'That's th-that's – it's just impossible,' he stammered. The gurgling sound his double was making in the car was the so-called "death rattle" – the sound made by a person as they die as saliva and bronchial secretions come up a throat that is unable to swallow. Doctor Richards turned his back on the nightmarish scene and started to run. He heard that red-headed man in the distance shouting, 'It's you! You died!' over and over until the doctor got out of earshot. He told his wife what he had seen, and she was understandably

119

stunned. She was now convinced that the whole weird matter was some supernatural warning. She told her husband to drive carefully in his car every morning when he set out for work. On the following Wednesday the ghost did not call, nor the Wednesday after that, and eventually the household of the Richards family settled down to normality.

A year later, a shocked Dr Richards met the red-headed man at a party thrown by a friend at a house in Cressington Park – so he was no ghost - and this man – an estate agent named William Mossman - invited him for a ride in his new red AC Cobra sports car, but the doctor declined, and begged the man not to drive whilst full of drink.

'Oh come on Richards, don't be a fuddy-duddy old man,' Mossman insisted, 'I'll drop you and Moira off. Childwall isn't it? In fact, how does this grab you: *you* can drive the bloody thing. It's an AC Cobra sports car and it's got a 7-litre Ford V8 engine – the fastest production car in the world! Can do 200 miles per hour. Insurance was sky high for the thing but worth every penny. It's a two-seater but Moira can sit on my knee!'

Another party guest - a cousin of Mr Mossman, a young man named Oliver, overheard the conversation between the doctor and the tipsy estate agent. Oliver was a police cadet, and in an officious tone he told his cousin, 'William, it is an offence, punishable on indictment or summarily, to be in charge of a motor vehicle on a road or other public place when unfit to drive through drink. A police constable may arrest without warrant – '

'Oh put a bloody sock in it Dixon of Dock Green!'

snarled Mossman. 'Been watching too much *Z Cars*! Go and get a blasted girlfriend!'

'William, can I have a word with you?' Dr Richards asked the estate agent, and led him by the elbow to a quiet corner of the house. He told William about the weird visits of a man who was his exact double to his Childwall home. He told him about the blood on his face and how he had led him to a red sports car which had crashed, and how he had seen himself dead at the wheel.

'You're not saying all this to scare me are you?' Mossman asked, evidently a little perturbed by the doctor's weird claims.

'I give you my word,' said the doctor, 'ask Moira if you want – she saw him too.'

'And you say the sports car was red?' asked the unnerved yet intrigued estate agent.

'Yes,' Dr Richards nodded.

'Come and have a look – it's parked outside,' Mossman tilted his head sideways and he and the doctor went to the front door.

'I *will* make a citizen's arrest – cousin or not!' warned young Oliver, thinking the men were going for a ride.

'Go and burst your pimples!' Mossman told his cousin and despite the presence of a vicar he gestured to Oliver with the V-sign.

Mossman led Richards to the little driveway at the side of the house, and there was the very same red sports car the doctor had seen that evening a year ago. The doctor went cold when he laid eyes upon the gleaming vehicle. He nodded, made a gulping sound, and said, 'Yes, that's the car William – no doubt about it; there aren't many on the road like that one.'

'Cost me two thousand,' said William Mossman, stroking the bonnet. 'You sure you weren't dreaming, old chap? Some dreams can be so realistic you'd swear they actually took place.'

'No, it was *no* dream,' said the doctor, 'it was a warning. It's giving me the creeps just seeing it – I better get back to my wife.'

William Mossman was scared into coming to his senses and he stayed overnight at the host's house and didn't drive home until the following evening. Doctor Richards believes he somehow prevented a fatal car crash – a crash in which he would have died and William Mossman would have sustained serious injuries. The mysterious, supernatural way in which the doctor was warned of that fatal crash still perplexes Mr Richards, who is now in his late eighties, and he thinks he'll never know the truth – not in *this* world anyway.

PLAIN JANE

Everybody saw Jane Trout but no one noticed her. She was petite, blonde, grey-eyed, and walked with a self-conscious stoop. Everyone heard her but nobody listened, and the 17-year-old trainee typist at the Dale Street fabrics firm was little more than a gofer, forever fetching coffee, cigarettes and sandwiches from a shop across the road. The girl had heard colleagues whisperingly refer to her as Plain Jane, and they often asked her about Joe, an obvious make-believe boyfriend of hers. They loved catching Jane out and making her blush when she couldn't remember when Joe's birthday was, and one of her co-workers at the firm almost drove the girl to quit one day when she told Jane, 'A liar's got to have a good memory, dear. A few months ago you told us this Joe of yours was born on 9 October, and now you're saying he was born on 3 September!'

Then it all changed for Plain Jane one September morning in 1968. The teenager was on her way to get the office staff their elevenses when she saw something glittering on the pavement at the Dale Street end of Manchester Street. It was a rose gold heart as big as Jane's thumbnail on a chain, and it had an eye made of tiny jewels on one side and some emblem shield featuring 8 red balls in relief on its reverse. Jain kept the gold heart and on her way back to the office she saw a tall broad-shouldered strong-jawed man in a finely cut pinstriped suit with a head of styled silvery-grey hair. She'd had a crush on him for weeks and she smiled at him but he strode past her without even noticing that she existed.

Jane did not know it but that jewellery item she had found on the pavement of Manchester Street was the Medici Heart – a mysterious talisman made for Catharine de Medici, a 16th Century Italian noblewoman and one-time Queen of France and the mother of three kings. She had been despised for her ruthless Machiavellian tactics, and she was also unlucky in love – until a Maltese occultist made her a special talisman – a rose gold heart with an eye of diamonds, and this powerful charm made everyone fall in love with Catharine. The Medici Heart has been found and lost again down the ages, and was allegedly worn by Elizabeth I, Marie Antoinette, and even Shakespeare's wife, Anne Hathaway. Jane Trout wore the Medici Heart, unaware of the talisman's unearthly history, and there was a tectonic shift in people's attitudes towards her. She went to fetch the coffee, ciggies and sandwiches the next morning wearing the 16th Century talisman and brought Dale Street's traffic to a standstill. Hot-blooded men beeped their horns. Her passing crush in the pinstriped suit stopped in his tracks and asked Jane: 'What's *your* name?' with a glazed look. A younger colleague with him said, 'Steady on old man, I saw her first!' and then a beautiful lady named Katrina, who turned out to be the head of a respectable local fashion-model agency, seemed besotted with Jane, and invited her to her office. Jane was very naive and thought she was going to be hired as a model. Instead, Katrina had a different type of proposal. 'Would you like to be my partner?' she asked, reclining back in her padded leather chair as she cast an admiring eye over the teenager.

'Partner?' Jane asked, baffled. 'I don't know the first thing about models or fashion I'm afraid.'

'I didn't have that *type* of partner in mind —if you catch my drift,' Katrina told her, and she smiled, then licked her lips, and it was as if she was licking the smile off her own face in an instant. She suddenly seemed deadly serious about the proposal, and her large dark eyes were fixed on Jane's face. The penny dropped ever so slowly in Jane's mind, and the girl got up and went straight for the door, but Katrina thrust herself upon her from behind and seemed out of breath as she pleaded with Jane to change her mind. 'I'm not interested, let me go!' cried Jane, as Katrina held her hand hard on the door handle. Jane pushed her away and almost fell down the stairs as she made her escape. She could hear Katrina begging for her to come back but the trainee typist ran out of the building, and as soon as she was back on the streets of Liverpool, her ears were bombarded with wolf whistles from every passing male, and a random dissonance of car horns. 'Cor, look at that!' said a tipsy man in his fifties passing by, his arm brushing against Jane, and his friend jokingly asked the young lady, 'Doing anything tonight darling?'

A gaggle of schoolboys, none of them over thirteen, shouted rude names at Jane and a few made obscene gestures to her, but one boy in spectacles detached from the pack and ran to Jane, who was walking along with her head bowed. The boy walked alongside her and said, 'My love is like a cabbage, divided into two, the leaves I give to others but the heart I give to you.'

The gang of schoolkids cheered when this piece of doggerel was recited at Jane and the boy walking with her leaned forward and said, 'I made that up just for you; can I have a kiss?'

'Shove off!' Jane pushed his face away but he kissed her thrusting palm and laughed. Then came more of the same lustful remarks from passing men, and this ostinato of trite comments and innuendo went on until she almost fell into the shop she visited five days a week for her work colleagues. The middle-aged man who always served her would hardly ever speak about anything besides price increases and the weather, but today he was looking at Jane Trout as if she was the Queen of England. As soon as Jane was able to collect her thoughts, she recalled the items she'd been asked to buy, but the man serving behind the counter seemed so distracted by Jane's face, he kept bringing the wrong items to her. When he eventually brought the right ones, he grasped Jane's hand as he took the payment from her and gazed into her eyes the way a boy does with his first crush. Jane did not like the way people young and old, of both sexes, were regarding her as some sexual object – it was just as bad as being ignored.

Jane eventually wondered if the heart-shaped talisman she had found was somehow responsible for her newfound popularity. On the following day she left the jewellery item in her purse – and she did not turn a single head; not one person gave her a second glance. As soon as she put the gold diamond-encrusted heart on, she became the centre of attention, and she realised that the heart had some sort of supernatural power, and this frightened her a little. The power of the golden heart seemed to increase as the days went by. Men and women fought one another, competing for Jane's love and a few lingered lovesick outside her Tuebrook home. Then the heart-shaped charm was mislaid somewhere in the kitchen, and with a mounting sense of horror, Jane realised she had accidentally thrown it in the pedal bin in the kitchen – and that bin had been emptied into the dustbin in the backyard. Jane went into the yard and saw, to her utter horror, that the dustbin had been emptied that morning. All interest in the trainee typist waned, and Jane burst into tears as she descended back into the world of her previous existence; a world in which she was as good as invisible amongst the good-looking females of life. About a week after the loss of the Medici Heart, Jane was running for the bus to work one morning, when a young man reached out to her from the open platform at the rear of the vehicle – and he grabbed her hand and helped her onboard. The man's name was Joe, and although he was not by any stretch of the imagination a handsome man, he had a great personality and he was a very caring soul. He got talking to Jane on the journey to her workplace and asked her on a date. Jane went with him to a cinema and then onto a pub on the first date, and he laughingly told her that his nickname was "Average Joe" because there was nothing really outstanding about him, in looks or personality. Jane said she disagreed; she told Joe he was a very attractive man and also very unselfish – which was rare in this day and age. She in turn told him how people called her

"Plain Jane" behind her back, and Joe shook his head and told her she was beautiful – but also shy – another quality that was rare amongst the people he knew. The couple later became engaged, then married a few years later, and they had many beautiful children, and as I put these words down today the couple are still married.

SOME ODD TALES

Just before I even get this chapter underway with its quiver full of odd tales, let me give you a perfect example of the type of odd tale I'm referring to in this section. Many years ago, around 2005, I was on BBC Radio Merseyside's *Billy Butler Show* talking about strange local tales concerning the paranormal when Billy put a woman on air who had called the station with a seemingly bizarre story. It concerned an area of the city I knew well: the Grove Street area of Edge Hill, because I grew up in that neighbourhood. The woman, named Karen, said that on the Friday morning of 21 September 1979 she was hurrying to her place of work – a certain Liverpool University building on Oxford Street where she was a cleaner. The time was a quarter to seven and the sun was just peeping over the horizon behind her. Karen, who was then aged twenty-four, lived with her mum and dad and brother Stan on Woodside Street off Wavertree Road, and Stan usually gave her a lift to the place where she worked, but he was ill with the flu on this morning and Karen, being unable to drive, had to walk a mile to get to the university building. At that time in the morning, Karen felt a bit uneasy walking to work; it was only just getting light and it was deadly quiet. The part of Grove Street Karen had to walk past had a reputation for being a red light area and it was common for kerb-crawling men to view any woman walking alone as a potential prostitute. So, as Karen walked down Grinfield Street, she was nervous as she neared the junction of Grove Street and Oxford Street. However, upon reaching the traffic lights at this junction she was relieved to see that the roads were dead. With the exception of an electric milk float whirring along the far end of Grove Street, there was no traffic and not a single pedestrian to be seen. Karen crossed Grove Street and walked up Oxford Street. She could see her workplace from here now and felt quite safe. To the cleaner's left there was a green space with a path cutting diagonally through it, and something moved on the grass here. For a moment, Karen thought it was two cats slinking about out the corner of her left eye, but when she turned her head left to look – she got the fright of her life. On the other side of the path running through the green stood two little figures, a bit taller than an Action Man doll – about fifteen inches tall, and they were apparently digging a hole with two little spades. Karen slowed down, and although she was scared at the sight of the little people, her curiosity was getting the better of her. The predawn lighting conditions were dim, and lent the surreal scene an even more sinister aspect, but then Karen saw that the two little figures were a miniature Frankenstein monster and a Count Dracula. They were digging away and Karen could hear faint voices as if the undersized men were arguing. The pint-sized Frankenstein monster suddenly turned to face Karen, and she saw his squarish greenish forehead and dark set-back eyes, and she tried to scream but her throat had closed up with fear. The Dracula figure also swung around and his pale face was presented to her. He looked startled, and Karen could even see his classic widow's peak. The two figures ran off into a hedge that bordered a sunken car park, and Karen tried to run, but felt a weakness in her knees. She was scared to look around because she thought the little figures might be following her, and when she reached her workplace a security guard named Paul asked her what the matter was because she looked so pale and he could see Karen's hands trembling. 'You'd never believe me,' she told the guard, to which he said, 'Was it a ghost?'

Karen just shook her head and although she had packed in smoking three weeks ago, she found herself cadging a cigarette off the guard because her nerves were that shot through by the weird encounter. Paul kept asking her what she had seen but she refused to tell him. When Karen had finished work she walked another way home because she was terrified of walking past that green at the junction of Grove Street and Oxford Street, and she never even told her parents or brother what she had seen, fearing ridicule. A week after this, Karen was in a canteen at work one lunchtime and she heard Maria, one of the women serving behind the counter, having a conversation with a colleague, and Karen's ears pricked up when she heard Maria say, 'They were like little dolls of Frankenstein and Dracula.'

Karen went over to the counter and said to Maria, 'What did you just say about Frankenstein and Dracula?'

Maria went all self-conscious and said, 'Oh stop earwigging Karen, nothing.'

The workmate Karen was talking to – a lady named Bernadette – said to Karen, 'She said that she saw two little men dressed up as Frankenstein and Dracula. She's potty!'

'Shut up, Bernie,' Maria said to her friend, covering her mouth coyly with her hand as she blushed.

'This wasn't that green on the corner of Oxford Street was it?' a gravely serious Karen asked Maria, and the latter seemed shocked. She nodded and said, 'Why? Have you seen them?'

'About a week back on my way to work,' said Karen, and she asked Maria a question that made the kitchen worker's eyes widen: 'Did they have little spades?'

Bernadette smiled and answered her friend's question for her. 'Yeah, she's just said that. Oh come on you two, have yous been taking drugs or something?'

Maria had seen them that morning at a quarter to seven on her way to work – and she had seen them in the exact same spot Karen had seen them a week ago. On this occasion though, when Maria saw them she did not scream – she just ran off and the little doll-like figures did not run away, but stayed put with their spades, watching her run away.

When Karen mentioned these sighting on air on the radio show, we received lots of calls from people who had heard about the little men, and we also received a call from a man named Stephen Viner Jones, who told us how, one summer morning in 1976 at round 6am, he set off for work from his home on Mulgrave Street, Toxteth, on his new Honda motorbike. Stephen worked at a pallet-making yard off Everton Road, and his route took him along Grove Street, passing the green where Karen and Maria would later see the bizarre miniature figures. On this morning at 6am, the visibility was good, and as Stephen approached the traffic lights at the Grove Street and Oxford Street junction he saw they were green – but then he saw something moving across the road ahead and could not believe his eyes – it was two little figures, a few inches over a foot in height, and one looked like a miniature Herman Munster with greenish skin and the other one was wearing a cape and a high collar. Stephen swerved to avoid hitting the creepy figures, which had been walking across the road from right to left – towards the green where they would be seen three years later. The figures ran off and Stephen almost lost control of his bike at the junction. He looked back and could not see the little entities, and for a while he thought he had hallucinated them.

Just what the little beings are is a mystery; we can speculate but we will probably never uncover their true nature. If they were elves or fairies, why would they dress up as Frankenstein's monster and a vampire? Perhaps they were just projections from something which likes playing with the minds of humans – it's really anybody's guess, and I often wonder if the little beings will be seen again.

Some of the stories that come my way - such as the previous one - are so bizarre I often file them away rather than publish them because I fear they may detract from the overall seriousness of the subject of the paranormal, but I have come to realise that such oddball stories do serve a purpose in the study of our local mysteries; they show us just how strange life and the universe is, and even within the textbooks they read in schools, colleges and universities today, we can see that this is a fact: the universe is truly bizarre. The science teachers in the old schools in the last century rarely mentioned the crazy world of Quantum Physics. The tutors in those bygone schools used to draw atoms on the blackboard as miniature solar systems with electrons orbiting the nucleus as planets orbit the sun – but today we know those chalked concepts of the atom were wrong. The pupils of today know things about Quantum Physics that would have been laughed at by the science teachers of, say, the 1970s, because they would seem so bizarre and ridiculous. Imagine two little football goals set up side by side in a gymnasium in 1971. We tell the assembled science class and science teacher that we want a volunteer to throw a football into the mouth of one of those goals. We get bemused looks, and a child thrusts his arm up and he is allowed to throw the ball into – let us say – the left goal. Now, we tell the class and teacher that on the subatomic scale, we can carry out the same experiment, only this time we have two rectangular openings parallel to one another like this:

[] []

These openings – or goals - can be in a thin sheet of metal. Now, believe it or not, when we fire an electron towards these two goals, it can go through the *two of them at the same time* and also interfere with its own path so it produces an interference pattern behind the slits on a screen. This is a proven scientific fact – but only on the atomic scale (up to molecules comprising around 810 atoms); even the most gifted footballer cannot kick a ball so that it goes through both goals at once while wiggling about on a bizarre wavelike trajectory which interferes with its own path. I am not going to fill the rest of this chapter describing the many other utterly bizarre and logic-defying things that subatomic particles get up to; there are dozens of great books out there and articles on Wikipedia for those who are curious to learn more about the topsy-turvy world of Quantum Physics. What I will do now is tell you about some of the odder tales I've looked into over the years – perfect examples of that much-quoted adage: 'fact is stranger than fiction'. I will start with a very odd incident which took place at one of Liverpool's internationally renowned venues. I have a plethora of mysteries concerning the Cavern Club in my files. I have the well-documented claims that the Devil appeared in person during an Ouija session at the club in the 1960s, and what are we to make of the discovery, in 1982, of a mysterious rectangular 8-foot-deep subterranean swimming pool, 120 feet long and 70 feet in width, hewn out of solid sandstone bedrock beneath the Cavern's foundations? Just who went to so much trouble to create an underground swimming pool has never been identified, but it could have been that wealthy claustrophiliac, Joseph Williamson, the Mole of Edge Hill. I have so many Cavern mysteries pigeon-holed away I may write a book on the subject one day, and I must say that some of the stories are very odd indeed, such as this one. The general consensus is that the incident happened one evening in early June 1965 because the American poet Allen Ginsberg had just visited the Cavern, proclaimed Liverpool to be the centre of the Universe and predicted that the Beatles would change the world. Around the time of the Ginsberg visitation, a beautiful red-headed American girl in her early twenties named Cheri visited the Cavern with a long-haired man of a similar age who, according to Bob Wooler (the Cavern's legendary compère and disc jockey), looked facially like a cross between Peter Sellers and Ringo Starr. Cheri introduced her friend, who was wearing a very expensive-looking tailored suit, as Richard, and said he was a big Beatles fan. The voice of Richard sounded artificial and tinny, and the words he uttered, in a bad imitation of the Liverpudlian accent, did not seem to synchronise with his lips. People also noticed that "Richard" seemed to have the matte complexion of a Lewis's mannequin, a wig of nylon hair, dead-looking eyes, and he danced jerkily and unnaturally as if Ray Harryhausen was animating him. People who were present while "Richard" was there told me he just didn't look or move like a bona fide human - as if he was some weird counterfeit person. Psychologists call this the "Uncanny Valley" effect, where something masquerading as a human just doesn't look right, be it a virtual computer person or a lifelike animatronic doll. Richard not only looked artificial, he made a whirring sound as the night went on, as if he was some robot. Then, around 11pm Richard started thrashing his arms about in a violent manner, and according to many witnesses, his head turned 180 degrees, and as girls screamed at the unearthly contortion act, he ran up the stairs with his head facing the wrong way, and Cheri hurried after him. Some thought it was all some mime act – a man pretending to be a robotic Beatle, but I have the feeling someone ahead of their time was testing a prototype android out that evening. Cheri and Richard were never seen at the Cavern Club again. The android – once only found in the realm of science fiction - was originally classified as a sophisticated robot designed to resemble a human, but with the incredible progress in electronics, computing, artificial intelligence and nanotechnology, a true android would really be the creation of a humanoid through a technological substitute of the natural chromosome complex; in effect an almost organic race of artificial humans that would be born fully grown with an innate lifetime experience encoded into their computerized minds (a hybrid of software and hardware). The ultimate goal would be to come up with a novel biochemical coding-system similar to our own DNA so the androids could ultimately reproduce. Would it be morally wrong to create such high-tech artificial slaves though? How far has research into humanoid robots and androids progressed behind closed doors? The progress has gone much further than we think, if the occasional leaked information is to be believed, and the research has been going on since the 1950s. I once investigated a very curious report of an alleged androidal being which was apparently being tested in Liverpool in the early 1980s. At around 2p.m., on the Wednesday afternoon of 15 September, 1982, a 29-year-old constable named Geoff Nesmith left the Traffic Police Headquarters on Smithdown Lane and embarked on the journey to his home in Moreton. Along the way, Geoff noticed Judy Greer, a girl he had dated once, standing on the corner of Brownlow Hill and Peach Street, on the campus of Liverpool University. Judy was now a student at the university.

Geoff pulled over at the small student shopping centre and wound down his window to greet Judy. The couple started talking, and Geoff left his car and walked with Judy into Bob's Newsagents to buy cigarettes and a magazine.

There were two other people being served in the newsagents, and they were an elderly couple. Geoff and Judy waited behind them, talking to each other, when something bizarre occurred. Geoff glanced through the newsagent's window and saw a gleaming black limousine pull up in front of his parked car. The windows of the sleek vehicle were so heavily tinted, the interior was not visible. A man wearing a smart blue suit and sunglasses emerged from the rear door on the far side of the limousine. Moments later, an identically dressed man left the vehicle from the other side and he was joined by the driver of the vehicle. The three men gathered at the rear door that faced the newsagent's window, and they leaned forward to help a fourth man out of the car. This man wore a trilby and a long raincoat. He left the car slowly as if he was suffering from some debilitating medical condition. He seemed very unsteady on his feet as he walked, and the three men accompanied him closely and acted as if they thought he'd collapse at any moment. The four men entered Bob's Newsagents and barged carelessly into the elderly couple. The man in the trilby who had been ushered into the shop stepped forward to the counter and grabbed the *Daily Express*. Geoff and Judy thought the man looked very odd. His skin looked artificial, and he moved his arms and legs in a completely unnatural way.

The newsagent held his hand out to the man and

said, '*Express?* Seventeen pence sir.'

There was no reaction from the man in the trilby. He stood rooted to the spot, and all of a sudden, a suspicious whirring sound emanated from his head. Simultaneously, his face became contorted and his eyes rolled in different unsynchronised directions. The 'man' was obviously some mechanical simulacrum of a human. The three men behind the mannequin-like figure were suddenly gripped with trepidation, and they muttered profanities under their breath as their hands seized the man in the trilby. A man got on each side of the figure and each man put a hand under its armpits before quickly carrying the fake-looking male off the premises, and into the limousine, which then sped off.

Geoff, Judy, and the elderly customers in the newsagents were astounded by the extraordinary proceedings. They all looked through the window of the shop and watched the three men guide the robotic figure into the back of the limousine. The men looked about then entered the vehicle, which drove off down Brownlow Hill. Stranger still, I lived in the Edge Hill district of Liverpool at this time, and I remember hearing a rumour about a human-looking robot that had allegedly been built at Liverpool University. Many people claimed they had seen this robot masquerading as a man. I distinctly recall one person say that she saw the figure sitting on a bench in Abercromby Park, throwing bread to pigeons in a mechanical manner.

Years later, Geoff wrote to me about the strange incident from his home in St Helens. Unknown to him, his former girlfriend Judy had also been in contact from her home in north Wales. Their stories

139

matched exactly. What exactly did they and other witnesses see that September afternoon in 1982? It has been predicted that the android-building business will become one of the greatest new industries of the 21st century, possibly rivalling the world's automobile industries. The main backer of android research is the military. A fearless, armour-plated android soldier with a self-destruct capability would be a dream come true for many of the world's armies. Most armies already use remotely-controlled bomb disposal robots, and the android is the logical successor to those robots. On the civilian front, android fire-fighters clad in fireproof material could go where no human fireman could go. The possibilities are endless. Today, the technology exists to create androids, thanks to the remarkable quantum-leap development of computer chips, but in the early 1980s, when the strange mechanical man was seen in Liverpool, silicon chip technology was much more inferior. Perhaps some group of electronics experts, working in secret, created a primitive android, and later tested it out by programming it to carry out the simple task of entering a newsagent's shop to buy a newspaper. This rudimentary mission probably failed through some technical malfunction. One wonders if the same conjectural innovators were responsible for the "Robot Ringo" incident at the Cavern. We may know more one day.

From the androidal we next move to the tripedal, and another odd tale, which harks back to the Liverpool of the 1980s.

Besides paranormal entities such as Spring-Heeled Jack and the Galosher Man (who could both run at superhuman speeds and jump incredible hyper-

Olympic distances), some very strange characters have visited Liverpool over the years. For a short while in 1983, a bizarre street performer appeared in the thoroughfares of the city. His face was painted chalk-white, he sported a yellow straw boater, a white and purple striped boating jacket, and appeared to be tripedal – possessing three legs. Some thought one of his legs was a sophisticated false motorised limb, but others who remember him swore he really was three-legged. He juggled, danced and also had a football on an almost invisible elastic thread that he would hurl at passersby to get their attention. I mentioned this strange performer on local radio once and a retired policewoman named Jane told me a bizarre tale concerning him. The performer left his battered old maroon transit van (emblazoned with a huge yellow smiley face) parked in the loading bay of a major store on School Lane, and when the authorities tried to tow the vehicle away it wouldn't budge. The van was making a faint humming sound but the police could not see what was generating the sound because the back door windows of the transit were painted on the inside with black gloss paint. When the tow truck finally lifted the van it spun violently and smashed into the truck, damaging it. Inside the transit van was a giant aluminium gyroscope powered by an electric motor, obviously set up so its axis would resist any attempts to move the van. The performer never returned to the booby-trapped vehicle and went missing for about a month. Why he had set up such an elaborate prank with the gyroscope was never established. In June 1983 the street artist was dancing to New Edition's *Candy Girl* on a ghetto blaster on

Church Street when one of two passing girls – 16-year-old Lisa Murphy - made fun of his three legs. He slammed the football on the elastic hard into the back of her head and continued dancing. Lisa swore at the eccentric performer and called him a "Freak of nature".

On the following Saturday Lisa and her friend Sue were walking through town on their way to buy records at Woolworths when a clown in an orange conical dunce's hat in an ankle-length dress grabbed the ice cream cone Lisa was eating and thrust it in her face. When Lisa swore at him he slapped her hard against the face then held her in a headlock, saying, 'Naughty naughty naught-naught girl!' as he sprayed her hair with orange paint. He then emptied a tube of itching powder down her neck and exclaimed, 'Oops a daisy!'

Sue recognised the violent clown – it was the three-legged performer her friend had mocked a week ago, and she saw his three shoes protruding from under the dress's hemline. As Lisa burst into tears the weird clown ran off singing *Row, Row, Row Your Boat*.

'Let's report him to the police, Lisa,' Sue told her sobbing friend, who was removing her coat so she could scratch her itching back and neck. 'No, I want to go home,' cried Lisa, and the girls had to pool their pocket money to get a taxi to Lisa's home, where it took three shampoo hair washes to get most of the orange paint out of Lisa's curly locks.

On Sunday morning, Lisa woke in her Tuebrook home and discovered to her horror that she could not open her mouth. It transpired that her lips had been superglued together, and when she looked in the mirror she saw her face had been made up as a clown. Straight away she thought of the weird three-legged street performer and shuddered; had he somehow got into her room during the night? The realistic possibility terrified the girl. Over the following month Lisa was attacked by the tripedal performer in disguises ranging from a nun to a monk, and the attacks took place in places ranging from Church Street in Liverpool to Southport's Lord Street. Lisa almost suffered a nervous breakdown because of the attacks, and the police were informed. The police said they had received other complaints about the weird street performer but he had proved to be very evasive when they attempted to question him. The sinister street artist eventually vanished from the city centre, never to be seen again. When I mentioned this peculiar case on a local radio programme, scores of listeners telephoned the radio station to tell how they remembered the creepy clownlike entertainer. One woman told me how she encountered the three-legged performer on Church Street when he was made up as a clown in a sailor's outfit, and he swiped candy floss from her three-year-old son, drenched him with a huge water pistol, then ran off laughing hysterically. A man named Norman who witnessed this cruel act ran after the freakish farcical buffoon, chasing him as far as School Lane, where the performer's Transit van was parked. The creepy comic climbed into the van, started the engine, and Norman tried to pull open the passenger door when the window of that door was suddenly wound down. The deviant's painted face appeared at the open window and he spat a jet of fire into Norman's face. Norman instinctively closed his eyes and the spurt of flame singed his eyebrows, burnt his fringe, and left him with a sore reddened forehead. The van tore off down School Lane and almost crashed into an oncoming vehicle as it swerved the wrong way onto Paradise Street. Someone out there must know the identity of that quirky, violent street performer – perhaps he is even reading these words himself...

From twisted urban street clowns of the 1980s, we move next to a very odd tale involving a night-time encounter with a royal bloodsucker in the 1960s.

At 7.20pm on the Saturday night of 2 February 1963, smart and pretty 15-year-old redhead Betty Jones arrived at the house of the Johnson family on Walton's Lancaster Street to babysit. Her charge for the evening was 7-year-old Brian, a very quiet and well-behaved child she had minded before without incident. She let him watch a police programme called *Hawaiian Eye* on TV, but put him to bed just after 9 o'clock. Betty then watched the telly and drank endless cups of coffee and nibbled her way through half a tin of assorted biscuits. The teenager watched the satirical late TV show *That Was the Week That Was* and the next thing she knew it was midnight. She looked out the window at the fog and wondered when the Johnsons would be home; Mr Johnson had said he and his wife would be back around midnight. The Johnsons came home at a quarter to one, and a palatic Mr Johnson stuffed two pounds in Betty's hand, kissed her, and then his wife slapped him. Mr Johnson said he'd walk Betty home because of the lateness of the hour and the thick fog, but his wife forbade his suspicious intentions and she walked the blushing babysitter to the end of the street and urged her to get home as quickly as possible. Betty assured Mrs Johnson she'd be alright, and walked off, heading for her home on Dunbar Street, half a mile away. On County Road in the murky limbo of fog, Betty thought she heard distant whistling. She looked about and saw no one. Not a soul was about on this freezing foggy morning. Betty then heard the approach of someone behind her whistling the old tune *Greensleeves*. The girl turned around and saw the silhouette of an overweight man around six feet in height coming towards her through the mists. He passed the teen, and then he stopped whistling, his heavy footfalls halted, and this stranger turned to face Betty – and he also blocked her way. To Betty there was something tantalizingly familiar about his round face and that beard and moustache, but she simply couldn't place the man.

'Abroad in the black hours maiden?' the stranger asked in a rich deep voice.

Not understanding the question, Betty just politely smiled and walked around the corpulent man, and as she did she noticed the red rose pattern embroidered on his tie. He sprung after Betty, grabbed her forearm and said, 'Maiden, your beauty beguiles me! Your gold-red hair and summer-blue eyes provoketh me! Come with me and be my love!'

'I'm spoken for,' said Betty, paradoxically close to swooning in fear yet feeling intoxicated by the attention from the lovelorn stranger. First Mr Johnson had kissed her – now this.

'Then why isn't the fool guarding you now?' asked the towering obtrusive man. His eyes widened and the lustful desire in them was intense. Betty felt as if she was dreaming. The stranger's eyes turned red – blood red – and this happened instantly.

'Oh!' Betty yelped, and tried to pull herself from the weird man's grip.

'Leave her alone!' cried a voice somewhere to the left of Betty in the fog. The teenager snapped out of some hypnotic spell, and her weird admirer gritted his teeth – *fanged teeth* – and turned to the silhouette crossing the road from the direction of St Mary's Church. It was a sprightly grey-haired man holding out a crucifix. 'He's a vampire!' yelled the man, 'And he wants his seventh wife! Don't you Henry?'

The beefy man let go of Betty and ran off into the fog, and the man with the cross implored Betty to get home as soon as possible. He told her something she could not comprehend, and to this day she remains perplexed by his words. The man calmly informed Betty: 'My dear, you almost became a blood cow for none other than Henry VIII. Yes, I know it's hard to believe, but that man is over four hundred years old – because he's a vampire.'

'Henry VIII?' asked Betty, close to tears. Now she realised why he had seemed so familiar; she had seen his face in schoolbooks read in the history lessons about the Tudors and the Wars of the Roses – but wasn't that a long time ago? She was understandably confused.

'Look, he's still there – he won't give up,' the old vampire hunter pointed to the pale face peeping around the corner of Church Road West in the swirling fog. 'See him?'

'Yes,' said Betty in a broken voice, 'I'm scared.'

'Come on, I'll drive you home,' said the old man,

beckoning the girl towards Bedford Road. She went with him and got into a Ford Zodiac. Right away Betty noticed the Dominican Rosary hanging from the rear view mirror, and the smell of something like church incense in the vehicle.

'What's a blood cow?' she asked, as the man started the car.

In a matter-of-fact way the saviour of Betty Jones replied: 'A blood cow is a person with a rare blood group who is kept alive by a vampire so he or she can keep drawing blood from them. The vampire feeds you iron-rich foods and makes you drink tomato juice and hibiscus tea to get even more iron into you. Blood cows usually become partial vampires themselves and can only go outdoors after dark.'

The old man also mentioned other things about the life of the vampire but Betty was in such a state she cannot now remember what the man said. She recalled seeing her father walking through the fog up County Road and telling the man to pull over, which he did, and Betty's dad – who had been on his way to the Johnsons house to collect his daughter – naturally wanted to know why she was in the car of a stranger. When Betty told her father she'd been accosted by a vampire – who also happened to be King Henry VIII – he was understandably sceptical – and he confronted the driver of the Ford Zodiac, asking him who he was and why he had Betty in his car. As soon as Betty left the vehicle the driver leaned across the passenger seat, slammed the door and drove off without a word of explanation. When Betty got home she asked her mother, 'Mam, what's my blood group?'

'Oh don't start all that baloney!' roared the girl's

father. He'd heard Betty's account of how she'd almost become the blood cow of Henry VIII because she had a rare blood group.

'AB negative – why?' Betty's mother answered.

'And is it rare?' Betty asked, highly anxious to know the answer.

'The doctor said it is,' replied Mrs Jones, 'I'm sure he said it's the rarest blood group – why?'

'She was in a car with some 'arl fellah who protected her from a vampire!' interposed Mr Jones in a sarcastic manner, before his daughter could reply to her mum. Betty reeled off her account of the meeting with the stocky vampiric Tudor, and her mother did not believe a word of it. She thought the so-called vampire had been working in cahoots with the old man in the car, possibly to abduct Betty and "have their way" with her.

For weeks, Betty was convinced that the royal vampire was watching her whenever she went out the house, and the girl refused to go out after dusk. Whatever and whoever the person was, the incident gave Betty terrible nightmares for years. Did Betty encounter a vampiric monarch from the Tudor period or was the whole thing some staged prank? The incident really does defy analysis, although there *are* tenuous links between King Henry VIII and vampirism; first of all, the father of the Tudor dynasty, a Welsh warrior named Ednyfed Fychan, had a strange liking for blood, and some claimed he drank it in battle and he seemed to go to enormous lengths to spill the blood of enemies in battle and smear it upon his hands and face. Whilst fighting against the army of Ranulph de Blondeville (the Earl of Chester) Ednyfed cut off the heads of three English lords and carried the heads – which were still dripping with blood – to Llywelyn, the Prince of Wales. There is also a strange vampiric rumour concerning the Henry VIII, the descendant of Ednyfed Fychan. When King Henry died in 1509, his enormous bloated body was a putrid mass of rotten flesh infected with syphilis and tuberculosis. The large corpse was placed in a lead coffin which was taken around the streets of London on a procession. Upon the coffin's arrival at Syon Chapel, it was noted that the lead lining had come apart through all of the shaking and jolting about on the rattling cart as it traversed the rough roads, and the blood of the dead king was dripping heavily out the damaged casket onto the pavement. When the plumbers arrived just before the dawn, they saw a strange animal resembling a black dog with huge fangs lapping up the puddle of Henry's blood. A strange cloaked man in black, who professed to be a mystagogue, is said to have remarked, 'Ha! The prophecy of Friar Petow has come to pass! Friar Petow didst say in the pulpit of Greenwich Church four years ago that King Henry, like King Ahab - the wicked seventh king of Israel – would have his blood licked by wild dogs – and the dark soul of this tyrant shall never rest! He shall walk the night for evermore!'

Some present objected to the treasonable outburst, and those loyal to the House of Tudor reached for their swords, but as the sun peeped over the rooftops at the break of dawn and dazzled the eyes of the angered men, the man in black seemed to melt away – and so did the strange black hound that had lapped up the pool of the dead monarch's blood. I wonder if Henry VIII is now some form of vampiric being who still has to 'walk the night'....

Our quest for the odder tales of the supernatural now takes us from the Walton of 1963 to the Birkenhead of 2001, to a Halloween encounter with some very odd entities which were interpreted by their victims – a couple of children - as witches – but heaven knows what they were. Before I relate this bizarre story, let me explain the physiological process of fear and the effect it had one of the young victims in this case. There is a condition known as vasovagal syncope which occurs when a person becomes so scared, blood vessels dilate and the heart rate rapidly slows, and as a result of the resulting drop in blood pressure and the slowing of the heartbeat, the person faints. I often hear people say ghosts cannot harm you and that it's the living you should be scared of, but poltergeists have inflicted serious injuries and some people have died from heart failure after encountering a ghost. Those with highly strung nervous systems – especially children – are particularly prone to psychological harm from paranormal beings, and a classic example of this allegedly took place at the Birkenhead branch of Woolworths on Grange Road in 2001 – at Halloween. That Wednesday afternoon, a brother and sister – Izzy (who had just turned 14) and 11-year-old Gareth - decided to visit Woolworths to get some sweets and Gareth had said he wanted to see if the store had fireworks as Guy Fawkes' Night was less than a week away. Brother and sister left their Claughton home around 3.30pm. Gareth had just got over a stomach bug and had been off school on this day, and Izzy had played truant and had been hanging round at her friend's home on Larch Road until she decided to go home under the pretence of returning from school. When brother and sister crossed Exmouth Street on their way to Woollies, Izzy said that as it was Halloween, they should have a race to the store, and whoever lost would be taken away by the Devil. Little Gareth shook his head and seemed scared at the suggestion, but Izzy sprinted off down Grange Road West with Gareth running behind her. Something bizarre then took place; a woman in a long black robe and a black hood darted out of Craven Street on the left side of the road, and she looked as if she was well over six feet in height with long pointed shoes. She was shrieking with laughter as she overtook a startled Izzy and Gareth. The weird woman ran into Woolworths, and Izzy and Gareth went into the store moments later.

The entire store was empty. No customers were about, and the two children could see no staff either. They walked around Woollies and were baffled as to why no one was serving at the counters. Gareth smiled and started helping himself to the Pick 'n Mix section, taking handfuls of sweets, but Izzy warned him that there were CCTV cameras recording everything. Gareth was a natural-born worrier and he put the uneaten sweets back. Izzy went to look at some CDs when Gareth grabbed her elbow and said, 'Izzy! Look, it's that weird woman again!'

At first the children thought the lanky woman in black had on a Halloween mask, because she had a nose like the puppet Punch and bulging, staring eyes encircled with black rings. She was singing a very strange song, and the words ran thus:

Whenever you see the hearse go by
And think to yourself that you're gonna die
Be merry kids, be merry!
They put you in a big white shirt
And cover you over with tons of dirt
Be merry kids, be merry!
They stick you in a long-shaped box
And cover you over with tons of rocks
Be merry kids, be merry!
The worms crawl out and the worms crawl in
The ones that crawl in are lean and thin
The ones that crawl out are fat and stout
Be merry kids, be merry!
Your eyes fall in and your hair falls out
And your brains come tumbling out your snout
Be merry kids, be merry!

The creepy woman with the grotesque caricature of a face then softly laughed, and it was a laryngitic chortle. 'Hello!' she shouted to Izzy and Gareth, and then she headed towards the frightened brother and sister. It soon became apparent to the children that this woman wore no mask – that ghastly pale face was a living one - and when she smiled she showed irregular and discoloured gravestone teeth. Gareth backed away and with rising panic in her voice, Izzy said to him, 'Let's get out of here.'

The teen and her brother not only found the doors of the store locked, they could not see the street outside – just a thick grey void of fog.

'Izzy! There's more of them!' Gareth cried, and his sister stopped trying to open the door and turned to see there were now five of these weird hag-like women. Izzy got out her mobile – but she could not get a signal, and she panicked. She and Gareth ran off and tried to find other escape routes from the premises but there were none. One of the black-clad women shouted, 'These two will make a fine meal! She's got brown eyes – they're very tasty brown eyes!'

'I'll put you in a pie, laddie!' cried another one of the weird 'witches' as she chased after Gareth. During the ensuing cat and mouse chase through the empty store, one of the terrifying entities caught Izzy and her cold claw-like hands gripped the girl's throat. Izzy screamed, and was so frightened, she passed out. She woke up on Craven Street twenty minutes later and found people encircling her. Someone told her they'd phoned for an ambulance. 'Where's Gareth?' Izzy asked, and became hysterical. 'Where's my brother?' the girl screamed and she ran off to Woolworth's where she found him in a terrified state in. He said he'd hidden from the creepy women in a photo booth, and when he came out of hiding he found they'd gone and customers and staff had returned to the store. The boy had then gone in search of his sister and had told several adults what had happened but they seemed to think he was joking, especially with it being Halloween. For many years, Izzy and Gareth suffered from lucid nightmares about the five figures dressed like witches – but what were the entities doing in Woolworths of all places? I do know a Baptist chapel stood on the site of the store years before, and various people who worked at Woollies over the years have told me the place was haunted, but what on earth were those spine-chilling crones? And will they ever return?

The following short odd tale was related to me when

I was a child, and took place near to where I used to play when I was a kid - the Botanic Park (where my Sherwood Forest stood in the form of a little wood). It's a very odd tale indeed, and it allegedly happened one December in the early 1970s, but I cannot explain it.

Grief affects people in different ways. When bouncers Hughie and Donny saw their neighbour Jimmy lying in his coffin at the wake, dead at the relatively young age of 45, they talked to him as if he was alive and well. These two doormen (and amateur boxers) each weighing over 16 stone, fought back tears as they gripped the rim of the coffin and surveyed their old drinking buddy – a confirmed bachelor they had shared a thousand adventures with. Jimmy had been the best man at each of their weddings. Now he lay there stretched out in his Sunday best with a slight smile on his face. Hughie took a fiver from his wallet and said to the corpse, 'Give this to the ferryman mate; take you safely to the other side,' and he tucked it in the inside pocket of Jimmy's jacket. A bottle of scotch later, the bouncers decided to go and "borrow" a hearse from the local undertaker, then put Jimmy and his coffin in the back of the vehicle for a last round of his favourite pubs. A so-called hardened criminal who objected to this 'distasteful' gesture was knocked clean out by Donny.

Hughie drove the hearse with the open coffin in the back and Donny told the lifeless passenger: 'We'll start with the Durning Jimmy lad! You loved that place. Then we'll call in at the Beehive and the Big House.'

The strange pub crawl went swimmingly, and the bouncers were not pulled up once, but several policemen must have wondered why a hearse was out at night. Drinkers who had known Jimmy came out some of the visited pubs and doffed caps and patted the hearse out of respect. At 11pm the doormen were returning home via Wavertree Road when they were finally pulled over by the police. There was a major altercation, and then a detective notified the sentimental drunks that Jimmy was not in his coffin. That evening, people who had known Jimmy well said he came into the Botanic pub, close to where the hearse was pulled over, and he assured those who had heard of his death that he was alive and well, but he looked off-colour. 'My last bevvy,' he said, and gave the barman a fiver (the money Hughie had put in his deceased friend's inside pocket to symbolically pay the ferryman to take Jimmy's soul to the other side), saying, 'Keep the change.' He sank that pint, then left, and they found his body sitting on a bench in the park across the road.

And now for what must surely be the oddest story in this chapter. In the 1950s at a certain well-known hospital in Liverpool, a pretty 6-year-old girl died from an overdose of barbiturate tablets after finding the bottle of pills in her auntie's kitchen cupboard and eating six of the colourful tablets, thinking they were sweets. The deceased child's auntie had been prescribed the tablets for insomnia and anxiety. During the post mortem of the child something allegedly happened that spread a raft of strange rumours throughout the medical profession and into the grapevine of public urban legends. There are many versions of the strange incident, but after many years I finally traced the witnesses down after discussing the bizarre and terrifying case on a BBC radio programme I hosted about local mysteries.

The coroner and his assistant laid the little girl's body out on the slab at the mortuary and the post mortem commenced. After the external examination of the child, a large Y-shaped incision was made in the body, starting at the shoulders and terminating in the pubic bone. As the skin was being drawn back, the coroner and his assistant distinctly heard a faint child-like voice say, 'I'm scared.'

The coroner then realised that something was moving about in the body of the deceased little girl – and this naturally startled him and the assistant. Bodies can occasionally move because of nerves and organs in a corpse on the dissecting table have been known to move about because of a build up of gas from decomposition – and sometimes the escaping gas makes some strange sounds – but this sounded like a human voice. The coroner moved the viscera aside and saw a pair of eyes emerging from blood and other bodily fluids. He recoiled in shock, holding his scalpel in a defensive posture. His first thought was that a rat had somehow got into the body of the girl while the corpse was in cold storage – but then he saw the *thing* raise its bizarre-looking head, and it was plain to see that this was not some rodent. The thing had globular eyes with blue irises, and these eyeballs were under an inch in diameter. The head these eyes were set in looked brown and leathery, and a quivering, toothless mouth was now visible. 'Don't hurt me!' The thing said, at which the assistant swore and stepped back from the corpse.

The unknown creature came out of a hollow in the

child's viscera and seemed to have crab-like limbs, possibly four of them or even more. The coroner, with all of his experience and medical expertise, was not sure what the thing was, and he wondered if the creature was an unborn twin of the dead girl that had developed within her; this was not unknown – but why would the thing look like a crab? The creature opened its mouth and closed its eyes as it make a high-pitched screaming sound, and the coroner told the assistant to go and telephone a retired senior coroner straight away. When this senior medical examiner arrived on the scene, the creature had retreated back into the corpse, but now and then it would peep out from the ghastly soup of blood and other bodily fluids at the medical men. The senior medical examiner killed the thing with a lancet, and it screamed and tried to get out of the body and made defensive movement with its crablike claws until it vomited blood then defecated, squirting a runny yellow fluid on the body. The coroner was advised by the retired medical examiner to say nothing about the incident for fear of upsetting the parents of the dead child. The older coroner's view was that the creature was indeed an unborn twin that had developed in the girl and had managed to live from her in some parasitic form, but how on earth had the thing been able to speak? The senior medical examiner allegedly kept the creature pickled in formaldehyde for many years and what became of the weird corpse is unknown.

The following tale is more romantic than odd, but deserves a place within this chapter because it is a rummy account with a rather astounding coincidence.

Beware, for the fickle Wheel of Fortune turns with the wind, and those at the top may find themselves crashing to the bottom and those who were sinking into Hell will find themselves in the highest reaches of Heaven. Larry took his good life for granted, and then in February 1973 after a divorce, bankruptcy and a suspended 18-month sentence for drawing huge cheques, knowing full well that his bank would never pay them, the businessman hit the bottle, then suffered a full-blown mental breakdown. He lost everything (including his sanity for a while) and ended up living on the streets at rock bottom. On this day he sat in his den – the alcove of a condemned building in a forgotten corner of a Liverpool slum on an old armchair someone had dumped, and he held a can of Skol lager lifted from a supermarket and toasted Mandy, the name he had given to the brunette in the faded old holiday poster on the wall of his alfresco hideaway. When he was weary or when the drink had softened the sharp edge of reality, Larry would look at Mandy and drift off into her poster world; the golden beach, crying white flecks of gulls in a china blue sky, blazing white-hot sun, and then the undischarged bankrupt would hold Mandy in his arms and kiss her and pray that he would never have to return to the cruel grey real world where he had nothing and nobody. He always returned in tears from the dreams. Then the tall wall of overgrown weeds that afforded Larry a measure of privacy was mown down by council workmen and he was moved on by the police. He returned every day to his former home to see Mandy and always kissed her paper face before he left. Then one day he made his pilgrimage to the poster and found a middle-aged woman tearing the face off his dream woman. Larry screamed for her to stop, and when that woman turned to face him, she looked familiar. It was, without a doubt, Mandy, only she was a lot older – but still so beautiful. The woman explained she was June Presnick, a former model, and she had posed for that picture on the old holiday poster, way back when she was 22. Now she was 55 and it hurt her, seeing her wrinkle-free fresh-faced younger self on that poster. Larry seized June's hand, kissed her knuckle, and with tears in his eyes he told her how her image had got him through the worst times of his life. He spoke of romantic incidents with Mandy in the world of his dreams, and June was really moved by his words. Her own life had gone into a decline since her divorce and her confidence had long been lost. Larry arranged a date with June and cleaned himself and his life up. She told him to call her by that name he had used – Mandy - and they ended up married. When the couple honeymooned on a beach in Sardinia, it was literally a dream come true for Larry.

And finally, in our last odd tale in this chapter, an incident takes place which begins with a man in an abject state of terror, but ends with him finding love.

In December 1976 a 39-year-old businessman named Paul Lyle was speedily reversing his new British Leyland Princess out of Arrad Street (a back alley running behind the Everyman Theatre) onto Hope Street when he accidentally hit a woman, knocking her down with some force. Paul panicked and tore off, peeling rubber as he jumped the lights on Hope Street. He glanced back once as the car swung left onto Mount Pleasant and saw the woman lying inert on the pavement with a knot of people around her. Paul cursed himself for reversing out of a back street onto a main road; it was something he normally wouldn't do, but a momentary lapse of reason and his mind being elsewhere had caused the accident. 'Why did she walk out into the road anyway?' Paul growled to himself, 'Stupid cow's just as much to blame as me!'

He parked the Princess on the narrow alley known as Cropper Street at the back of Lewis's and wondered what to do. A confusion of thoughts raced around his mind. Did he get away fast enough without some do-gooder getting his registration? Could he go to jail if she died? He'd hit her with some force and she didn't get up after the impact. Should he go and see solicitor Rex Makin and explain what had happened?

'Why did the stupid bitch walk out without looking?' he yelled to himself, and then he tried to calm down and started to slowly breathe in and out. He got out the car and went into Lewis's department store in shock, walking the floors in a daze. As he pretended to browse the hi-fi section he heard a woman's voice behind him cry out, 'You road hog!' and he turned to face her and saw a pretty young lady approaching.

'You knocked me down! You killed me!' she cried, and Paul backed away, perspiring and confused. No one else paid any attention to the ranting woman. 'What are you talking about?' asked Paul, his throat as dry as sandpaper.

'You knocked me down on Hope Street you bastard! *That's* what I'm talking about!' the young lady roared.

Paul turned and ran out of Lewis's. He jumped into his car, started it, and thought about the woman he'd knocked down. How had she found him? Why hadn't she sustained any injuries?

He drove his car homewards up London Road, just wanting to put all of this nightmare far behind him – but the woman appeared in the passenger seat, giving him such a fright he went through a red light.

'Go to the Royal Infirmary, and tell them what you did or I'll haunt you for the rest of your life!' the apparition threatened - then vanished. Paul was so distracted by the ranting ghost he crashed into roadworks and was taken to the Royal infirmary with fractured ribs. Whilst recovering at the hospital he asked a nurse if a woman had been killed on Hope Street in a hit and run incident.

'She isn't dead - she's in a coma upstairs,' said the bubbly nurse, 'her name's Jane Edwards'.

'I thought I heard about her being knocked down and killed on the radio before I crashed, see,' said Paul, and he was eager to know more about the condition of Jane Edwards but the nurse told him to rest. Paul later sneaked from his hospital bed and found the ward where Miss Edwards was lying in a comatose state. She had the same face as the 'ghost' which had visited him. He went to the young woman's bedside, squeezed her hand, and in tears he said, 'Jane, I am so sorry.'

Jane's eyes opened, and she smiled, and whispered, 'Thanks for coming to me.' She made a full recovery and never told the police that Paul had knocked her down. She started to see Paul and eventually they married. Jane had vague memories of floating out of her body after the accident and looking for Paul in an angry state. It was as if she was, for a while, a living ghost.

THE STOLEN SATURDAYS

I've changed a few names in this strange story for legal reasons. Stephen – the person who found himself at the centre of some very strange goings-on in this account - was interviewed at length by myself and several other people on air on a local radio show when I had a slot talking about paranormal mysteries, and during further re-interviews years later he did not change one detail of his account.

In the 1990s, a 22-year-old opportunist thief from Norris Green named Stephen Runcett saw 77-year-old widow Rosie McAllister struggling to carry two full carrier bags of shopping on Utting Avenue, Walton. The pensioner had just been to Asda and was trying to make the arduous journey to her home on Sandyville Road, 400 yards away. Runcett asked Rosie if he could carry her shopping but she gave a faint smile, shook her head then put the bags down while she had a breather. Stephen picked them up and said, 'Come on, love, don't be proud,' and she believed he was being chivalrous and told him where she lived. When they got to her door, she tried to give him 50p but he refused. He said he was late for a Job Centre appointment and explained how he made an unofficial living as an odd job man to earn a few bob, and how he wanted to find a job desperately, just so he could afford to get a place of his own. Rosie asked Runcett if he could fix her television; it had sound but a blank screen. Runcett said he'd have a look after his appointment at the Job Centre, and when he returned, around 2.30pm, Rosie gave him tea and biscuits. Runcett wore a pair of driving gloves as he removed the back of the television set; he said he was wearing them for safety reasons – in case he touched a live wire. He looked at the components in the back of the telly, talked of capacitors and the cathode ray tube, and then he said, 'Ah, that's the problem. One of the valves has gone kaput.'

'Oh, well how much is a new valve?' asked Rosie, adding, 'I haven't got a clue about those types of things.'

'Probably just a fiver, Rose, I'll buy it, love,' Runcett told her.

'No you won't, Stephen, you're unemployed,' replied Rosie, heading towards the sideboard, 'I'll pay, and you'll be needing bus fare.'

Runcett watched the old lady open the drawer in the sideboard, and there was an old biscuit tin full of rolls of money; each little roll tied with elastic bands. Rosie unravelled a ten pound note from one of the rolls and then she closed the tin and closed the drawer.

'Who's that?' asked Runcett, gazing at the window of the living room.

Rosie went to the window saying, 'Who did you see?'

'Some tall man was looking in the window,' said Runcett, and he nodded to one of the walls and said, 'and then he went that way. I think he might be headed for your front door.'

'Wonder what he wants?' the old lady said, and went into the hallway to the front door. She opened it and saw that there was no one there. She returned and said,

'Not a soul there.'

'Listen Rosie, do me a favour,' said Runcett in a very sombre tone, 'when I go to town to get this valve, don't open your front door to anyone. There are some bad people knocking about, love. I've got a bad feeling about that man who passed the window before.'

Runcett left the house and said he'd be back in about an hour – but he never returned, and Rosie discovered that her £1500 savings had vanished from a box she kept in the sideboard. She immediately suspected Stephen Runcett and recalled how he'd inveigled her to go to the front door after he claimed he'd seen a tall man passing the window. She realised he'd just done this as a ruse so he could take her savings from the drawer while she was out of the living room. She reported Runcett to the police but the police couldn't prove Runcett was guilty as he had worn gloves in the house and he hadn't even touched the tea or biscuits kind-hearted Rosie had made him that day. Runcett also had an alibi about being somewhere else, and this was backed up by his mother and her neighbour. Furthermore, the police could find no trace of the money Runcett had apparently stolen, and he proved he had even just borrowed money off his uncle – so how could he have £1500 stashed away? The police told him they'd be watching him like a hawk from now on because they believed he was guilty of the heinous theft of the pensioner's savings. Runcett countered the police's threat by saying he'd sue them for harassment if they started leaning on him. When Rosie identified Runcett at the police station, she said, 'I curse you! I hope someone takes things you value in your life!'

Strange things happened to the thief Runcett after

that curse was laid upon him by Rosie. Runcett finally asked Claire, a girl he'd admired for years if she'd go on a date with him, and she said she was free Saturday. He went to bed Friday night in a smug state and when he turned the bedside lamp off and closed his eyes he thought of all the places he'd shop tomorrow morning to get clothes for the dream date – starting with All Mankind, then C&A – and at some point Stephen fell asleep. He awoke to sunlight streaming through the curtains onto his bed, and he remembered that this was the day he'd be going out with Claire. He went downstairs, switched the radio on, then the kettle, ready to make himself a cup of coffee – when he heard the DJ on the radio say: 'What a beautiful sunny Sunday morning it is.'

'Saturday you plantpot!' Stephen condescendingly said to the radio – and then he heard church bells. The penny still didn't drop. He turned the telly on and saw *Countryfile* with John Craven. That programme was usually on of a Sunday, Stephen thought. He turned on the Teletext feature of his TV as he wanted to have a look at the racing pages – and he noticed the abbreviation for Sunday at the top of the screen: Sun – but he still didn't realise what day it was. Then the DJ on the radio reminded the listeners that Mark Goodier would be presenting the UK Top 40 show from four o'clock. Stephen knew the Top 40 Show on Radio 1 always went out on a Sunday and his stomach turned over. Was this really Sunday? Stephen got dressed and dashed to the corner shop – and there were all the Sunday newspapers laid out on the counter. He asked the shopkeeper: 'It's not Sunday is it?'

The man behind the counter returned a quizzical

smirk and said, 'Yeah – all day. Why? What day did you think it was?'

'Saturday,' gasped Stephen Runcett. 'I must have slept through the whole of Saturday.'

'Had you had a good few the night before then?' the shopkeeper asked with a crooked grin.

'No,' answered Stephen, 'all I remember is going to sleep on the Friday night. I was supposed to take a beautiful bird on a date on Saturday; what am I going to tell her?'

'The truth,' suggested the shopkeeper, 'they call it a lost weekend. I had a few in my younger days, overdoing it with the ale.'

'I was stone cold sober though,' murmured Stephen, heading out of the shop, and when he got onto the sunny but cold street he thought, *Is there something wrong with me? Have I blacked out or had some seizure in my sleep?*

He walked past a telephone call box then halted, and walked back to it. He had to tell Claire what had happened. He heaved open the door and went through his jacket's inside pockets till he found her number on a crumpled Post-It Note. He dialled, and after several rings she answered.

Every word felt painful as he said: 'Claire? It's me Ste. I'm sorry about yesterday – '

'You sober now then?' Claire interposed.

'Claire, I was asleep!' protested Stephen.

Claire gave a short fake chuckle and said: 'With who? Look, just forget it Stephen – you're a bit small anyway; I only like men who are taller than me.'

'Claire, I give you my word – I went to bed Friday night and woke up about half an hour ago. I'm actually worried I might have some brain condition!'

'You'd have to have a brain in the first place, love,' replied Claire, coldly. 'Now stop calling me because I hate liars, got that shorty?'

'Claire, you're being unreasonable. Claire?'

She'd hung up.

The week flew over and Runcett reached Friday evening feeling a little uneasy. Would he go to bed again and wake up on Sunday? He convinced himself that the lost Saturday was some one-off incident, perhaps down to a lack of sleep. He got into bed just after midnight on Friday night and looked forward to the match on Saturday afternoon; going the game would do him the world of good with such an anxiety-ridden week behind him. He switched off the bedside lamp, closed his eyes, and for a brief moment he saw a tall man with short slicked-back hair in a finely-tailored suit plucking little square sheets with dates on from a daily calendar. It was a typical nonsensical excerpt from those types of dreams one has before sinking into the strange world of sleep.

Runcett awoke to church bells. That told him that the same thing had happened again, and he shot out of the bed, went downstairs and turned on the TV. Yes, the Teletext told him it was Sunday, and *Breakfast with Frost* was on the telly, and that programme – which always bored Stephen to tears – was on each Sunday. Once again Stephen went to the corner shop but he didn't go in this time because he could see the Sunday papers advertised on the news boards outside the premises.

Now Stephen Runcett felt scared. He walked slowly back to his flat and thought about the strange condition. If it was some sort of neurological disorder,

167

why would it always strike at the same time? There seemed to be something almost *supernatural* about all this – something spooky, and then, out of the blue Stephen recalled the curse of Rosie McAllister that day in the police station when she had identified him; she had said: 'I curse you! I hope someone *takes things you value* in your life!'

Was Rosie McAllister some witch? Runcett wondered. Saturday had always been one day he looked forward to – going out to pubs and clubs, going to the match – and now – well, it was as if something was stealing his Saturdays. It was so bizarre, no one would believe him. For the first time in his life, Runcett ventured into a church and caught the last few minutes of a midweek Mass. He lingered around after the service and made his way to the priest's quarters. The priest was a kind-looking old man with wireframe spectacles.

'Hello; can I help you?' the priest asked with a smile. 'This is out of bounds to the public – '

'I'm sorry father,' said Stephen, 'but I've got to see you – just for a few minutes – please? It's about something really strange that's been happening to me.'

The priest nodded and there was a pause. 'Yes – go on,' he said.

'Something is stealing the Saturdays from my life,' Stephen told him, and smiled awkwardly, 'and I don't expect you to believe me. I wouldn't believe it if it hadn't happened to me.'

'Something is stealing you're – did you say "Saturdays"?' said the priest, narrowing his eyes behind the lenses of his glasses. 'I don't understand.'

Stephen's eyebrows shot up and he nodded. 'It – it's

mad, I know but the gist of it is this: I go to bed Friday night, and when I wake up, it's Sunday morning, and it's been happening week after week. I was supposed to go on a date with a girl one Saturday, and I didn't wake up till the Sunday and she naturally didn't believe me.'

'And you're not on medication – er, tranquilizers or anything like that?' the priest queried, holding his cleft chin between his finger and thumb. Stephen shook his head. 'No Father, and I rarely drink, and definitely don't do drugs – and er, I don't have any medical conditions.'

'It's quite an odd one,' said the priest, and then he looked Stephen straight in the eye and said, 'Tell me, why do *you* think you're mislaying your Saturdays?'

Stephen couldn't say he thought the woman he'd stolen £1500 from had cursed him, and a nervous tic fluttered on his face. The priest noticed this facial twitch.

'I haven't a clue,' replied Stephen, avoiding eye contact with the holy man, 'but I thought it might be something weird, like; something supernatural.'

'Oh, I see, like a *curse*,' the priest said, and there was a dim smile on his lips.

'Yes, but I don't know why anyone would curse me, Father,' said Stephen, feigning bafflement.

The priest seemed to know the truth of the matter, because he said: 'Well, if you think it *is* all down to a curse, and if you feel you might have been cursed because you wronged someone enough to drive them to curse you, you must make your peace with them and make amends.'

'Make amends? For what?' Stephen asked, feeling a

little annoyed at the suggestion. He imagined the priest would say some prayer to lift this terrible curse.

The priest took a step nearer to Stephen Runcett and said: 'Well, say you had done something wrong to someone – like stolen money from them, for example – then you'd pay them back.'

Stephen gulped. 'But I haven't, Father, and I'm a bit narked actually, because you're making me feel as if it's all my fault.'

The priest just stood there. He said nothing in reply.

'No wonder the churches are empty if this is how you treat your flock, Father. See ya!' Stephen told him in a raised voice which echoed down the sandstone-walled corridor. He turned and marched out of the church.

Later that day in a pub, Stephen got talking to a very attractive barmaid named Linda, and she kept letting him know she was single and constantly touched his hand as she told innumerable stories about funny things that had happened to her over the years. Stephen knew the missing Saturday syndrome would ruin any chances of a steady relationship with Linda, and so he never asked her out – but she asked him out instead. 'Are you doing anything this weekend?' she asked him.

'The only days off I have are on Wednesdays,' he claimed.

'I work all through the week here and the only day I'm due off this week is Saturday,' she told him.

That was the end of that, Stephen thought, but then he had an idea. He bought a huge alarm clock from a shop in Old Swan and set it for 8am Saturday morning. He went to bed that Friday night and wondered if such a loud alarm clock would wake him in the morning. He had a strange dream of that well-dressed man again – the one he had seen pulling dates from the daily calendar in that short surreal dream before he dozed off for 24 hours. This time the man started speaking to him in a rather well-spoken voice.

'Ah, Stephen, you must be wondering why you keep skipping Saturdays,' he said, in an echoing voice. All around was a black ominous void of empty space.

'Yes – I am wondering,' Stephen replied, looking about, 'is it something to do with me stealing that old woman's money?'

The debonair man nodded. 'Yes it is, and unless you pay back the money you took from that old lady, you will never experience a single Saturday again.'

'It's wrong!' Stephen cried out. 'It's wrong what you're doing to me; who are you to steal days from my life? Who are you, anyway?'

The man laughed and looked at something in mid-air that was manifesting itself from a small cloud. It was a collection of dates from that daily calendar, and each one of the leaves of square paper had the word "Saturday" upon it with the name of the month and the date. These pieces of white paper with red and black dates upon them fluttered about like butterflies. They multiplied until there must have been about two hundred of them.

'There are 53 Saturdays in this year, and you're going to lose half of them, and next year I'll take all of them,' said the man, 'and I know how much you love your Saturdays Stephen; all that drinking with friends and dancing at the clubs and your pharmaceutically-enhanced one-night stands, and how you love shouting your head off at the match. You'll be doing without all that unless you give Rosie her money back.'

Stephen gritted his teeth. 'You're wrong! I'll get a mate to stay over on Friday nights and he'll shake me awake on Saturday morning!'

'You're good as dead on Saturday,' said the man, and he snapped his fingers and all of the fluttering dates vanished. 'That alarm clock won't work either – you won't hear it. Your heart's beating now at its slowest rate. Gabriel's Horn couldn't wake you.'

'Who are you?' Stephen asked, seething yet a little afraid of the all-encompassing black void.

'Pay the money back and you'll get your Saturday's back,' said the man, and he vanished.

Stephen awoke screaming and gulping for air. He sat up in bed and listened to his heart pounding. He got out the bed and heard the church bells again. He picked up the big alarm clock and smashed it against the wall. Enough was enough. He was forced to go to a loan shark to get £1500 so he could pay back Rosie McAllister. He secured the loan – and was told he'd have to pay back £3500 spread over six months. Stephen Runcett knocked on Rosie's door and when she answered she tried to close the door on him, but Stephen placed his foot in the door and said, 'Rosie, here's your money back! I'm sorry I took it but I was in debt! I'm sorry!'

The old woman threatened to call the police, but Stephen threw a bulging padded envelope containing the £1500 into the hallway, and then he left. On Thursday evening, Claire – the girl he had stood up because of his mysterious comatose condition – walked into the pub. She said the man she had been dating was violent and that she'd left him. Stephen bought her a drink and Claire started to warm to him again. By 11pm, Claire and Stephen were drunk, and he asked her to come back to his place, and he promised he'd sleep on the sofa – which he did. On Friday night, Stephen slept with Claire, and when he awoke, it was 8am – on a *Saturday* morning. He knew this because a passing young man was shouting to someone: 'Are you going the game this savvy?'

Stephen almost burst into tears when he heard that cry out in the street, and when Claire woke up she asked him what the matter was.

'It's Saturday,' he said in a choked-up voice, 'Saturday; what a beautiful day.'

After that morning, no more Saturdays were stolen from Stephen Runcett.

A CAULDRON OF
WITCHY TALES

No book of mine would be complete without some story of a witch or two; well, here's a cauldron full of such tales.

I've had to change a few details for reasons of confidentiality in this strange and touching tale, but the rest is all true. The peculiar telephone calls started a week before Christmas in 2010. Always when Angela was out of the house, always after the December dusk had fallen on Gateacre. The landline would ring at the Halewood Road home of 35-year-old Angela and her 40-year-old partner Matt, and Matt was usually the one who received the annoying and somewhat sinister calls from someone who sounded as if she was in her sixties or even older, and she never gave a name – until this particular wintry night. At 9.45pm the latest nuisance call was answered by Matt's sister Erin, and when she asked who was calling, a female voice had replied, 'It's just Grace – Matt will know who I am. Tell his partner Angela to go to her first little home at midnight on Christmas Eve, and she will surely find happiness. Good evening.'

Around 10pm when Matt and Angela came home

from an evening out at a local Indian restaurant, Erin told her brother about the call she'd received whilst minding the house. 'Matt, a woman named Grace telephoned, and she said something really odd – she must have been drunk or something – but she said something about Angela finding happiness if she goes to her first little home at midnight on Christmas Eve.'

'What?' Matt shot a puzzled look at his sister, then angled his head to Angela, wondering if she could make sense of the bizarre message, but Angela just returned a very uneasy expression as she tried to take in the gist of the strange message.

'Grace,' Erin replied to her brother, 'she said you'd know her.'

'I've never heard of a woman of that name before,' said Matt, shaking his head. He took off his coat whilst gazing tensely at the cordless telephone on the shelf next to the TV. 'It's got to be that anonymous caller again,' he decided, 'and if this goes on I'll have to notify the police.'

'Or just change our number,' suggested Angela, and she vanished into the kitchen to make some coffee.

'Why should we change our number?' asked Matt, 'I say if she keeps on calling we should report her to the law.'

Erin, on her way to help Angela in the kitchen, asked her brother as she passed him: 'What's the point of the calls?' And what did she mean about Angela going to "her first little home"?'

Matt shrugged as he picked up the remote and turned on the TV with the gentle touch of a soft rubber button. 'It's always about Angela,' he said, 'always some garbled message about her. What was the

175

last one? "Tell Angela someone's thinking about her an awful lot." I can understand if it was kids playing pranks but the caller sounds as if she's getting on a bit.'

Erin went into the kitchen as Matt watched the TV. 'Wonder who it is, eh?' Erin said to Angela as she spooned the ground coffee into the percolator. 'Did that make any sense about you going to your first little home, Ange?'

Angela shook her head. 'My first little home was a tiny semi in Halewood where my mum raised four of us, and it was knocked down years ago. Doesn't make sense. Probably just someone's idea of a joke.'

'She sounded very sincere,' Erin recalled, 'and well-to-do; well-spoken.'

'Well, let's just hope she stops her barmy calls soon,' sighed Angela.

Erin suddenly had an idea. 'Hey, did you ever try tracing the call by dialling 1471?' she asked, and although Angela nodded, Erin decided to go into the lounge, where she picked up the telephone and dialled in the code that would hopefully supply her with the telephone number of the person who had been making the nuisance calls.

'She withholds her number, Erin!' Angela shouted from the doorway of the kitchen, but Erin's eyebrows rose and she smiled. She said, 'She hasn't this time, get a pen! 0151...'

Angela remembered the number and dialled it. There was no answer, but when she went to make some coffee, Erin redialled the number and a man answered, and as he spoke, there was a bleeping sound – and Erin could hear traffic noise and the faint sounds of voices. She'd called a public telephone box, and the old man told her that the telephone box in question was the one at the junction of Belle Vale Road and Grange Lane. The old man said he had seen no one in the call box and hung up, thinking someone was pulling his leg. So, Angela now knew that the last call Grace had made was at a telephone box less than 300 yards from her house, but that still didn't throw much light on the telephonic mystery.

Christmas Eve arrived, and as usual, all the wrapping of the presents was left to Angela while Matt drank wine and ate tube after tube of Pringles as he watched the *Have I Got News for You Christmas Special*. He became sarcastic in drink, and kept making little remarks about a mole Angela had on her cheek. It wasn't even really noticeable, but she was self-conscious about it, and it really hurt her when he joked about it. Finally, at 11.50pm, as Matt was singing rude verses to the carol singers on the telly (as the Midnight Mass was broadcast from the Metropolitan Cathedral that year), Angela exploded, and she threw one of Matt's gifts at him and turned the air blue with insults about his bad breath, his spreading bald spot and his 'interfering father' and then she went and put on her coat and stormed out of the house. There was a heavy snowfall that year and Angela trudged through a thick blanket of virgin snow in her slippers as she heard Matt shouting for her to come back, but she ran, and started to cry. Upon reaching the Junction of Halewood Road and Belle Vale Road, Angela's subconscious suddenly came up with a memory which threw a lot of light on Grace's enigmatic comment about the "first little home". Back in 1991, when Angela was just sixteen, she had dated her first boyfriend Stephen, who had also been sixteen, and they used to huddle together in that red telephone box – the one around the corner that Grace had called from. Yes! She remembered it now. Stephen used to jokingly say, 'This old phone box is our first little home Angie. Now, we could put the sofa over there, and the cooker there, and the fireplace is here,' and he would pretend to hold his palms out to an imaginary coal fire. And then he kissed Angela one night in that phone box and solemnly told her: 'I love you Angela, and my Gran told me once, that there's no love like the first love. I hope you'll always be mine, girl, because I know I'll always be yours.'

And then Stephen's family had to move away to another area – to Wigan. But it was as if they were going to Florida those days. Stephen visited Angela for a while, and then somehow he lost touch, and Angela was broken-hearted for months afterwards.

The rusty metal tongue of an old clock chimed the midnight hour somewhere, and now Angela had tears in her eyes. She crossed the road and looked at that telephone box. She went inside and saw a curious thing – a sprig of mistletoe had been tied to the door-closing mechanism by someone. The sight of this mistletoe really caused Angela's heart to ache.

She heard the sound of feet crunching in the snow outside. Had Matt come after her? A face peered in through the panes of the telephone box. It was Stephen. He'd hardly changed; he was just a bit stockier. The door heaved open. 'Angela!' he said, and he smiled and his eyes did too. 'What are you doing here?'

'I could ask you the same,' she said, and she saw his

eyes narrow as they saw the tears rolling down her cheeks.

He coughed, then said: 'I just had to come here tonight – to this phone box – I drove from Aigburth; that's where I live now. Do you remember what we called this phone box?'

She nodded, and the two of them simultaneously said, 'Our little home,' then they laughed, and they embraced, and snow started to fall. She told him about Matt, and he told her about the woman he'd split from six months ago, but she didn't tell him about Grace until after they were married in the following year. He knew no one named Grace, and she was never heard from again after that night, and I thought she might have been some matchmaker somewhere up there in the Great Beyond, but I have since been told by a very old woman that it was a witch who steered two lost soulmates back into one another's arms. Many years ago, back in the 1950s, there was a kind old eccentric woman named Grace who was often seen walking up Gateacre Brow followed by a clowder of cats – all strays she fed, because Grace was a real animal lover, and some called her the Cat Lady. Some of the older folk in Gateacre Village remembered that Grace had been associated with a real-life coven of witches, and that at the age of forty, Grace had left the coven to marry a man who proved to be untrue. She became a recluse after she discovered he had cheated on her. No one recalled Grace passing away, and there are no records of her death, but if she was active in 2010, she would have been a century old or more – but witches have been known to extend their lives with their craft.

Halloween is traditionally a time we automatically

associate with witches, and the Halloween of 1974 is a very memorable one to a certain female who was inaugurated into the world of witchery that year.

On the Wednesday night of October 30 1974 at 11.50pm, a teenaged couple sat in a parked car on Prenton's Marlborough Grove. The couple were Eric Godwin, an 18-year-old trainee chef and his girlfriend of two weeks, 16-year-old Maureen Appleby, who was still at school. 'What have you parked here for?' Maureen asked, looking through the windows of the BMW – a car Eric had borrowed from his father. 'I live in the next street, Kings Mount,' she told a smirking Eric as he leaned towards her, his lips puckering.

'Yeah, well, I thought we could have a bit of nooky time here first,' he said in a very sleazy manner. Maureen leaned back, shrinking away from him with a look bordering on disgust. He still had chewing gum in his mouth. 'Stop that, Eric,' she protested, pushing her hand against his bare chest. He'd unbuttoned his shirt because he imagined the sight of his naked chest would get Maureen going. 'I told my mum and dad I'd be back at eleven, and it's nearly twelve. They'll go spare,' said Maureen, glancing up at the full moon hanging over a deserted Marlborough Grove. Something flitted across the lunar disk, startling the girl. It was not an owl – it was too big to be any night bird or bat – and that silhouette had looked like a person!

'Eric, something just went past the moon!' she told her lecherous boyfriend, but he pushed her into the seat and started kissing her neck. 'Eric! Did you hear what I said?'

'Yeah, it's been a satellite or something,' came his muffled reply from under her chin, 'romantic this, isn't it?'

There was a sound of shrieking female laughter somewhere in the distance, and Maureen pushed Eric's smooching face away and he looked around, expecting to see someone on the street – but instead he saw shadows flitting across the road, pavement and walls of the houses – moonlight shadows that were being cast from above.

'Eric! Look!' yelped Maureen, looking wide-eyed at the night sky through the windows of the car. There was a woman, mostly in silhouette, with a faint tracing of silver from the moon around her face and bare legs, flying slowly across the clear Persian blue sky. She wore a knee-length skirt and her hair was up in a bun, and she was now moving her arms in semicircular movements and kicking her legs about so it looked as if she was doing the backstroke through the sky. The whole impression was mesmeric to Maureen but it frightened Eric, who kept swearing in shock. His hands seized his throat and he rasped, 'I've swallowed me chewy! It'll wrap around me heart!'

Marlborough Grove is on a slant, so when a panicking Eric took the handbrake off and missed the biting point of the engine, the BMW lurched forward and stalled, and Maureen pointed skywards, yelling: 'There's another one look! Eric – look!'

'I don't wanna look!' yelled back her terrified boyfriend.

This second airborne female was not in silhouette; she was fully illuminated by the moon, and Eric and Maureen could see her long red hair and the white nightie she was wearing as she flew just above chimney pot level with her arms stretched out ahead and her toes pointed as if she was springing off a diving board. She only looked young and petite. The BMW tore off down the moonlit road and swung onto Woodchurch Road, narrowly missing a beeping Hackney cab. Maureen was enthralled by the flying girls but Eric was making the sign of the cross and muttering some prayer. Then, as the car halted at the lights at the Balls Road junction, Eric nodded to Oxton Congregational Church and said, 'Protect us Lord from these witches!'

Maureen found herself giggling, and an annoyed Eric asked, 'What's funny about that you stupid mare?'

'I thought witches were just things out of fairy tales,' said Maureen, her face lit up with joy, 'I can't believe we've just seen them! Wait till I tell our Jane – she's into all that witchcraft and love-spells stuff.'

Jane was Maureen's older sister, and Eric had said she was weird because she always dressed in black.

'That's it, isn't it?' Eric said, as he moved off with the changing of the lights, 'it's bleeding Duck Apple Night now isn't it?'

'Tomorrow, it is,' said Maureen, but Eric shook his head and said, 'Which is now; it's gone past midnight.'

'Oh yes, so now it's the witching hour,' said Maureen, 'it's usually between one and two in the morning but when the moon is full, it starts at midnight, especially at Halloween.'

'Your barmy sister been down your ear-hole then?' Eric said, switching on the radio to listen to the *Night Ride* programme on Radio 1 to calm his nerves.

Maureen tapped his fist on the gearstick. 'Take me home Eric, my parents will have murder with me for staying out this late.'

'I'll take you back soon,' laughed Eric. 'We're going to a quiet little speck by the park, having a bit of romantic how's your father – '

The car suddenly lost all power and something stopped it on Oxton Road. As Eric tried to restart the BMW, the passenger door opened, and Maureen saw the girl in black standing there. It was her sister Jane, smiling. 'It's time you joined us, sister of mine,' she said, and gently pulled a startled Maureen out the car. Eric leaned across the passenger seat to see who it was – and saw the stranger was Jane – and she and Maureen and a red-haired girl went up into the air. He almost fell out the BMW and went cold with fear as he saw those two witches on either side of Maureen, holding her arms as they flew through the sky shrieking with laughter. Eric never went near Maureen again and later moved to Liverpool. Maureen's children – all girls – are also part of a coven in South Liverpool now.

Most witches – unless you try to harm them or theirs – are usually friendly nature-loving folk, but some witches of the past have been known to resort to the Black Arts to get what they want – even long after they have gone to their grave...or met their fate at the burning stake...

In the autumn of 1997, the National Trust said that a spate of recent television costume dramas had helped to make historic houses and gardens the most visited tourist attractions in Britain. Little Moreton Hall – a half-timbered moated manor house in Cheshire – featured in ITV's version of the DeFoe classic *Moll Flanders*, was one such attraction, and it was visited by the Leigh family from Birkenhead one afternoon in October 1997. The youngest of the family was 19-year-old Heather Leigh, a girl who was not into history and had only accompanied her parents and 21-year-old brother Brian because she had been badgered into coming. Heather, a Goth, normally sat in her room all day listening to heavy metal or hanging with friends at Quiggins in Liverpool. When Heather visited Little Moreton Hall, which was built between 1504 and 1610, she had a strange feeling of *déjà vu* – as if she had been there before. She had not watched *Moll Flanders* on the telly and had most definitely never set eyes on the historic dwelling before, and yet the girl felt at home in the place. When the family had visited the hall they visited a local antiques shop before setting out on the 53-mile-journey home. At this antiques shop, Heather's father bought an onyx ring emblazoned with a gold letter H for £100 and gave it to his daughter. The owner of the store said he believed the ring was very old, possibly dating back to the Jacobean era (1567-1625) but he knew nothing of the ring's origins. An old man had sold it to him ten years back.

As soon as Heather put this ring on, her personality seemed to undergo a drastic change. She was usually outspoken and loud but now she was quiet and shy. She was prone to thrash out power chords on her electric guitar in her room, but her brother Brian was surprised when Heather started to pick strange haunting tunes on the instrument. She wrote a curious verse in a writing pad which Brian read. It went:

I know a little girl sly and deceitful

every little tittle-tat she goes and tells the people
long nose, ugly face
ought to be put in a glass case.
If you want to know her name,
her name is Heather Lee.
Please Heather Lee,
keep away from me,
I don't want to speak to you, nor you to speak to me.
Once we were friends, but now we disagree.
Oh Heather Lee,
please keep away from me.
It's not because you're dirty,
it's not because you're clean,
it's because you are a witch, and you shouldn't be seen.

The word *witch* stood out to Brian in the strange verse, and the copperplate handwriting bore no resemblance to Heather's normal spidery scrawl. On the following morning Brian heard raised voices in his sister's room. His mother was shouting, 'What have you done to yourself?' Brian went to see what was going on and got the shock of his life. His sister normally had her shoulder-length hair dyed blue with purple streaks – but now she had long red hair – and Brian asked if it was a wig. His confused mother said, 'No, it's not a wig – it's real – and I don't know how her hair grew that long overnight!'

Heather was also wearing a long black velvety dress, and a choker necklace of gold, embedded with a variety of gemstones and pearls. Heather sat there on the edge of the bed, closed fists on her lap, gazing down at the floor. When Brian asked her if she was alright, she looked up at him – and he noticed she now had blue eyes. His sister's eyes had been olive green. 'Heather's gone,' she told Brian in an unfamiliar soft voice. Her nose ring was absent, and all of the pale foundation Heather had worn was also gone, along with the dark lipstick.

'Gone where?' Brian asked, thinking his sister had suffered some breakdown.

'To the stake,' came the spine-tingling reply, in a weird accent reminiscent of a Lancashire brogue, 'gone to burn, instead of me.'

'Mum, her tattoo's gone,' said Brian to his mother, drawing attention to the back of Heather's left hand – where the girl usually sported a tattoo of a lemniscate - the infinity symbol. The 'new' Heather refused to leave her room, and Brian felt a shiver run down his spine when he heard her singing *Greensleeves* as she strummed and picked chords on her guitar. He visited a priest and told him of the unearthly, unaccountable change in his sister, and the priest visited Heather then spoke to her distraught parents. Mr Leigh recalled how the change in his daughter had occurred after she had put on that old onyx ring, so the priest resolved to remove it from the teenager, and red-headed blue-eyed Heather screamed and clawed at the face of the holy man as he removed the old onyx ring. Over the course of an hour, Heather's red hair became shorter and changed colour, and before the shocked eyes of the family, the old Heather returned, her eyes now green, and the tattoo on her hand reappeared, along with the girl's usual attire – black tee shirt and dark-grey jeans. The returned Heather sobbed and hugged her mother and rambled on about people 'in the old days' trying to burn her alive at a stake – for being a witch.

The priest kept the onyx ring, and said it had been a 'gateway to possession'. Heather had nightmares about the sinister ordeal for years, and on some occasions she was heard to sing *Greensleeves* in her sleep.

The last tale seems to suggest that some old witches never die, they merely fade away for a while until they return from the great unknown beyond the grave for something they want – in this case a couple of children...

At 8.30pm on the Wednesday evening of 31 October, 1990 – Halloween – Mr and Mrs Gregson told their 7-year-old son Jake and their 5-year-old daughter Jodie to behave for the babysitter Charlene and that mummy and daddy would soon be back – around half eleven at the latest. It was the first time the couple had been out in three months. Charlene let the children stay up till 9.20pm, and then she sat downstairs reading *Just Seventeen* magazine and occasionally looking at the mildly amusing Jasper Carrot stand-up and sketch show *Canned Carrot* on the telly.

What happened next will probably never be explained. Charlene suddenly saw something shadowy out the corner of her left eye; it looked like a very thin female in pure silhouette, but before the babysitter could turn to see what it was, she felt overcome by something which caused her to faint, and she slumped sideways onto the sofa. Upstairs, Jake was lying in bed, looking at the full moon through a gap in the curtains when he heard his sister next door scream. The boy sat bolt upright in bed and shouted his sister's name. 'Jodie! Are you alright? Jodie!' he cried, and getting no answer he then called for Charlene. Next door he could hear strange bumps and unidentifiable sounds. Jake opened his bedroom door and saw a quivering long black leathery cloaked object stretched out on the carpeted landing, about six feet in length. He slammed the door shut and hid under his bed, where he screamed, 'Charlene! Help!'

The bedroom door slowly opened with a faint creak and then Jake saw someone, or something that was obviously pretending to be Charlene, moving along the floor. It peeped under the bed at him and facially it resembled Charlene but the eyes glowed and the mouth was huge. Its raspy voice said: 'Come out, it's only Charlene! Don't ye be frightened of me now Jake.'

Jake crawled further away under the bed, and then he heard Jodie's frantic and muffled voice coming from inside the terrifying mimic. 'Yes,' the thing said, 'she's in here,' and it patted the bulging belly of its long greyish body. The weird woman then snarled at Jake and reached out, trying to grab him with bony fingers tipped with long yellow nails. 'It won't hurt, you'll just go asleep!' the woman informed Jake. Her eyes started to give off an orange glow like the light from the bar of an electric fire. These eyes made Jake feel sleepy. 'So you can come into Mama like a good boy,' the weird lady said, and her voice had a strange echo to it, 'And then you shall be with your sister, all gobbled up and safe with Jodie, and then ye shall be born again Jakey, and I shall be your Mama!'

'I want my mummy,' Jake said, crying.

'Open your eyes and listen to me Jakey!' cried the ghastly-looking woman. And then she said an unintelligible repeating phrase which sounded like:

'Addy-addy-on-kon-kay...Addy-addy-on-kon-kay! Addy-addy-on-kon-kay! Don't you *dare* look away!'

And as she came out with this strange gibberish, Jake could hear his little sister's muffled screams coming from inside the unearthly intruder. 'Addy-addy-on-kon-kay!' the creepy lady said as her arm seemed to unnaturally lengthen so her hand could close in on Jake, who was feeling very sleepy as he looked at the woman's incandescent orange eyes.

There was a sound downstairs; the door opened and Jake recognised the voices of his mother and father. They were arguing and yet it was music to the besieged boy's ears.

'Don't you shout to them or I'll kill them too and eat their hearts and make jam from their brains!' the woman cruelly warned.

'Mummy!' screeched Jake, 'Daddy! Help! Help!'

The face of the wizened woman crouched on the floor seemed to shrink to something skeletal – almost insect-like, and then it vanished.

Jake crawled from under the bed and found Jodie fast asleep nearby. She had no memory of the traumatic unearthly incident, and Mrs Gregson had cross words with Charlene for being fast asleep when she was supposed to have been minding the children. No one believed Jake's story, and when the boy's mother told an elderly neighbour named Mrs Bright about her son's incredible yard, the old woman made the sign of the cross and said, 'Oh, he's telling the truth love. That night, I was trying to get the cat to come in become some boys were letting off fireworks, and I saw her.'

'Saw who?' asked Mrs Gregson with a nervous smile

on her lips.

'It was a woman, all in black, with long white hair, and she wore a cloak,' answered Mrs Bright, and her trembling hand rose and she pointed her index finger to the sky. 'And she was as thin as that, honest,' she said, looking at her finger.

'Go way,' said Mrs Gregson, dismissively.

'Before God in Heaven!' said an annoyed Mrs Bright, 'She was standing on the windowsill of that window up there – ' she said, pointing to the window of Jake's bedroom. 'She was clinging on, and I was that scared, I just went back in. I'd only glanced up to see what the cat was looking at.'

'Well if you're telling the truth, why didn't you call the police? It could have been a burglar,' said Mrs Gregson, looking up at her son's window.

Mrs Bright nodded, 'I'll tell you why. When I came out a few minutes later out of curiosity I saw she was gone, and I just knew she wasn't one of the living. She struck me as an old hag, like an old witch. The moon was out and there was just something hanging in the air that night.'

In all the years Mrs Gregson had known old Mrs Bright she had never known her neighbour to lie or speak of anything remotely supernatural, so she was left quite unnerved by the old lady's testimony.

Not all witches are shrivelled old hags of course – why, some of them are quite beautiful, like the one in the following story – a story that was personally told to me by the teacher mentioned in the tale.

In 1977 a new English teacher we shall call David Roberts (not his real name) started work at a certain well-known college in Liverpool. The teacher he had replaced had died and was not missed by any of the pupils or staff. He'd been a slovenly man of 63 who used to blow his nose on handkerchiefs then dry them on the classroom radiators. Mr Roberts, at 39 was much younger than his predecessor and days after taking up his post at the college he handed out books by Marvell, Chaucer, Byron, Larkin and Lawrence and told his 30 pupils to write a "flowery" 2000-word essay on someone's love life – real or fictional.

Erica de Brigue, a certain pretty 18-year-old pupil with a cascading blonde Farrah Fawcett hairstyle, wrote a realistic story about the double life of an English teacher named David who embarked on a steamy affair with his sister-in-law. The descriptions of the sexual acts carried out between the teacher and his brother's sister were very graphic in Erica's essay. The pupils were supposed to read out their own essays but when the teacher came to Erica's desk, she told him a very sultry and well-spoken voice: 'Ah, be a dear and read my essay out please. I have a rather sore throat.'

Mr Roberts rolled his eyes, and picked up the six-page essay from his pupil's desk, then started to read it out loud – and then, to his utter horror, the teacher realised that it was about *him*. In real life he *was* having an affair with his brother's wife, and her name and his name and every detail in the shocking story by Erica was factual; it was simply beyond coincidence; Erica obviously knew about the affair in great depth – but how? Roberts stuttered to a halt and saw Erica eyeing him knowingly with a sadistic grin. He was saved by the bell, which sounded the end of the lesson. Roberts told Erica to stay, and when they were alone he asked her if the essay was real or fiction.

'Oh, it is very real Mr Roberts - based on a man I know,' Erica replied, her accusing green eyes burning through the teacher. He felt as if those beautiful olive-green eyes were X-raying his very soul. He found this Erica de Brigue so beautiful, so seductive, yet he felt there was something dangerous about her, and he just couldn't put his finger on what it was. David Roberts decided he'd try and find out just who this girl was.

In the following week, as rain lashed the windows of the classroom, Roberts told the class to pick one of the Seven Deadly Sins as the basis of an essay. For the heathens among you,' Roberts said to the class as he sat on his desk, 'the Seven Sins are – '

'Sir, your flies are undone,' said Erica, and the class erupted into laughter and suggestive 'Oohs!''

'Alright, grow up!' said the teacher, getting up off the desk and quickly turning around to yank the zipper up. He turned back to face the class, blushing slightly, and continued with his challenge to the pupils. 'As I was saying, the Seven Deadly Sins are anger, envy, greed, sloth, pride, gluttony and lust. Seven words you can use for the theme of your essay – and I want your work on my desk on Monday morning – got that?'

Some of the pupils nodded and smiled, but most grumbled at the challenge, finding any essay to be a chore, especially one that had to be based on one of those sins. Erica chose "anger" and wrote a story about a highly-sexed man named David who has an affair with his sister-in-law Catharine but dies when his angry brother Martin discovers the affair and blasts him with a shotgun. The brother of David Roberts – Martin - was a farmer and possessed a shotgun, and his wife was named Catharine – the woman David was having an affair with – and yet again Erica's story matched every detail of the teacher's real-life affair. The killing in the essay was described as happening this coming Sunday, the day David was due to visit his brother, and upon that day, Martin confronted his teacher brother and said he knew about his affair with Catharine. Martin reached for the shotgun, saying, 'Get ready to meet your maker, you bastard!' but David delivered a powerful upper cut to his brother's jaw and knocked him out. The shotgun went off as Martin hit the ground and its two barrels blasted the air close to David's right ear, deafening him. He stood there in shock, and realised that in a very warped way, Erica de Brigue had saved his life by forewarning him of Martin's intent to blast him to death.

On Monday morning, Erica's chair was empty. No one in class remembered her and she could not be traced. I traced her by her unusual surname: she was a witch of old, born a long, long time ago, and once went under the name of Jehenne de Brigue (and sometimes Jehenna; La Cordière and Eriqua de Brigue) – until the year 1391, when she was tried for witchcraft and burned alive at the pig market in Paris – but not long afterwards she was apparently seen alive and well and was identified in her new 'guise' (for she could alter her features by transfiguration) by her beautiful and very distinctive green eyes. She is probably still roaming the world today and resorting to all sorts of mischief. If you see a girl with unusually vivid green eyes – beware - it could be her...

Witches come in all shapes and sizes, all colours, and some are born witches – and these are the most powerful – and most dangerous - type. In 1957 in

Kirkby, a family from Scotland Road moved into the newly-built houses on Leeside Avenue, and the youngest member of this family was 10-year-old Iona, a girl regarded by even her own parents as odd. She hated going to bed at night and often stayed out after dark, frightening other children her age with ghost stories and some weird and gruesome tales. The child was fascinated by witches and told her mother that she had been born before and had been a Lancashire witch. Iona's mother just thought her child had a vivid imagination, but one day the girl came home with a huge black cat.

'Where on earth did you find that thing?' Iona's father asked, when he saw the oversized feline in the back garden.

'His name is Haussibut,' replied Iona casually, 'I found him among the graves outside St Chads. He used to belong to a really bad highwayman but – '

'Shush!' came the noise from the cat, and it lifted its paw to his mouth, as if to gesture 'be quiet' to the girl. This humanlike sound and gesture really unnerved Iona's father, and he said, 'You're not keeping him, I'll tell you that for nothing!'

'No, he's keeping me,' said Iona with a smile, 'you see Haussibut is training me – '

'Shush! Said the cat, Iona turned to face him and the overgrown moggy subtly shook it head and narrowed its huge green eyes.

'You take it back where you found it or I'll go and see Killer Jones,' threatened Iona's nervous father. Killer Jones was a local man who hunted rabbits and had a cold-blooded fondness for shooting small animals with an air rifle.

'We'll hang Killer Jones and send his soul to the pits of Hell if he even looks at Haussibut,' said Iona, defiantly, her little fists clenched tight at her sides, and the cat made a strange rhythmical hissing sound – as if it was chortling. Iona's father hurried inside the house and told his wife about the strange cat and of the violent words of their daughter.

On the sunny but chilly Friday afternoon of February 8,1957, Iona and three new friends she had acquired were in the back garden playing when a boy of eight years of age named Michael climbed over a fence and started taunting the girls. Iona's mother watched the proceedings. Michael put his thumb to his nose and wiggled his fingers, blew a raspberry at the girls, then shouted, 'Toorally, oorally, oorally ooh! They want four monkeys at the zoo, so I'd apply if I was yous, you ugly-looking monkeys!'

'Come here and say that you little squirt!' Iona retorted, and Michael spat on the grass and effected an exaggerated 'hard-knock' walks as he marched to the girls. When the boy was about six feet away from the youngest girl – Jane Fairley, his head seemed to whip back and he fell to the floor unconscious, as if he'd been punched by someone, but none of the girls was near enough to lay a finger on him. Iona told her three female friends to stand around the inert Michael and to do and say what she did. Iona pressed her palm on the boy's forehead, and the 3 hands of her friends were laid on that hand, and Iona's mother opened the window of her kitchen and listened to the strange words spoken so solemnly by her daughter:

Voici un corps mort

Raide comme un bâton,
Froid comme le marbre
Léger comme un esprit,
Lève-toi au nom de Queen of Elphen!

This strange incantation was recited first by Iona and then by the three other girls about six or seven times, and then Iona crouched and placed her two index fingers under the shoulder of the prone boy, and the girl on the other side of the child did the same, and Jane Fairley, was directed to place her two index fingers under the right ankle of Michael, and the girl facing her did the same with the lad's left ankle. Iona slowly stood up, and the other three accomplices did the same – and Iona's mother gasped, 'Oh Jesus,' because she saw the unconscious boy slowly float in mid air about a foot over the heads of the girls. He moved slowly upwards and one of the girls laughed, but Iona said to her, 'No, Paula, be quiet or he'll fall!'

Iona's mother ran through the kitchen, opened the kitchen door, and when she rushed to the four children, there was no sign of Michael.

'Where is he?' Iona's mum asked, looking up into the blue sky. 'How did you do that?'

'He called us names,' said Jane Fairley, and her two friends positioned themselves in front of Iona as if they were ready to protect her from her mother. Michael was found minutes later, crying his eyes out in the upper branches of a tree about a hundred yards from Leeside Avenue. The boy, having a fear of heights, had awakened at rooftop level and had thoroughly wet himself. He never ventured near Iona and her little 'coven' again, and would often cross the road if he saw any of the 'witches' coming his way. Iona's mother heard her daughter recite more of her ominous spells, and she noticed how many of them referred to a "Queen of Elphen" – and when she asked Iona who this was, her daughter said she was a Queen of the Elves who helped witches.

'You're not to spout this mumbo-jumbo any more, Iona,' her mother told her, 'you're not a witch and you're going to have people laughing at you!'

'The stupid priest spouts mumbo-jumbo every Sunday!' Iona yelled at her mother, 'No one laughs at him do they?'

Iona's mum asked her husband if anyone in his family had ever messed about with witchcraft, and he recalled how his grandmother often read tealeaves and often cursed people. 'Maybe she takes after her, love,' Iona's father wondered.

As Iona got older she became quite pretty, and in 1967, at the age of twenty, she became very attracted to a 30-year-old local businessman named Gene, but he was already engaged to a 25-year-old Lydiate woman named Jo. Iona became that fixated with winning the heart of Gene she followed him to a nightclub in Liverpool one Saturday evening with her coven - which now numbered nine. Iona is said to have done everything within her supernatural powers to seduce Gene, and when she danced at the club, many admiring eyes were locked on her. She tossed her long silky hair about as she writhed to the music and danced suggestively around Gene, who now seemed to be totally captivated. After the dance, he just had to ask Iona what her name was, even though his fiancée Jo was at his side. Iona told him, and she mentioned she lived on Leeside Avenue and had seen him walk past her many times. Jo was enraged by this blatant flirtation and she clutched Gene's hand and almost dragged him off the dance floor to the bar, where she gave him a right earful. He said he was sorry and that the drink had gone to his head. 'No, that Iona has gone to that thing between your legs more like!' Jo seethed, and seemed ready to throw her drink in the wandering eyes of her boyfriend, because he was still making furtive glances at Iona, and almost everyone else in the club was also gazing at the girl.

That night as Gene made love to Jo, she said, 'Tell me you love me, Gene, please tell me!'

'You know I do,' Gene said, and kissed his fiancée.

'Say my name, and tell me you love me!' she insisted.

'I love you Iona – ' he said, and realised the slip, and Jo pushed him off her.

Not long after this Jo became pregnant to Gene, and the latter promised her he would never look at Iona or even talk about her again, and the couple decided to marry, and even had grand plans for a big wedding in one of the city's cathedrals (Jo was Protestant and Gene Catholic) but Gene continued to make the occasional reference about Iona and how he'd seen her on his way to or from work, and Jo would always remind him about the promise he'd made to stop mentioning – and thinking – about her. The weeks went on without any definite date set for the wedding, and Jo told him that her baby bump would be showing in a few months, so Gene got on the phone and called the vicar of a church and made all the arrangements. Jo cried when they got the date ironed out, and said she was so happy – now she *knew* how much her fiancé loved her – and her unborn baby. The couple went out to celebrate the forthcoming wedding and told many of their friends at the club about the date and informed most of them that they'd be receiving the invitations soon.

But Iona turned up that night, and she really turned heads, for she seemed immensely more beautiful than she had before. Jo was absolutely distraught when she saw the girl, and urged Gene to leave, but he was in such a daze as he gazed at Iona, he didn't seem to hear a word his fiancée said. Jo grabbed his face with her hand on each cheek and turned his head so he faced her. He looked hypnotised, and seemed to break out of some spell.

'Gene! You promised me – remember? You swore you'd never look at her again. I'm carrying your baby!' Jo took hold of his hand and placed it on the very slight bump in her abdomen. He saw his fiancée had a tear in her eye.

'Oh! Oh Jo, I'm sorry – forgive me.' He embraced Jo and kissed the top of her head, but still he turned and took a sly glance at Iona, who was now dancing within a circle of admirers in the middle of the dance floor.

To keep Gene away from Iona, Jo sat with him among her friends – four other couples – in a corner of the club, and they chatted about the wedding. Jo told her friends how she was going to have her hair done exactly like Audrey Hepburn's hairstyle in *Breakfast at Tiffany's* as Gene had a thing for the actress, which raised a lot of laughs and playful banter – but then the smile was wiped off Jo's face when she looked to the next table, just five feet away; Iona was sitting there, apparently eavesdropping on the conversation. Jo turned her back on her rival, but when she looked back at her fifteen minutes later, she could not believe her eyes. Somehow, in the space of a mere quarter of an hour, the beguiling girl had somehow acquired a pearl tiara comb and it was set in the exact chic updo of the Holly Golightly character Audrey Hepburn had played in *Breakfast at Tiffany's* but much stranger still, the face of Iona now resembled Hepburn. It was eerie to Jo, yet at the same time she felt sick with jealousy. Gene turned to ask his fiancée what she'd like to drink when he noticed Iona, and he remarked to Jo, 'Hey, now that's a coincidence; doesn't she look like – ' but then his words trailed off as he recognised the Audrey Hepburn lookalike.

'Yes, it's *her* – 'Jo said through clenched teeth, 'she's trying everything she's got in her bag of tricks to get you Gene. Let's go home.'

'Are you *sure* it's her?' Gene asked with a perplexed look.

Jo grabbed his hand and squeezed it hard. 'Yes, you know very well it's her – she's got the same cheap tacky dress on. Now let's go home!'

'Look, Jo, just ignore her!' said Gene, squeezing his fiancée's hand back. 'Why should that little minx drive us away from our friends?'

'Minx?' Jo gave an agonised chuckle at the mention of the word, 'You mean slut don't you?'

'She's not ruining our night – and it *is* our night, Jo,' said Gene, 'so let's stop running away from this attention-seeker and start enjoying the night.'

Ten minutes after this, Gene got up to go the toilet as Jo was showing off her engagement ring to her friend Mandy. The minutes passed, and Jo looked towards the dimly lit corridor which led to the toilets on the far side of the room. A friend named Charlie got up and jokingly said, 'I'm just going to powder my nose.'

Jo tapped his arm as he passed and said, 'Charlie, can you tell Gene to hurry back here? He's been gone for ages.'

'Ah, missing him are you?' said Charlie, and he nodded and walked away towards the corridor. When he tried to push open the door of the gents he found it partially obstructed by the backs of several men. There was a crowd in the toilet, and Charlie became aware of a rhythmic sound coming from one of the cubicles. 'What's going on in here?' he asked a young man who was gazing at the door of the toilet cubicle with a twisted smile.

'Some fellah's getting his oats with a bird in there, lucky sod!' replied the youth.

Charlie looked around, thinking he'd see Gene, but he was nowhere to be seen. Charlie relieved himself at the urinal, washed his hands in the basin as he listened to the sounds of a man's grunts and a woman's groaning coming from the toilet cubicle. 'Not very romantic is it?' he asked a shocked older man who had just come into the gents, and then he walked back towards the table to rejoin his friends. He had assumed he'd see Gene sitting there. Instead he saw the worried face of Jo. 'Where is he?' she asked, and Charlie shrugged. When he reached the table he said to Jo: 'He's not in the toilet. He must have gone to get a round in. Here, you won't believe this but there's a randy couple in the gents, and they're at it like hammer and tongs.'

'Oh no,' muttered Jo, and she grabbed the tabletop to support herself. She seemed unsteady on her feet.

'You alright Jo?' asked Mandy and Charlie simultaneously.

She walked to the corridor, went to the gents, pushed the door open, and a man said, 'You're in the wrong toilet, love,' but Jo ignored him and she fought through the crowd of curious men and when she reached the door, she saw the 'engaged' sign and started to sniffle, thinking of her engagement. She said, 'Gene – are you in there?'

She heard a muffled, unintelligible male voice – and she thought it sounded like Gene.

'Don't stop, carry on! Carry on!' said a female voice behind the door.

'Gene!' Jo screamed at the door and started to pound upon it with her fists. 'Open the door!'

'No, no, no – please! Gene, no!' said the female behind the door.

There was a rattling of the handle, and the door opened, and all the men cheered.

Gene came out, his face smeared with lipstick, and his tie was loose and his shirt was in disarray. His flies were open. He seemed to be in a trance, or drugged. 'Jo,' he said in a low voice.

Jo screamed and pushed him aside and lunged past him. She saw Iona sitting on the toilet seat with her knickers at her ankles and there was a smile on her face – a face glistening with perspiration. Jo seized the girl's updo and shook Iona as if she was a rag doll. She tried to smash her head against the white enamel tiles of the toilet walls, and it took three men to drag her off Iona. A bouncer came into the toilet and dragged

Jo backwards from the men's toilet. He threw her onto the cold rainy street, despite the protestations of Jo's friends and then the bouncer grabbed Gene by the lapel and he asked him: 'Are you some animal? Doing that in the toilet you dirty bastard! You should be ashamed of yourself! Come on!'

He threw Gene out onto the street and he fell over Jo, who was lying in a huddle on the rain-slicked pavement, crying her eyes out. Gene haled a hackney cab and he and his friends had to drag Jo into it because she kept saying she didn't want to go home with him. She threw her engagement ring away and it was never found. A diamond blade could not have cut through the tension in the air back home. Gene swore he could not remember how he had ended up in that toilet making love to Iona, but his best friend said, 'I find that really hard to believe Gene, and I feel like giving you a hiding mate. You've got a beautiful lady here for God's sake!'

'No, *had* - ' said Jo, sitting in an armchair, gazing at the floor, her face streaked with mascara. 'I'm leaving him, I've had enough. I'll get a termination.'

'No!' Gene cried at Jo, and his friend made a fist and looked as if he was going to strike Gene.

'Why not?' Jo screamed back at Gene. 'You're obsessed with that dirty trollop! To do what you did in a – in a toilet of all places – it's just depraved. You need help Gene, you really do.'

Gene and Jo's friends left by four that morning, and Jo slept upstairs and Gene slept on the sofa. Jo got little sleep, and when she awoke at 10am, she found Gene sitting on the edge of the bed. He held a carving knife – at his wrist.

'What are you doing?' she asked, eyeing the blade, glinting in the morning sun.

'If you leave me, I swear to God I will cut my wrists, and I will put this knife through my heart, Jo! You've got to believe me – I can't remember how I ended up in that toilet with – with *her*!'

'That's not fair, Gene, don't do this to me!' Jo said, her bulging eyes on the blade, which was now pressed into his wrist. She saw its edge dig into the blue veins and she felt her heart palpitate.

'I know this sounds like some cop-out Jo, but I've been thinking about Iona, and I really think she's a witch. I think she's got some sort of hold on me – '

'Alright, but just put that knife down Gene, remember you're going to be a father. What would I tell our child, eh?'

When Gene heard Jo mention the baby he closed his eyes, he shook, and tears oozed from the flickering lids. He let go of the knife and Jo grabbed it and threw it under the bed. Gene fell forward onto her, his head on her bosom, and as he sobbed she stroked his head and thought about what he'd said about Iona being a witch. She recalled the way she had changed her hairstyle in the club and how her face seemed to have undergone some sort of transformation – a drastic change that could not have been achieved by make-up alone, not within such a short amount of time. Was she an actual witch? Then perhaps Gene really was the victim in all this; she probably had some power over him. She knew what Gene was like in drink – he just smiled and became sentimental – he was certainly not the type to do what he did to Iona in a toilet. As far-fetched as it seemed, that had to be the answer.

'Gene, I think I believe you,' said Jo in a broken, choked-up voice. He stopped crying and lifted his head. When he faced her she saw how red and flooded with tears his eyes were.

'You believe me?' he asked.

Jo stroked back his fringe. 'Yes, I think we need professional help on this – a priest or something. Or maybe we should just get away – as far away from here as possible.'

'Thankyou – for believing me,' said Gene. 'It must have been absolutely horrifying for you, but if you think about it, if I'd had that type of lust for her, I could have just met up with her miles away at a hotel. I swear to God Jo, I just remember going into the gents, and then – '

Jo placed her index fingertip on his lips. 'It's alright Gene, let's not even think about it because I believe you. Let's try and find a way to keep this evil hussy away from us.'

As the days went by the couple somehow became even closer than ever before, and on some nights Gene shook in his sleep and broke out in a cold sweat as he suffered lucid nightmares about Iona chasing him. Then something very disturbing happened in the following months. Jo was shopping with her sister Sandra on Church Street when Iona approached her. She wore a chocolate-coloured beret, a lemon yellow Aquascutum coat. She cheekily reached out and placed her hand on Jo's baby bump and said, 'I'll have that!'

'Get off me you bastard!' Jo roared, slapping Iona's hand away, and her sister Sandra recoiled at the reaction in shock. Jo was normally a very quiet and easygoing girl.

'That's the slag I was telling you about!' Jo told her stunned sister and they watched Iona disappear into the milling crowds. On the following day, Jo awoke with terrible stomach cramps. She believed she was having a miscarriage and Gene drove her to the nearest hospital. Tests were run and the news was even worse than the couple expected: there was no baby – it had all been a phantom pregnancy.

'That is impossible,' sobbed Jo.

The specialist – a Mr Gregory - who had thoroughly examined Jo was adamant. 'It's a false pregnancy – also known as a hysterical pregnancy, and the actual official name of the condition is pseudocyesis,' he said, 'and you experience morning sickness, you gain weight in the abdominal area.'

'My period stopped! I am pregnant, my doctor told me!' Jo ranted and the tears ran down her face. She looked lost and Gene worried about her state of mind; she looked as if she was on the edge of a nervous breakdown.

Mr Gregory sighed and looked at his private notes in a green folder. 'Your period stopped because of something called amenorrhea – which can be caused by many things including stress, but from the looks of it, it would seem that you're now starting your period – and that should be proof that you are not pregnant. I'm sorry, but this is more common that you might think.'

That night Gene and Jo lay in bed, nuzzled against one another. Every now and then Jo would shake as she softly cried, and Gene would just whisper, 'It's okay babe.' He longed to say 'We'll try for another baby' but thought it would be insensitive to come out with that while Jo was getting over the loss – imagined or real, he could not tell, and he wondered if Iona had somehow taken the unborn baby when she had placed her hand on Jo's bump and declared: 'I'll have that!' The wedding was put on hold in a type of limbo because neither wanted to even talk about marriage – the whole phantom pregnancy incident had taken the veneer clean off the prospect of the white wedding.

Time is a great healer, and a month later, a measure of normality had returned to the couple's life. Spring was arriving now and Gene took his fiancée to the city centre of Liverpool to do some shopping, as such shopping expeditions always cheered Jo up. As the couple were entering a shoe store on Church Street, they saw a pregnant Iona coming out. She patted her bump and said to Jo: 'I told you I'd take it.'

She then walked on out of the store and Jo tried to grab Iona's hair, but Gene held her back and Jo screamed, 'Let me go! She's got my baby! She's got my baby! Let go of me!'

A crowd formed around Jo and Iona looked back and smiled at Gene as he fought to restrain his hysterical fiancée. A policeman on his beat ran to the screaming woman and said, 'Calm down love! What did you say about someone having your baby?'

'Her! She took my baby!' Jo pointed into the crowd but the policeman couldn't make out who she was singling out.

'No, officer – ' Gene tried to explain but his fiancée shouted over him.

'Her name's Iona and she stole my baby! Stole it out my womb!' Jo told him and burst into tears.

'Out your...womb?' the policeman's eyes thinned and

he looked Jo up and down, and then his eyes travelled to Gene's face.

Gene winked at the policeman and said, 'It's okay constable.'

'It's not okay!' shouted Jo, and then her eyes rolled back into her head and she passed out in Gene's arms, all down to the shock of encountering Iona with what she imagined to be her baby. The policeman went to call an ambulance.

Gene and Jo decided to move over to Wirral in an effort to get away from Iona, and they never set eyes on her again. Gene's mother saw Iona pushing a pram through Kirkby one afternoon but it contained nothing but a doll, and the young lady's pregnancy never came to anything; had she been wearing padding, just goad poor Jo, or had her condition been caused by witchcraft? It really is hard to say. Gene eventually married Jo in 1971 and the couple had three children, all girls. What became of Iona, I do not know.

HE FOUGHT A GHOST

Many years ago in Liverpool, a certain bouncer named Paul was hired as a doorman at a city centre pub on Friday and Saturday nights, and after these shifts were completed he'd have a Coke and a twenty-minute rest at the pub before helping out at an all-nighter club just a stone's throw away. Because Paul was a regular churchgoer, his colleagues used to call him St Paul, and one Sunday morning after the pub had emptied at 1.15am, just the barmaids, the landlord and his wife remained behind, and Paul told them how his faith had saved him when he became a violent drunk years back. 'Exactly five years ago this morning,' he told Mike the landlord, who was sipping from a half-pint glass of Peroni, 'exactly almost to the hour, I saw the light. I was at war with the world. I was a coke head, I was seventeen stone though, drinking and eating my way to a coronary.'

'I remember,' said Mike, and he almost smiled and looked as if he was going to say something but was too scared to. 'I remember you driving the motorbike with the chainsaw that night.'

Paul paused and looked pensively at the bar counter, head bowed for a thoughtful moment. 'Yeah, but that was a case of fighting fire with fire. I had to resort to that; that's the only language they understood.'

'Chainsaw on a motorbike?' queried Azzalia, a curious 20-year-old barmaid who halted her glass-collecting at the tables.

'Sounds worse than it was,' said Paul with a grin, 'but

all it was like, was me nicking this drug-dealer's Kawasaki and driving it into the club he owned.' Paul imitated the sound of a motorcycle accelerating and slid his closed fist over the bar. 'Smash! Right through his lackeys on the door; all overweight ponces trying to dive out the way but they weren't even fit enough to dive. Smashed one of their pelvises in didn't I Mike? Dead funny it was.'

Mike nodded and by the grave look in his wide eyes he seemed to be recalling the horrendous attack.

'And you had a chainsaw?' asked Azzalia, seeming impressed by the account.

'Yeah but it wasn't like a massive one – ' answered Paul, as if he was trying back pedal.

'It was big enough,' said Mike, and he took a loud swig of lager.

'Nah, it was just a 37cc one,' insisted Paul. 'It took that nancy's fingers off because he tried to grab it. Common sense says if you see a chainsaw coming towards you –'

'At sixty miles an hour though – ' added Mike.

'Well, even so you get out the way,' Paul continued, 'I was aiming at that prick's neck anyway. He had to learn to play the guitar with his left hand after that. Anyway, I got my own back on that pusher blurt running the club and destroying kid's lives.'

'And then you saw the light,' said Jacqui, the older barmaid with a trace of mockery in her intonation.

Paul looked her up and down in a rather condescending manner and slowly nodded. 'Yes, I did, actually, and this is how it happened. I went home after a long shift, and I just felt – well – hollow is the only word to describe it. I'd split up with my latest bird; was going through birds faster than the KFC – and I was coming down off the pills and the ale, on a real downer I was, and I was thinking of suicide all the time. I just didn't care. I knew it was only a matter of time before I'd kill someone. Anyway I saw this old DVD on the coffee table – don't even know where it came from; the bird said it wasn't hers. It was *Jesus of Nazareth* with er – God - what's-his-name – Enoch?'

'Robert Powell,' said Mike the landlord.

'Oh, what an actor,' said Paul, closing his eyes and shaking his shaved head. He opened his lively eyes and asked the barmaids: 'Have yous seen it? *Jesus of Nazareth*?'

'Is that the one where he fancies Mary Magdalene?' queried young Azzalia.

Paul grimaced as if there was car battery acid in his Coke. 'No! That's blasphemous shit, that! This is the real thing; Jesus as he really was, dead kind and deep like, and I sat there watching it, and it was like a shaft of light had come down from Heaven onto me. My eyes were just opened. I had to watch the whole series. It's hard to explain but it was like a spiritual awakening.'

'I know what you mean,' said Azzalia, picking up the drinking glasses again, 'I was like that when I first heard Pink Floyd's *Dark Side of the Moon*.'

'*Dark Side* is like fuckin' Milli Vanilli compared to this, love,' Paul replied.

'Doesn't he put it eloquently?' Jacqui asked the landlord and his wife with a lopsided grin.

'Well, I saw the light,' Paul went on, 'and it was like a laser beam from Our Lord shining right into my bonce, honest. And I changed. Stopped all the drugs, drinking, shagging for shagging's sake – pardon my French ladies – but I'm just telling you how it was. And I go to church every Sunday now. And I have this on everywhere I go, look.' Paul loosened his tie and unbuttoned his shirt.

'A bullet proof vest?' Jacqui asked, tongue in cheek.

'Do you write those jokes in the Christmas crackers?' a piqued Paul asked the sarcastic barmaid. 'No, not a vest – this protects me even more.' He fished a small golden crucifix on a chain from his hairy chest. 'They take the piss out of me because of my faith but I don't care. They won't be laughing when they all get thrown into Hell – into the Lake of Everlasting Fire.'

'I don't want to go to Hell,' said a worried Azzalia, 'I'll have to start going to church.'

'Yeah, you better had,' said Paul putting the cross back in his mat of chest hair. 'You could get run over tomorrow, and if your name's not in that book, St Peter's not gonna let you in, is he?'

'Oh don't say *that*!' Azzalia looked at Jacqui and asked, 'Is there a Hell, Jacqui?'

'Yeah - this world,' said Jacqui in an uncharacteristically sombre tone, 'the real Hell is probably like Ibiza in comparison.'

As Jacqui spoke, everyone heard a tapping and scraping noise in the room, and they saw it was a piece of chalk writing block letters on the darts blackboard all by itself. Azzalia screamed. Because the topic of conversation had been about Hell, she imagined the Devil was chalking the words.

"THIS PUB IZ DAMMED" the piece of chalk wrote, then fell to the floor.

'*What* on earth did that?' gasped the shocked

212

landlord Mike, and Paul calmly said, 'A spirit that can't spell.'

'Ooh!' Azzalia dropped one of the glasses she'd been holding and it shattered on the floor. 'Something just touched me!' she cried, and her hand felt her bottom and she looked behind her.

'Calm down everyone,' said Paul, looking around, 'it's because we were talking about God. It's been the other fellah that.'

'Who?' Mike asked.

Paul pointed to the floor. 'The guy down below. The Devil, Mike.'

Azzalia clung onto Jacqui from behind, making the latter yelp. 'I don't want to go to Hell!' said the young barmaid in a high-pitched voice.

'You'll be alright love,' said Paul, 'start going to church and get a crucifix.'

'Rub that out!' said Irene, Mike's wife, pointing to the weird chalked message on the darts blackboard. Mike stayed rooted to the spot, obviously scared to go near the spooky graffito.

'Here, I'll rub it out!' Paul spat on his fingers and rubbed the four words out on the board. 'Now calm down will yiz? It's just Old Nick having a bit of a joke.'

'Why pick on this pub out of all the hundreds boozers in this city?' Irene wanted to know.

Paul looked at his watch. It was 1.35am. He was due at the club. 'Well, folks, I better be making tracks, so I'm gonna have to love you and leave you,' he said, and seeing as the four people around him were all still looking at the blackboard, he added, 'And stop worrying about all that. Have faith and *he* won't come back here.'

Paul left the pub and made his way to the club, thinking about the chalked message, but pushed it aside in his mind. He now had the coked-up troublemakers of *this* world to contend with.

On the Monday night, a long spell of poltergeist activity commenced at the pub. The counter flap lifted and fell by itself, bottles were smashed against walls, beer glasses exploded, customers were pushed about by unseen hands and there were phonecalls made to the pub by someone in a raspy mocking voice who would say, 'Death to you all.'

A medium was brought to the pub and she said the spirit causing havoc was someone who was definitely connected to an employee of the pub. Azzalia went pale when she heard this. 'I don't know anyone who'd come back and haunt me,' she said, and Jacqui was sceptical of the medium. She thought she was just making it all up.

'Is there an employee here named Paul?' the well-spoken psychic suddenly asked the landlord.

Mike nodded. 'Yeah, he's a doorman here – why?'

'Well, I can't quite get the name of the spirit you see,' explained the medium, 'But it told me its name sounds like Paul.'

At that point, the lights went out in the pub for a moment then came back on.

'I'll tell him to come over,' said Mike, producing his mobile phone. 'Just hang on a minute.'

Paul happened to be playing pool at a pub a few minutes away, and he came straight to the pub to 'suss out' the medium. He found her, in his estimation, to be genuine. When she told him the disruptive spirit had said it had a name like his, he told her: 'I thought it might be him. His name was Saul – he was on the doors with me years ago, and we had a really big mad falling out. He died in a car crash this time last year. He was one bad man, and I mean bad.'

'I remember him,' said Mike, 'the fellah who doused that lad with petrol because he wouldn't accept the smoking ban in that club.'

'Yeah, that was Saul; they used to call him OTT,' reminisced Paul, then he explained to the medium: 'Over the top – OTT. He was into the occult. He burned the Bible once in Sefton Park and urinated in a font in a church. He told me he wanted to kill this girl on a church altar, and because I said he was sick he got a sledgehammer and smashed my 'arl fellah's headstone in.'

'No!' said Irene, throwing her hands to her face, 'So it was him! It was in the papers.'

Paul nodded. 'Yeah, Irene, I got told, like, but I was in hospital at the time with my self-inflicted liver condition and Frankie the Rope tried to hang him on my behalf in Newsham Park but the rope snapped. He had the Devil's luck, literally.'

'Oh my, I don't think I want to get mixed up in all this!' said the shocked medium. She seemed unsteady on her feet.

'Oh, no, I'm a born again Christian now, love,' said Paul desperately trying to reassure the appalled medium. 'Can I get you a glass of wine or anything? Please don't judge me from my past, I'm a changed man now, honest, love.'

'No thank you, and I really must be going,' said the nervous psychic.

'Before you do go,' said Paul, 'can you give him a

message? Saul?'

'He's listening in now,' she said, looking at the ceiling.

Paul smiled and announced, 'Well Saul, meet me tonight – at midnight if you like – in the spot where we last had a scrap, and we'll have it out man to man instead of you scaring innocent people in here!'

The bell behind the bar rang three times by itself.

Paul waited at midnight on poorly-lit Brooks Alley (which runs off Hanover Street and turns sharply into School Lane). As the fearless bouncer glanced up at the moon, something shoved him hard into a wheelie bin. He felt as if a car had hit him, such was the magnitude of the force that had smashed into his side. He got up, stunned and disoriented, and saw a man made of pure shadow standing about twelve feet away – and the silhouette was recognisable as Saul's outline with its long neck and the skittle-shaped body.

'So, you showed eh?' laughed Paul, and he recalled his dad's smashed gravestone and charged at the ghost like a rhino, head down, imagining there'd be some impact – but the silhouette merely vanished and Paul's head hit a brick wall which left him with an agonising pain in his neck and a numbness in the top of his shaven head. He swore, picked himself up, and as he went to turn to face his old foe, he received a vicious kidney punch which left him on his knees. He then heard a faint gravelly voice close to his ear say, 'You said I was sick. I'm with my master now. There's a life after death with him.' It sounded as if Saul was making a concerted effort to speak.

'Get back to Hell you bastard, you *are* sick!' was Paul's reply, and he managed to get himself up with one knee on the ground when he actually felt something pass through his back and touch his heart. The pain was as if a glowing poker had prodded his heart. He cried out in agony. Still, Paul's anger drove him to stand, and he turned, swearing, and saw the ghastly skeletal form of Saul in the body of that shadow. The eyes looked very sad in their black sockets, and they glowed with a faint red light.

'He allowed me to come back for a chance to kill you,' said the hoarse voice of Saul, and his hands, blacker than charcoal, grabbed at Paul's throat and started to squeeze. 'Come to Hell, Paul..come on!' said the grating voice.

'Lord protect me!' Paul said, and the words came out like a croaky whisper as the resurrected Saul tried to crush his windpipe.

Amber light flooded the alleyway, and Paul saw a tall luminous figure appear, surrounded by a golden aura with the colours of the rainbow fluctuating around its edges. It reminded him of the Northern Lights. 'An angel – has come!' Paul said, trying to smile, and he managed to punch Saul's face, but the head felt as light as polystyrene foam, and Saul smiled, showing his crooked dark green teeth. 'That's my master! He *was* an angel!' murmured Saul.

The angelic-looking visitant was very handsome, with radiant blue eyes which shone and glinted like boron-blue diamonds, and the hair was golden and shimmered. The suit was white and satin-like. Whoever he was, he looked at the proceedings with a bland almost uninterested expression.

'God is mightier than the Devil!' declared Paul in a scratchy, fading voice, and he felt that old anger he used to feel in his dark days well up inside of him. How dare this piece of excrement try to dent his faith – this would-be child killer who wanted to snuff someone as a sacrifice; the bastard who smashed his beloved father's gravestone! Paul grabbed the hands throttling him, pushed them from his throat, and somehow he bent those hands back till they snapped at the wrists. He found himself talking in a incomprehensible language that started as profanities and became some strange tongue. There was a look of utter terror now in Saul's decayed face. The hands broke at the wrists as if they belonged to a carbonized statue, and then Paul found himself smashing in the head of the deceased bouncer with his fists. He knew the power coming from within was not of this world, but from God. And then he began to understand what he was saying; he was talking in tongues, the language of the angels and the Holy Spirit, and he knew he was plugged into the same lethal mountain-levelling energy source that had divided the Red Sea and powered the Ark of the Covenant, and he was slightly afraid; he had not experienced fear for a long time. The glowing man standing behind the battered remains of Saul turned and vanished in a flash of blue light, and Paul heard Saul begging for mercy in a dwindling voice.

'No, please Paul, we were friends, please have mercy on me, please!'

In a voice that thundered and echoed throughout Brooks Alley, Paul roared, 'There is no redemption from Hell! Go below, and stay below in the fires forever!'

'Oh no, no, please Paul, I beg of you!'

'In the name of Jesus Christ, depart!' said Paul, and

now his voice had become human-sounding again, and he saw a red luminous crack open in the road, and for a moment he saw thousands of writhing naked bodies of men and women, all screaming for one deafening moment among an incandescent orange glowing mountain range. He was looking into the pits of Hell. Saul fell down into it all minus his hands, with his most of his head caved in, and then the great crack in the road closed up, yet Paul could smell the awful sulphuric aroma for a while as he staggered away.

When he returned to the pub, Azzalia touched the back of his hand and was about to ask him if he was okay but she screamed out and said his hand was hot. Blisters formed on Azzalia's palm and she fainted from the pain. Paul eventually felt the power and the heat leave his body, and he told the landlord he was giving up his job. He said he wanted to stay away from violence. He asked the barmaid Jacqui if she'd like to go for a meal with him on the following night and at first she shook her head and seemed dumbfounded by the change in Paul's nature, but she eventually started to date him, and they later married and settled down in Chester.

THE AUGURY MAN

In 2009, a 16-year-old girl named Zoe fell in with a Liverpool gang called The Jacks, and part of the initiation ceremony into this crew was to ride a lift up to the13th floor of a specific block of flats at exactly 3am and knock on a particular door before going back down via the lift. The thirteenth floor of the high-rise block was said to be haunted by a shadowy man who appeared each morning at precisely 3 o'clock. Some thought he was the Devil and others said he was an omen of death. Zoe had to video her mission on her phone to prove she had gone through with it. Marcus, the 18-year-old gang-leader of The Jacks, arrived at Zoe's street at 2:30am in his car with two lackeys, and the girl was driven to the multi-storey apartment building. They arrived there a few minutes before three, and at that time in the morning the place was dead. Zoe pressed the special red button on the main entrance door of the flats which allowed access to the postman, and she hurried across the thin durable grey carpet of the hall with her phone videoing the proceedings. Outside, Marcus was driving away. Zoe went to the lift door and summoned the elevator. It arrived, and there was a rather over-long pause before a faint bell pinged and the doors lethargically opened. The interior was clean and well-kept. Zoe filmed the elevator floor indicator LED as it climbed in steps, and then the lift stopped and after another drawn-out pause, the doors parted ever so slowly on the thirteenth floor – to reveal a stark black silhouette of a man who seemed to be well over six feet in height. Zoe panicked and pressed the down button but the lift wouldn't respond.

The man was about twenty feet away at the end of a corridor, gazing out a window that went from the floor to the ceiling, and Zoe thought about rushing out of the elevator to the stairs, but the stranger turned and faced the frightened girl. He was black, with closely cropped hair, and he wore a long dark coat to his knees. In a deep rich well-spoken voice he recited Zoe's full name – Zoe Cassell Jones – then added, 'Unless you do as I say, you'll be famous – a household name.'

Zoe was puzzled by the statement, but the man said something which really shook her.

He walked towards her as he spoke. 'In three days' time you will be murdered. Do you understand that?'

Zoe stood glued to the spot in the lift, her gloved hand at the buttons. She pressed the down button but that elevator would not budge.

The tall eerie black-clad figure halted just a few feet from the entrance to the inert elevator and looked at the frightened teenager. His eyes were blank, emotionless, and he said: 'Your killer will never be found, and your face will be over all the news. He punctures those eyes of yours with a knife. That will be his trademark, and he will do that to seven other girls he kills after you.'

'I'll call the bizzies!' Zoe warned, and the man didn't react. 'I'll phone them!' she reiterated and looked at her phone, but it was blank. Not even her screensaver was visible.

'I'm trying to save you young lady,' said the man, 'and if you don't take my advice, the name of Zoe Cassell Jones will be as famous as Mary Jane Kelly and Sharon Tate, although you won't even know who they were. I tried to warn them, just as I'm attempting to warn you now!'

Zoe swore and ran from the lift and upon reaching the door to the stairs she pushed it and discovered to her horror that it wouldn't budge. The eerie tall man walked towards her and intoned, 'Zoe, you must avoid Marcus from now on, or he will have an argument with you and kill you. He will then become a serial killer who takes seven more lives.'

'Leave me alone!' Zoe cried, her back pressed against the locked door. Then she screamed: 'Help! Help!

The black man vanished right in front of her, confirming what she had vaguely suspected – that he was a ghost. Zoe then fell backwards onto the floor as the door behind her suddenly gave way; now it had mysteriously unlocked itself. She heard voices of residents and the sounds of bolts being drawn back and latches being clicked off. They'd hear her screams, but she had no intention of hanging about. She ran out of the building and made her way home. She looked at the video she'd taken, and there was the tall man in black, visible for a few moments after the elevator doors had opened, but then the video ended there - when the phone had, for some unknown reason, lost power. She showed the video to Marcus and when she told him about the man's prediction regarding him stabbing girls in the eyes, he reacted quite strange. Marcus told Zoe she had faked the footage and said he *would* start stabbing girls in the eyes – and that he'd start with her eyes if she didn't admit to making the bizarre story up. Zoe was shocked at his over-reaction and she became so terrified by the ghost's prediction she went to live with her uncle in Bristol, even though her parents begged the girl to stay in Liverpool to go to college. Zoe recalled the two names that sinister black man had mentioned - Mary Jane Kelly and Sharon Tate. She discovered that Mary Jane Kelly had been the most horrifically mutilated victim of Jack the Ripper – and she almost retched when she saw the online pictures of the murdered woman lying stripped to the bone on her bed in 1888. Zoe also felt sick when she saw a graphic photograph of the body of Sharon Tate, one of five people murdered by members of Charles Manson's "Family" – along with her unborn baby, on 9 August 1969.

Zoe recalled how that tall dark stranger had said he had tried to warn Kelly and Tate – which would mean he'd have to be very old indeed, as Kelly had died back in 1888. That man had looked no older than thirty-five.

The entity Zoe met that morning has been encountered before, always advising people how to avoid a gruesome death, and I know of several such cases where the person issuing the warning matches the exact description of the Augury Man. In 2004 a 14-year-old girl named Szu (short for Szulita a Hungarian first name) was sitting on a bench on Lime Street Concourse while her father and older brother were buying books and magazines at the station's branch of WH Smith. Szu had just bought an artichoke, olive and tapenade baguette, and before she could even take a bite, a tall black man in a long dark trench coat slapped the baguette out of Szu's hand. The girl looked at the stranger and she felt anger initially, but when she saw the wide, bulging eyes of the man, she became afraid, and looked towards WH Smith, hoping she's see her father and brother coming out, but they were nowhere to be seen.

'Don't eat those things again or you'll die!' said the man in a very well-spoken voice. 'There's sesame in them, and you're allergic to sesame! You *will* die a horrible death if you eat one of those!'

Szu got up slowly from the bench and ran across the concourse to the bookshop to tell her father about the deranged black man, and as she looked back, she saw a scruffily-dressed man who had been begging at the station earlier on pick the baguette up and shout something racist at the black man. The girl located her father and brother in a queue and told them what had happened. By the time Szu's father came out of WH Smith the stranger in the trench coat had gone. Szu's brother thought the incident was funny and this caused a row between him and his father which caused the two of them to sulk during the train journey to Manchester. Szu told me that a year after this she went to France with her family and saw a girl around her age collapse in the street after eating a similar baguette which contained sesame. The girl almost died, and Szu recalled the man at Lime Street station warning her of an allergy to sesame, so she went to her doctor and he arranged for an allergy test. It was discovered that Szu was allergic to several foodstuffs – including sesame – and she was subsequently issued with an EpiPen – a pen-sized device that can inject a measured dose of epinephrine (also known as adrenaline) into the carrier to treat anaphylaxis – a serious, severe allergic reaction. But how did that black man who knocked the baguette out of Szu's hand know that she had an allergy to sesame? He could have been someone with a mental problem – but something tells me he could have been the ubiquitous and highly mysterious Augury Man. In July 2016, a pretty 15-year-old girl named Natasha Ednan-Laperouse died in a hospital in Nice after collapsing on a British Airways flight after suffering a severe allergic reaction to sesame she'd consumed in a baguette. Natasha had eaten the baguette – which had been purchased from the main Pret a Manger shop in Terminal 5 at Heathrow airport – and the girl had not been aware that the baguette contained sesame because there was no ingredients listing on the wrapper.

Some years ago I was in a second hand bookshop in Liverpool when the owner introduced me to a young lady who was a fan of the *Haunted Liverpool* books. Her name was Eloise. She said she had a strange story for me. In April 2013 she was to go to a wedding in Manchester with three of her friends, and a former boyfriend – Abel - had offered to drive the girls (who lived in the Halewood area) to the Manchester church where their friend Dominika was due to wed. Abel was to transport the girls to the wedding in his beloved vintage 1973 Volkswagen Camper Van, and he said he'd do the job for nothing, as long as he could go to the wedding reception. Eloise told her mother Carol about the travel arrangements to get to Manchester and Carol insisted on having a look at the Camper Van. Abel said it was completely roadworthy and that he'd spent a small fortune having parts welded and had even paid for a Volkswagen mechanic to look it over, but Carol said she had bad feelings about the van and practically called Abel a liar. Carol said she'd pay for Eloise and her friends to get to the wedding by train, but Eloise told her to stop interfering and they had a big row. Abel then tried to persuade Eloise to hook up with him again and he said he was getting broody and wanting to have kids. Days after this, Eloise was laying on her bed, watching YouTube videos when she dozed off. She had a terrible nightmare. She found herself walking about naked in a cold spacious room of stainless steel tables, white tiled walls and a bare mustard-coloured floor. This floor was ice cold beneath her bare feet, and she walked around, trying to find something to cover herself with and trying to find a way out of the room. Eloise said she rarely had dreams where she could smell things, but she could smell some potent antiseptic aroma in this dream. She saw her friends, lying naked on the stainless steel tables – and realised they were dead, and from the shocking stitched-up scars on their bodies, it was obviously some mortuary.

'Eloise,' said a man's *deep voice* behind her.

Eloise turned and saw a tall black man, well over six feet, standing there with a long black or possibly dark blue coat which went almost to his ankles. She instinctively covered her breasts with her hands, then placed her hand over her vagina and tried to cover her bosom with her hand and forearm. 'Who are you?' she asked, and she could feel her heart pounding.

'What will be, will be, unless you do as I say,' said the man, looking her in the eyes.

'Who are you?' she cried, ready to become hysterical

– when the hand covering her bosom felt something in the cleavage – something like a thread. She looked at her chest and saw she had a long stitched-up scar like the bodies of her dead friends, and in shock she looked back at the black man standing there and he half-closed his eyes and gave a slow knowing nod.

'You mustn't get in that van,' he said, 'you mustn't get in that van. Listen Eloise! Listen! You mustn't get in that van!' and he kept repeating that last sentence over and over as Eloise turned and tried to run down a corridor which went miles into the distance.

Eloise woke up with a start, and she was so affected by the nightmare, she cried. She went to the bedroom of her parents and told them about the graphic nightmare.

Her annoyed father rubbed his bleary eyes and moaned, 'Oh my God, Eloise, you're waking me up because you had a nightmare. Are you for real?'

'Come here love,' said the girl's sympathetic mother, getting out the bed to hug her.

'She's going worse,' mumbled the girl's father, his words muffled under the duvet.

Carol took her daughter downstairs and said, 'Now, listen – and I mean it – you're definitely *not* going to the wedding in that fellah's van. I'll pay for you and your mates to go by train. Don't try and overrule me this time Eloise or I swear I'll cause a scene – '

'Mam! Let me get word in edgeways will you? I'm not going in his van after that dream,' Eloise assured her, and then she started crying. 'I saw my friends dead and I had this scar mum.'

Carol hugged her daughter hard and patted her back.

'She's not still going on about that, is she?' Carol's

husband groaned from the landing as he went to the toilet.

Carol mouthed a profanity and gave him the V sign, and Eloise smiled as she wiped the tears away.

Eloise and her friends went to the wedding reception by train – and that same day, Abel was driving around Halewood in his Camper Van when the front right tyre blew. He crashed into a skip and sustained minor injuries – but had that tyre blowout occurred on the M62, with the van travelling at 70 mph, it's possible that the nightmare of Eloise might have come true.

Long before Eloise was born, back in February 1975, the Augury Man seems to have issued another spinechilling warning. The recipient of the warning on this occasion was a young businessman from Knotty Ash named Richard. He was an accountant who had landed a well-paid job for a London-based investments firm, and now, after studying the COBOL programming language (developed specifically for business) on a friend's Honeywell 1200 computer for over a year, he was a very able programmer, and COBOL programmers in particular were in great demand with amazing salaries on offer. One such amazing salary was there for the right person if they passed a basic interview and aptitude test at a firm based in London at Finsbury Circus, and Richard was due to go to this interview when he returned to the Capital on 28 February 1975. After the interview, which would take place at 9.30am, Richard would travel a short distance to have lunch with his girlfriend Aimee, who worked for the Provident Mutual Life Assurance Association just a few hundred yards away in the Moorgate area of London. The couple planned to get married in the summer, and Aimee, wanting some financial security in married life, hoped Richard would get the high-paid programming job.

On the evening before the interview, Richard had his tea with his parents and younger brother, and then he caught a cab to Lime Street to get the train back to London. He dozed off during the 200-mile journey and had a strange dream in which a silhouette of a man appeared, walking out of a tunnel. Richard couldn't see the man's face or make out the colour of his clothes because there was a light shining in the tunnel behind him, and eventually Richard realised that the light was an approaching train, and the man was walking along the tracks. 'Do not catch that train to Moorgate!' the approaching shadowy figure shouted to Richard three times in a deep resonant voice – and then he vanished, and the train came thundering towards Richard and he awoke with a start, crying out and making other passengers in his compartment jump. He thought about the warning he'd heard in the dream, and recalled that he would have to get the tube to the nearest station to his interview – which happened to be Moorgate. After the train arrived in London, Richard went to his Highbury flat and telephoned his fiancée Aimee to tell her of the strange dream, and she seemed worried and said that perhaps he should get a hackney cab to the interview. Richard said that was ridiculous when Moorgate Tube Station was right on top of the building where he the interview would be held. That night, Richard fell fast asleep, and he was only asleep for a few minutes when he heard the wailing laughter of two women. The laughter from each woman seemed to harmonise and yet it sounded

229

eerie and the strange thing is that when Richard awoke from his sleep he still heard the laughter for a few seconds. He went to his window and looked out onto the street. It was after midnight now – Thursday night into Friday morning, and Richard expected to see some young men and women returning from the pubs but the street was eerily empty and silent, and a yellow waning gibbous moon hung over the London skyline. So what had he just heard? Was the strange laughter perhaps from someone's TV set in one of the flats next door or below? Richard returned to his bed, shook the pillows to make them comfy to his weary head, and he was soon lost in the wilderness of sleep. This time he had the very same dream as the one he'd had on the train, the silhouette in some sort of trench coat walking ahead of a speeding train in a tunnel, and again this man said, 'Do not catch that train to Moorgate!' only this time he ran right up to Richard, and now he could see that the mysterious warning-giver was a black man. 'Richard, do not get on that underground train or you'll spend an eternity underground! Do not get the train to Moorgate!'

The man vanished and there was a terrific crash, followed by screams and people groaning, and then once again, Richard heard the two women, clearer than before, their hysterical laughter echoing in the tunnel in harmony – and Richard shot up in bed, his face covered in a film of perspiration. 'I – I don't believe this! All I want to do is get a good night's sleep! These bloody nightmares!'

Richard then did something he always avoided when he had an important appointment to keep in the morning – he drank a few glasses of whiskey. He soon dozed off, and there were no more nightmares. The alarm clock awakened him at 7.15am and he made himself a bacon, eggs and beans breakfast, drank a cup of coffee, showered, shaved and was out the door to catch the 8.37 from Drayton Park. Richard thought about the warnings in the dreams and of his fiancée's concern, so he decided to take the rear carriage, even though it was packed with rush-hour commuters. As the tube train moved off, Richard thought about the interview and the questions they might ask him, and these thoughts occupied his mind throughout the nine-minute journey to Moorgate – where something horrific took place. The train arrived at Platform 9, and people thought it odd that it was not decelerating – but speeding up! The train smashed into the dead-end tunnel, and in the resulting carnage 43 people died. The first fifteen seats of the first carriage, and all within them, were crushed into a space measuring less than 2 feet by four feet. The driver was killed instantly and to this day, no one knows why he did not stop the train. Witnesses on the platform said he was staring straight ahead, and one witness said his eyes were bulging as if he had realised the train was about to smash into the dead end of the tunnel. Richard, being in the last carriage, received only a few scratches when he was thrown into the other passengers, and he crawled out of the carriage, and in the pandemonium he heard a very familiar sound – two girls being dragged out of the wreckage of the second carriage were laughing hysterically in shock – and their laughter had a very weird, echoing and harmonious quality to it. Someone slapped each of the girls to calm her down and the laughter stopped. Richard went cold when he realised he had heard that laughter the night before in what must have been some form of premonition. In a state of shock he actually made it out of the Moorgate Tube Station and he passed the heroic responders of the ambulance, fire service and police force as he found himself laughing himself now. 'I should have listened to him; what a fool,' Richard muttered to himself, 'well I can't keep them waiting,' he continued, fighting through the crowds of curious people swarming down to the scene of a crash that had been felt at street level. Richard arrived for the interview, and the boss of the firm said, 'Damn the bloody interview; give that lad a cup of hot sweet tea!'

A nurse in the building examined him, and said Richard was just suffering from mild shock. He was given the job as programmer without completing any aptitude test or interview, and in June of that year he married Aimee. To this day, Richard does not know why he, of all people, received a warning from beyond regarding the horrific Moorgate crash, and he has not had any warning nightmares since that day. I do not profess to know who the Augury Man is, or why he should choose to try and save the lives of certain people, but if he happens to warn *you* then please do as he advises...

THE WINDOWLESS ROOM

I've changed a few names in this bizarre and unsettling story for legal reasons. In March 1996, a 22-year-old secretary from Formby named Gina Williams started work at a rather large well-known firm in Wirral. She typed accurately at 60 words per minute, had an in-depth knowledge of Microsoft Word and Excel, and she was also fluent in French and German. She'd only been in her office some twenty minutes when a 24-year-old employee named Colin Evans came in with a tin of Quality Street and sat on the edge of her desk. 'That's for you, Gina,' he announced with a smile, plonking the tin on the new secretary's desk.

'Aww, what for?' Gina asked, looking at the tub of sweets, and Colin said, 'Ah, just to welcome you to this place - *Anus Mundi* I call it.'

'Which is Latin for – no don't tell me,' replied Gina, 'something to do with somebody's bum.'

'The arsehole of the world,' said Colin, and he tapped on the tin of sweets and said, 'Can you save me a purple one?'

'I'll share them with you for elevenses with a coffee,' Gina promised.

Colin smiled, looked at the secretary's hair and remarked, 'Rare to see a real blonde nowadays.'

'Ha! I top it up a bit,' said Gina, and then she saw the cross face of her boss Tony King glaring at Colin through the window in the door. That door opened inwards and King calmly said: 'Colin, I'd like a word with you.' He then walked away from the door into the depths of his spacious neon-lit yellow-walled office.

'Wonder what Ming the Merciless wants?' said Colin, under his breath, and he went into the boss's office with Gina giggling faintly behind him.

King sat at his desk opposite Colin and with a face emotionless as stone he said: 'Stop bothering that new girl out there. You're a married man and we uphold a moral framework in this firm. I heard all about your illicit liaisons after the office Christmas party, and you've really gone down in a lot of people's estimations because of your extramarital affairs.'

'What's my private life got to do with anybody?' a flabbergasted Colin asked, and a nervous tic twitched under his right eye.

'When it's in the workplace – in my hours - it's not private anymore; and it effects productivity, and let me just tell you your name might be on the next list of redundancies. Now wake up and smell the coffee eh?'

'Tony – ' Colin began, struggling to put his beehive brain of buzzing thoughts into words.

'Mr King,' said his boss, looking at a pink form on his ink blotter with a ballpoint's tip poised over it.

'Mr King then - are you are telling me that a bit of harmless banter between me and the opposite sex will jeopardise any prospects of promotion?'

'From now on – yes!' Tony King slammed the pen down on the form, 'Look, I know you think you're Hugh Grant with that ridiculous floppy hairstyle of yours, and you're after anything in a skirt – but you're here to work; this isn't the *Love Boat* Evans!'

Colin closed his eyes, formed a painful smile on his lips and shook his head. 'I'd understand where you were coming from if I was a Government Minister, the deputy Governor of the Bank of England, or a Ministry of Defence chief sleeping with a Russian agent but I do not see how my career will be curtailed by having a polite chinwag with Gina out there.'

Tony lunged forward over the desk and ranted: 'It lowers morale among my employees, and they expect people further up the ladder in this company to have integrity, and if your wife knew the way you were carrying on she'd never sleep with you again!'

'I better go before I say something I'll regret!' Colin said, recoiling backwards from the desk with a screech from the chair's castors. As he turned to open the door, King shouted to his back, 'So knuckle down Evans and do what we pay you to do! I won't warn you again!'

Evans slammed the door and marched past a blushing wide-eyed Gina.

At noon, Colin Evans couldn't believe his eyes when he happened, in passing, to look through the window of Gina's office. Tony King and Gina were doing a very energetic dance, and when they stopped he heard King say, 'Fancy a girl your age knowing how to do the cha cha!'

'Dirty old hypocrite!' growled Colin. He realised now that the anti-adultery sermon his boss had lambasted him with had purely been King's way of keeping him away from the new secretary because *he* wanted her!

Colin watched the affair blossom between his married 60-year-old boss and 22-year-old Gina. Colin had asked Gina a few times in the canteen at lunch if the boss was pressurising her into being his mistress, and Gina had said that she genuinely liked him. She went for mature men, especially ones who were successful in their vocations. Tony King took Gina to various hotels in Lancashire, Wales and Cheshire three times a week for months, but then Colin heard a rumour; Mrs King's brother Graham had paid a private detective to catch his brother-in-law red-handed. Graham had never got on with Tony King after discovering he'd had a number of affairs behind his sister's back over the years.

One blustery June evening after work, King pretended to give his secretary Gina a lift home in his Lexus luxury sedan, but the couple were headed for a hotel in Chester. Noticing his car was being followed by a suspected private detective in a maroon Mini, Tony King went on a meandering route in an effort to shake him off. He raced through Thurstaston and headed for Heswall via Telegraph Road and turned left into the car park of a small hotel with a mock-Tudor facade. King waited, grinning. A minute later the private eye's Mini flew past and continued down Telegraph Road.

'Lost him at last,' gloated King, and he and Gina went into the quaint little hotel. In the hotel lobby, Gina asked, 'Am I really worth all this cloak and dagger business, Tony?' and King said, 'Oh, yes you are my dear,' and he kissed her. The hotel receptionist said: 'Good evening, you're obviously after a room, but er, I am afraid we are overbooked. There *is* a room of sorts on the third floor, but it's really not suitable – not up to standard, so to speak.'

'Whyever not?' queried King, unconsciously squeezing Gina's hand.

'Well, the room is in the middle of being renovated and it's had the old windows bricked up and there's just a rather basic double bed in there. It's all substandard, although we did let it to a couple who got stranded during those awful blizzards – '

'Is it available or not?' an impatient Tony King asked.

'Well, if it's something of an emergency, then we'd only take five pounds, which gives you an idea how basic things are up there,' replied the receptionist and he gave a big toothy smile.

King looked sideways at Gina, and he thought about that private detective searching for them outside in the night. 'Yes, we'll take it,' said King, 'you can't get a decent packet of cigarettes for a fiver nowadays. That's an incredible offer. Er, after we've unpacked could you send up a bottle of champagne?'

'Yes, but the only champagne we have is – ' the receptionist began.

'Oh, any will do! Here's your fiver,' King took out his wallet.

The receptionist beamed a warm closed-mouth smile and held his palms up to reject the offer of payment. 'No sir, pay in the morning; we *know* you're not going to do a runner. Room 9, it is, let me get the key.'

The windowless room was spacious with tall saffron-coloured walls, a double bed, and bare floorboards. The couple unpacked and cuddled on the bed. They waited for the champagne to arrive...and waited – so King looked for a telephone or some intercom to call reception – but there was only a small low table with nothing on it. A quarter of an hour elapsed and the champagne still hadn't arrived, so King went to see what had happened to it but found there was now no knob on the door, so he couldn't get out of the room. 'This place is Jerry-built,' he said, looking at the hole in the door where the knob had been. 'Where the hell is it?' He hammered on the door with his fist and shouted but no one came. 'Oh, this is ridiculous!' he moaned, 'Is that receptionist deaf down there? You'd think one of the other guests would go and tell him someone's banging.'

Gina giggled at the mention of that word.

'No, not that type of banging,' said King with a leering smile, and he stroked Gina face, 'not yet, anyway.'

'Let me see if they'll respond to a female voice,' suggested Gina, and she got off the bed and went to the door and shouted: 'Hello? Is there anybody there? Help! I'm being ravished by a sex maniac!'

'Stop that, Gina! They'll have the law on us!' Tony pulled her away, picked her up, and carried her to the bed. He chuckled. 'This could only happen to us. No one would believe it – stuck in a hotel room with no windows and we can't get out.'

'What if I want a pee?' mused Gina.

'Have a look under the bed and see if there's a po,' Tony got up from the bed and pushed at the door. 'It won't even budge a millimetre,' he said, then shouted, 'Come up and open this bloody thing!'

He turned and was startled to see Gina close behind him. A moment ago she'd been lying on the bed.

'Tony, guess what?' she whispered.

'What? Why are you whispering?' he asked, slightly bemused.

'Don't look up, but I just looked at the ceiling over the bed and there's a hole in it and someone's eye was looking through.'

'What?' Tony King automatically glanced up.

'I said don't look up,' Gina whispered. 'I don't like this one bit.'

'Yes, I can see the hole – are you sure someone was looking through it?'

She nodded. 'I could see the eye. There's a bloody Peeping Tom up there. He must be in the attic.'

'What was that?' King looked to the wall behind his mistress. Something creaked there.

'Tony, let's go somewhere else,' said Gina, glancing at the black spot in the ceiling, 'this place is giving me the creeps.'

'If no one comes up here in the next ten minutes, I am going to kick that door in,' Tony decided, 'and I don't care if I kick it off its hinges. They – '

There was a creaking sound from the wall behind Tony, and this time it was a lot louder.

'Oh my God, Tony – look!' Gina pointed to the bottom of the wall where it met the bare floorboards. 'It's moving! This wall's moving!'

'How can a wall be moving?' Tony asked, trying to smile.

'It is! Look close at the bottom of it! It's moving ever so slowly, ' said Gina, and she placed her hand on the wall in question. 'Tony, what's going on?'

He stooped and looked at the bottom of the wall. It *was* moving very slowly, and he estimated that the entire wall was moving forward so it covered about an inch every fifteen seconds. He tried to stop the advancing wall by leaning against it, but even his sixteen stones of weight could not stop that wall inching forward.

Tony went back to the door and strained his throat shouting for the hotel staff! And then Gina yelled out: 'Look! It's going faster!" Now the wall was touching the bed.

'We're going to end up crushed to death, aren't we?' gasped Gina, hand over her mouth as she eyed the relentless wall pushing the bed and its frame along.

'Don't start panicking, Gina!' Tony shouted at her, but he seemed very nervous all of a sudden. He pulled the mattress off the bedstead and stood it up, perhaps hoping that the wall would have to flatten the mattress before it flattened him and Gina.

Tony had left his Nokia mobile in the car; otherwise he'd have called the police now.

'Oh my God, what are we going to do?' Gina's trembling hands grabbed at Tony's arm, and Tony looked up to the ceiling – to that hole – and roared, 'And you're watching this eh? Is that your game? You'll get done for this if anything happens to us!'

The moving wall reached the bedstead and slowly crushed its wood and metal frame.

Tony charged at the door and slammed the soul of his shoe against it, but it didn't budge and it felt as if he had kicked a sheet of metal – as if that door had been reinforced!

He looked up and said, 'The light is sunk into the ceiling see? So the walls can pass over it! This has all been planned! Some bastard has planned this!'

Gina fell to her knees, gasping for air. 'I can't breathe!' she shouted, and felt her throat.

She clawed at Tony, gasping, hyperventilating, and she pushed him aside and kept pounding her small fists on the immovable door.

She fainted, and Tony put his hands under her armpits and pulled her to her feet. He held her to his chest, but then the wall pushed into her, and so he had to position her next to him. The two of them stood there, backs to the wall, and that approaching wall was shoving the toes of his shoes so he had a duck feet posture. Tony looked upwards and saw the face of a grinning man looking through a hatchway where that hole had been. It was the face of that receptionist he had spoken to earlier.

'You better stop this or you'll be done for murder you bastard!' Tony King warned him, but the wall pushed hard into his beer belly, and now it would be difficult to breathe.

'Thou shalt not commit adultery, eh?' said the face in the hatchway.

Gina came to and groaned, 'Tony! Help me!'

Tony felt – and heard - his ribs crack, and the pain was so excruciating, everything faded into a silent blackness as he passed out.

The couple were found later that evening on a grass verge on Telegraph Road, next to the Lexus with injuries that were thought to be consistent with a hit and run incident. At the hospital on the following day after the morphine levels had dropped a little, Tony found it painful to even speak, but he made it clear he and Gina – who was recovering in another ward – had not been run down by a car. He described the hotel and when Gina recovered from her injuries, her story matched Tony King's in every single detail.

A police inspector told the couple there was no mock-Tudor hotel – no hotel at all for that matter – anywhere on Telegraph Road.

King, fearing the incident was some supernatural warning against adultery, stopped seeing Gina, and every now and then, until his death in 2012, he would go in search of that "torture hotel" – but always failed to find it. The strange thing is that the private detective following King and his secretary on the night of the incident recalled passing a hotel on Telegraph Road. I have heard of phantom buildings before, and they are often to do with timeslips, but no hotel ever stood on that stretch of Telegraph Road, so the case remains a baffling mystery.

THE INTERDIMENSIONALS

The demon, in popular thought, is associated with possession and is usually automatically linked with religion and occultism. The demonic being is assumed to be a malevolent spiritual entity who can act as a tormentor to those who have been condemned to Hell, as well as a persecutor of someone living in this world who is usually a devout follower of the more orthodox religions, but of course, the Universe with its countless worlds in time and space is bound to have some beings that are frightening to our eyes, and should these beings intrude upon our planet or our dimension, it is likely that some will classify them as demons. The demon in literature and film is rarely depicted as a complete human; it is often a hybrid of the human and an animal, often with claws, pointed ears, horns, cloven feet and glowing red eyes, and the typical demon of this type is to be found in the fantastical paintings of the Dutch/Netherlandish artist Hieronymus Bosch (1450-1516). Real demons of this type surround us, but thankfully they live on a different scale of size to us. The microscope and scanning electron microscope has opened up a peephole to a kind of Hell inhabited by grotesque and alien-looking dust mites – some of which are happily munching away on the skin of your face right now. Then there are those terrifying entities that look like something of Ridley Scott's *Alien* films – the Demodex – long eight-legged crawlers that live in your eyelashes and come out at night to chew the dead cells on your eyelid, sup the spare oil in your follicles and lay up to 25 eggs in those licked-dry follicles. Your pillow is a veritable savannah upon which bloated elephant-like beings with eight spindly legs and nightmare jaws graze each night, but being microscopic, these monsters are not perceived by you, even when they crawl all over your head at night foraging for skin flakes and drinking your tears. Even a single human sperm, produced in billions in one sexual act, would terrify us if magnified from the cellular level of existence to the large-scale macroscopic world you and I inhabit; the sperm would resemble a violently thrashing, blind, bulbous-headed serpent, much longer than an anaconda and able to whip you to death with its powerful flagellum. All the things that seem cute – even the humble caterpillar, have demonic faces and these beings would be killed on sight if they lived on our scale of size. These are just beings that live on the human body or inhabit the everyday environment – and heaven knows what other strange and nightmarish beings – big and small – exist in other dimensions or on the billions upon billions of worlds out there in the cosmos. This leads me to believe that some so-called demons may not be connected to any earth-based religion at all, but may actually just be intruders from other realities – denizens from the other worlds and dimensions of this strange intriguing universe; beings which I term "the interdimensionals". When the Spanish Conquistadores came into contact with the Incas for the first time, the latter greeted them as "white gods" – or "Viracochas" – because of their pale skin. Viracocha was an ancient pale-skinned deity to the Incas, so their beliefs led them to believe that the European Conquistadores were of his kin, and should some interdimensional being appear in our culture dressed similar to Christ or the Virgin Mary, some would believe they were experiencing a holy visitation. The possibility that some "demons" are merely interdimensional beings should open up some minds and free them from their theological chains. So, with an open mind, let us first look at the "FaceTime Demon" case.

Fatal insomnia is a very rare disorder in which death occurs from a few months to years when the thalamus - a symmetrical structure of two halves in the centre of the brain – is damaged or degenerates. The person with this form of incurable insomnia finds it impossible to sleep and after experiencing frightening hallucinations, weight loss and dementia, invariably dies. In most people the thalamus is healthy and when we sleep, the brain blocks out external stimuli through a screening process in the thalamus. If someone mentions your name or a word you class as important, or if you were to smell smoke, your thalamus would wake you up. The thalamus also listens out for other possible dangers, such as intruders in your bedroom, and this brings me to the 3am Phenomenon – an inexplicable awakening from sleep at three in the morning and the feeling of someone being there – even though nothing physical is present to account for the alert. The phenomenon has been reported to me on numerous occasions and most serious students of the paranormal will know about this intriguing cognitive process. In 2016 a 22-year-old girl in Birkenhead was rushed into hospital after hyperventilating because she was intensely afraid of something supernatural which kept calling her on her mobile – and this thing even appeared in her room. At first the girl – named Jessica – received anonymous text messages warning her of fatal accidents and all sorts of terrible illnesses. She suspected an ex-boyfriend named Geoff and even reported him to the police and they advised her to block the sender's number – but Jessica explained that there was no visible number to block. Jessica went to a solicitor, who explained the offences of Malicious Communications and Harassment, and he asked to see the distressing text messages – but somehow, they had been deleted from Jessica's mobile. Jessica's mother, father and her best friend Naomi had seen these messages, but the solicitor said without them there was no basis for any case. Then the number of text messages increased, and one of them read: 'If you will kindly kill yourself, you will be my servant in the afterlife. I have 37 servants attending me. They all killed themselves to be mine.'

Then two names were mentioned in a follow-up text message, and these names were of two friends of Jessica who had taken their lives some years ago in their teens. Jessica almost had a breakdown when these messages continued for months, and one morning she walked half a mile to the waterfront via Alabama Way, and threw her mobile into the Mersey. Days later, Jessica's dad bought her an iPhone – and not long after the persecuting text messages started again. The first one said, 'You naughty twat! Throwing away a good phone, but you can't escape me!'

Again the sender's number wasn't accessible, and then things got worse, because someone – or something – FaceTimed Jessica. This happened at 3am when the girl suddenly awoke with a mounting sense of panic. The iPhone buzzed. It was someone called "Arawn" wanting to FaceTime Jessica. The bleary-eyed girl accepted the call, thinking it might be a friend named Aaron – but the face that appeared on the phone's screen looked terrifying. It was a red face with black almond-shaped eyes, a pointed chin, fangs and a classic Dracula widow's peak. The caller screeched with laughter and told Jessica she was going to die soon in a car crash. 'If you try to hang up, I'll appear in your bedroom!' the person warned. Jessica tried to hang up but the face remained on the screen – and then it appeared in her bedroom by the curtains – a glowing red head. Jessica knew it was real because it cast its scarlet light on walls and furniture, and when she closed her eyes she could perceive the after-image on her retina. The thing's maniacal laughter was so loud, Jessica's father knocked on the wall, thinking his daughter had her TV on at full blast.

The ghastly face flew towards Jessica and she passed out from intense shock. When she awoke her mother and father were standing over her. Despite hearing the strange laughter in Jessica's room, her parents could not believe their daughter's account of the apparition. Jessica's doctor persuaded her to visit a psychiatrist, and the specialist said it was possible that the young woman was suffering from persecutory delusions. However, "Arawn" visited Jessica again a week later, and this time, when the girl's mother barged into the room at 3am, she saw the weird red luminous face vanish in mid-air. Jessica became so afraid on the following night, she hyperventilated and was taken to hospital. The entity then left text messages on the girl's phone, but eventually stopped contacting her. This "FaceTime Demon" has been reported by other people, not just locally but across the world. Some of the incidents may be the work of hackers in scary masks, but I did discover that 'Arawn' is a very mysterious and ancient Celtic God of suicide. Years before the FaceTime entity plagued Jessica, another disembodied red glowing face haunted the bedrooms of two girls living seven miles apart. This was in 1979, and the victims were a Childwall Valley Road girl named Pauline, aged 14, and her best friend Donna, aged 13, who lived on Sinclair Avenue in Widnes. They had both attended the same schools until Donna's family moved to Widnes, but the girls still met up in town when they could and now Donna's father had had a phone installed (and an extension put in his daughter's room) so the two friends spent a few hours each day on the line to one another, talking about boys mostly, and clothes and the things girls in their early teens chat about. One evening around 7.30pm in May 1979, Pauline was supposed to call Donna, and the latter's father Terry told his daughter she was running up a phone bill calling her friend all the time. 'Donna, Pauline's parents have both got good jobs and they can afford to pay their phone bill,' said Terry, 'I'm just a dustman and your mum's a dinner lady, and we've got a lot of bills to pay this month. So let Pauline call you.'

Eight o'clock came and went, and Terry peeped in at his daughter and felt sorry for her. She was sitting there on the edge of her bed, looking at the telephone.

'A watched telephone never rings, they say,' quipped Terry.

'I hope nothing's happened to her, Dad, she always calls me when she says she will,' said a despondent-looking Donna.

'Call her then, love – go on, put your mind at rest,' said Terry, smiling sympathetically. He had an older daughter Judy and knew how fast kids grow up, and he thought how innocent this was, two young friends chatting over the phone.

'Thanks Dad!' said Donna, and she lunged at the phone and started to dial Pauline's number. Terry smiled and left the room, closing the door softly behind him.

A man Donna had never heard before answered. 'Yes?' is all he said.

'Oh, I hope I've dialled the right number – is that Pauline's house?' asked Donna.

'Yes, you must be Donna,' said the man, and he spoke in a low and sombre voice.

'Yes, is she okay?' Donna asked, fidgeting with the coiled lead of the handset.

'Donna, I'm afraid I've got some bad news,' said the unknown man.

'Yeah?' muttered Donna, already feeling a bit taken aback by his words.

'Pauline was knocked down and killed on Childwall Valley Road,' he said.

'No – oh no, she can't have – are you sure?' Donna almost fell off the edge of the bed. She felt dizzy and sick and her heart pounded.

'Donna, I'm sorry,' said the man. 'But yes, I'm afraid she's dead. A bus went over her head – it was horrible. Her brains popped out of her skull and went all over this man as he walked his dog.'

Donna dropped the phone and ran sobbing out of her bedroom. She almost fell down the stairs because she was blinded by her tears and couldn't see the steps. Her mother and father closed in on her and grabbed the hysterical girl.

'Donna, what is it?' asked the girl's mother, Eileen, and at the same time Terry said, 'Come on love sit down!' And he guided her onto the sofa where her mother hugged her and tried to make sense of her rambling, disjointed words as she cried her eyes out.

The girl shook in her mother's embrace and tears cascaded down her face onto her mother's cleavage. 'Bus – went over her – and her brains – oh – oh mum – no! Pauline – she's dead, killed!'

Her father somehow got the gist of what had happened but he tried shouting at his daughter to calm her down. 'What are you saying? Calm down love! Donna!'

There was a knock at the door, and Terry went to answer it. It was his neighbour, an old woman named Mrs Davis.

'Is everything okay Terry?' Mrs Davis asked, 'Only I could hear Donna crying from my garden.'

'Come in Mrs Davis, she's in there,' said Terry, nodding to the living room door, 'we're trying to make sense of what she's crying about.'

As Mrs Davis hugged the girl from one side and Donna's mum Eileen hugged from the other, Terry went to the telephone in the hall and dialled Pauline's home. The girl's mother Beryl answered, and Terry asked, 'Hi love, sorry to bother you, but is Pauline alright?'

'Yes, she went out with her cousin to Blackpool this

afternoon and she's not back yet,' replied Beryl, then she asked, 'ah, is Donna missing her? Pauline told me to ring Donna to explain where she was but I completely forgot.'

'Yes, that's all it was – yes – er, thanks. Bye now – bye.' Terry put the phone down and wondered what all the hysterics from Donna was about. When he told his daughter that Pauline was fine and that she'd just gone to Blackpool for the day with a cousin, Donna shook her head and said he was lying.

'Why would I lie, love?' Terry asked his daughter. 'I've just spoken to her mother and she has assured me her daughter is fine and well.'

Donna blew into a tissue and said, 'Dad, some man at her house told me! He said a bus had run over her and that her – ' the girl tried to describe the way Pauline had died but became choked up.

'Terry, phone Pauline's mum again and make sure – ' Eileen was suggesting when Terry over-reacted.

'No! I'm not phoning her again! She'll think I'm tappy! Let Donna speak to her – it's her mate's mum!'

'I can't!' said Donna and she started crying again.

'Here, I'll call her then,' said Donna's mum, Eileen, springing up off the sofa and marching to the hallway. 'What's her number?'

Terry sheepishly went after her and recited the number.

Seconds after Eileen dialled, the phone call was answered. 'Hello? Beryl? It's Eileen – Donna's mother. My husband phoned you before to check if Pauline was okay. Oh, she's there now? Can you put her on, please?' Eileen placed her palm over the mouthpiece and shouted to her daughter who was being comforted

251

by old Mrs Davis. 'Donna! Pauline's just come home now. Here she is.'

Donna wandered out of the living room into the hallway in a daze, red-eyed, dabbing her nose with a piece of crumpled tissue. 'Well what was that idiot talking about? Saying she'd been run over?' Donna wanted to know. She spoke to Pauline, told her about the man who had answered the phone at her address in Childwall, and how he had claimed she had died in a most gruesome manner.

'Donna, my Dad's working nights,' said Pauline, 'there's only me mum here. Maybe you got the wrong number.'

Donna shook her head. 'No, he said to me "You must be Donna" as if he knew we were friends. How would a stranger know my name?'

'You're scaring me now, Donna,' said Pauline. 'I'm tired with walking round Blackpool all day. I'll call you tomorrow.'

That evening, Terry told his daughter his theory behind the 'misinformation': 'Look, it's simple. You called Pauline's house but probably misdialled a wrong number. The fellah who answered it probably had a daughter or even a niece named Pauline, and *that* Pauline happens to have a mate named Donna.'

'So tomorrow then, we could hear about someone named Pauline who's been run over by a bus,' said Terry's wife, Eileen.

'Yeah, but say the person lives down in London?' Terry replied.

'He had a Liverpool accent,' Donna recalled, 'so I don't think your explanation's the right one, dad.'

'There *are* Liverpool people in London, Donna,'

replied Terry.

'Oh let's just forget it,' said Eileen, rolling her eyes, 'it's probably been some cross-line thingy and then some joker with a warped sense of humour has made up that horrible stuff about Pauline dying.'

'But he knew my name though,' said Donna.

'Your mum's right; let's just forget the whole thing,' suggested Terry, 'because there will be a rational explanation but we'll probably never know what it is.'

Three days later, Pauline telephoned Donna at 7pm. She had heard a bit of juicy gossip about a girl they both knew, but a man answered the call, and he did not sound like Donna's father Terry. 'Who's that?' Pauline asked.

'Tim,' said the man, 'is that Pauline?'

'Yes, is she there?' Pauline asked.

'Yes,' said Tim, 'she's here but she's not alive. My name's Tim Phoenix – Chief Inspector Tim Phoenix. Donna has been found hanged, Pauline.'

'What? No, she can't be!' Pauline almost dropped the handset in shock – and then she recalled the incident three evening's back when someone had told Donna that she had died under the wheel of a bus. She became suspicious, and said, 'I don't believe you.'

'Sorry? What was that?' Tim asked, sounding as if he was somewhat surprised by the girl's comment.

'Are you the idiot who told Donna I'd been run over by a bus?' Pauline asked.

There was a telling pause.

'You don't believe me, eh?' said Tim. 'Look love, I think you hanged your friend and I'll be calling round to your place in a few minutes to make an arrest.'

'Go ahead,' said Pauline, 'and I'll have the police

waiting for you! They can put you away for impersonating a policeman!'

The voice of Tim suddenly changed – it became very deep and had a weird mocking quality to it as it said: 'Die! Die Pauline!'

'You idiot! I'm going to report you!' Pauline shouted at the sinister practical joker.

'You're a Catholic and Donna's a Protestant isn't she?' asked Tim in a silly voice.

'I'm going now and the police will be able to trace your call!' shouted Pauline, ready to hang up.

In a gruff voice Tim warned: 'You hang up and I'll eat your grandmother Betty! She's here in Hell with me, aren't you, Betty?'

Betty had been the name of Pauline's late grandmother. This claim by "Tim" really threw the girl.

'Pauline, do as he says,' said a familiar old female voice – the unmistakable voice of her deceased grandmother Betty. 'Do as he says love - he's got me in a horrible dungeon down in Hell!'

'Nan?' gasped Pauline.

'Catholic, Catholic ring the bell!' said Tim in a weird voice, 'When you die you got to hell!'

'I'm reporting you now!' cried Pauline, feeling confused and sick after hearing her grandmother's voice.

Tim then laughed and shouted: 'Protestant, Protestant, quack, quack, quack! Go to the Devil and never come back!'

There was then a female scream that made Pauline's stomach somersault – and then she heard her Nan's voice cry: 'Oh! He's cutting my fingers off with a saw!'

And then the line went dead in the middle of another scream.

Pauline ran downstairs to her mother and burst into tears. She told her mum about "Tim" claiming Donna had hanged herself, and how he had said he'd eat her grandmother in Hell. Suspecting some sick hoaxer was at work, Pauline's parents went to the police and a GPO engineer was sent out to investigate, but despite a thorough examination of the phone line which served Pauline's home and a systematic inspection of the telephones themselves, the engineer could find nothing wrong with the line and nothing amiss in the electronics of the telephones. No one had tapped into the line or wired anything up to it. A further investigation of the state of the telephone line at the exchange end ruled a cross-line out as an explanation for the telephonic nuisance, so the mystery went unsolved – but the mysterious caller returned with a vengeance in the following month.

This time it was Donna's turn. One Sunday evening at precisely 8.15pm when the girl's parents went out for a drink at their local pub, the telephone started to ring. Donna was reading a magazine at the time, and when she answered the call she thought it might be Pauline, but it was the unfamiliar voice of a man, and he asked her to commit a sex act which shocked the girl. She slammed the phone down and wondered if it was that strange phone pest up to his twisted tricks again. The phone started ringing again, and this time it was Donna's mother, Eileen.

'How are you pet? Everything okay?' she asked.

'Mum, someone just phoned and when I answered he said something really rude – something he wanted me to do!'

'Oh no, it's not *him* again, is it?' said Eileen.

'I think it was, but he'd disguised his voice again,' said Donna, and she shuddered as she looked at the window. She'd forgotten to draw the curtains and wondered if he was out there watching her.

'Well, your dad and I will be home soon, love,' Eileen assured her.

'Okay mum, see you soon,' said Donna.

'We might find you dead though when we get home,' joked Eileen.

'Oh – don't say *that*, mum, that scared me then,' said Donna, taken aback by the bad taste of the 'joke'.

Eileen's voice slowly deepened. 'Yes, with your throat cut, and you hanging upside down by your ankles, with your blood dripping all over the carpet. Ah well, the carpet's red anyway.'

'Oh! It's you again!' Donna realised with fear welling up from the pit of her stomach that the freak was now impersonating her mother. She put the phone down on him but it started to ring. The girl backed away and considered running out of the house.

There was a loud bang at the window, and Donna screamed.

It was the neighbour, old Mrs Davis. She smiled through the window and gave the thumbs-up gesture. Donna ran to the door, slid back the bolt and undid the Yale lock's safety catch.

'Sorry I gave you a start, love,' said the old woman, 'only your mum and dad told me to check on you. Is everything alright?'

'No, Mrs Davis, that creep called again – the one who has been causing all the trouble,' said a very anxious Donna, and she beckoned Mrs Davis in.

'Oh you mean that barmpot messing about on the phone?' she asked, and the telephone started to ring.

Donna jumped with fright and looked at the telephone on the half-moon table in the hall. 'Could you answer it please, Mrs Davis? I'm scared in case it's him again!'

'Yes, alright love, I just lift it to my ear don't I?' she asked and picked up the handset awkwardly. She looked at Donna and smiled. 'It's him,' she mouthed without saying a word, and listened. Donna could hear the unbalanced caller talking in a high-pitched voice but she couldn't make out what he was saying.

'G'way you cracked bastard!' Mrs Davis said to the caller, adding, 'and the same to you with bells on!'

'What did he say?' asked Donna, her eyes were huge and full of fear.

'Oh he's definitely a crank, that one. I'd take no notice if I were you love, but he said he's going to appear in your room all hours in the morning,' replied the elderly but feisty woman, 'and I tell you what pet, he sounded away with the mixer to me. You tell your mum and dad about this when they come in – or you can stay in mine if you want. Tell your dad to make sure all the doors and windows are locked.'

'Do you want to stay and have a cup of tea and some cake, Mrs Davis?' Donna asked, and the woman grabbed her hand and squeezed it and said, 'Take no notice of that lunatic. It's probably all talk. He won't come here because he knows the police'd have him. Go on then, love, strong with just a drop of milk and two sugars, and what cakes have you got?'

Donna had never been so glad to have company.

Mrs Davis stayed with her till almost 11pm and at 11.30pm the teenager's parents returned home and found their daughter in a terrible state. She had been sitting in a corner in the kitchen with a steak knife in her hand. When her parents heard about the telephone tormentor now making sexual suggestions to Donna and describing her hanging from her ankles with her throat slit, they resolved to go to the police first thing in the morning.

Donna hardly slept that night because of the threat the voice had made to visit her 'all hours in the morning' – and he kept his promise. Around 3am, Donna awoke because she thought she heard a sound in her room, and as soon as she opened her eyes, she could make out a glimmering red light at the foot of her bed. It was undulating and radiating in spikes for a few moments, and then it grew brighter until something resembling a glowing pinkish red mask formed with sloping black eyes and a black smiling crescent of a mouth.

'Hello!' said a voice which appeared to come from this apparition. 'I told you I'd come!'

At that moment, Donna connected the ghostly glowing reddish face with the persistent weird caller, and she tried to let out a scream but she felt as if her throat had closed up. She grabbed a paperback book lying on the bed and hurled it at the face, but the glowing visage flitted out the way at an incredible speed, and then it darted towards Donna and stopped dead, hovering over the bed about a foot away from her face. Before the girl got out of the bed and ran out of the room, she could see that the face of the thing had a pointed widow's peak and the eyes seemed to consist of a black quivering sludgy liquid.

Donna fled from the room but as she ran down the landing towards her parents' room she saw a red ball of light appear in the air, and this sphere of luminosity turned into that unearthly grinning face. It said something that sounded like, 'Peekaboo!'

Donna was so afraid, she climbed over a banister to get onto the stairs and almost fell. She was now able to let out a scream, and she could see the that the hallway was illuminated by the pinkish light from the floating disembodied head, but as she reached the bottom step the light from the entity faded and Donna switched on the hallway light and looked back up the stairs. She heard footfalls and seconds later her father appeared at the top of the stairs dressed only in his underpants and he shouted down, 'What's up?'

Donna struggled to find the words to muster a coherent explanation for a moment, and then she yelled back: 'Dad, some horrible ghost – a face – just a head – appeared in my bedroom and chased me!'

'Are you sure it wasn't all a nightmare?' Terry asked.

Donna shook her head and started to cry.

Donna slept with her mum that morning and Terry slept in his daughter's bed and assured his daughter whatever the thing was, it would not return. But the thing not only returned on the following night, it also haunted Donna's friend Pauline at her Childwall home around the same time. Donna awoke in her bed after feeling someone kissing her palm. She opened her eyes and saw a side view of the disembodied glowing head with a pink aura around it. Its nose was pointy, and the eyes were closed as the thing kissed her palm and fingers. Donna screamed, pulled her hand away from the floating head and again ran to her parent's room. She expected the thing to appear in front of her again but this time it didn't. The girl's father, Terry rushed into the room and thought he saw something luminous with a red halo flit out of Donna's bedroom via the closed window. After that night, Donna saw no more of the creepy entity and received no more telephone calls from it, but the next morning, Pauline called Donna and told her that the red face had appeared in her kitchen around three in the morning and her father, who had just returned home from a long night shift, had seen the thing look at him with an expression of hatred before it flew backwards through a window. Then Pauline had heard a weird voice calling her name in her bedroom, and she had seen a smiling face looking through what seemed to be red flames in front of her wardrobe. Pauline reacted by hiding under the blankets. She then heard the uncanny-sounding voice shout out, 'Spoilsport!'

When Pauline peeped over the edge of the blankets she had seen that the room was in darkness and there was no sign of the mysterious and terrifying intruder. Neither of the girls ever encountered the mysterious red glowing face again. The descriptions of the entity and its persecutory nature via the telephone are strikingly similar to the entity which would stalk Jessica thirty-seven years later in the 2016 case. A priest was contacted by the parents of Pauline in the 1979 case and the clergyman expressed his belief that the entity that had haunted Pauline and her friend had been some "agent of the Devil" – in other words, a demon – because it had claimed to be torturing Pauline's late grandmother in Hell – but the entity might equally have been some trespasser from another dimension. Pauline assured me that her beloved grandmother had been a very kind and churchgoing lady who had led a blameless life, so what on earth would she be doing in Hell anyway? There's a question mark above the red face entity in my files, and I just can't accept it as a bona fide demon. The same classification is assigned to the weird being featured in the following account.

In January 1978, a 49-year-old Liverpool man named Ken Wheeler received a lump sum redundancy payment when he lost his job upon the closure of the Clyde Iron Works in Scotland. He moved back to Liverpool, but went into a spiral of depression when a group of fair-weather friends kept asking him to go out on pub crawls. Drink had been the cause of so many failed relationships in Ken's life, he decided to move somewhere quiet and spent a little time on his own so he could evaluate his life. He moved to Wirral and rented a house on Birkenhead's Bidston Avenue. With his modicum of newfound wealth Ken started to drink heavily, often whilst ruefully reflecting on that messy divorce from Rhona a few years back; a split caused by drunken behaviour that had led to domestic violence; he hadn't laid a finger on Rhona but he *did* smash a few TVs and break up a lot of furniture and plates during the rows. By the end of January, Ken seemed to have the drinking under control, and he set himself a goal in an effort to deal with the cold turkey – writing. He'd always harboured a secret ambition to be a novelist, so he bought a simple manual typewriter, a desk and bookshelves which he filled with all sorts of tomes, dictionaries and a complete recent set of the *Encyclopaedia Britannica*. Ken purchased an old brass face grandfather clock from an antiques shop for £100 and a transistor radio to keep him company in his study during the long hours of the night. But what would be the subject of his novel? He pondered upon all sorts of possibilities, but decided to write what he knew about – a man with a drink problem working at the furnaces of a Scottish iron works, set in the early 1970s. Just writing the first paragraph of the autobiographical work was harder than Ken had anticipated, and every time he struggled to find the words he went down to the kitchen, took the bottle of Bell's Whisky from the cupboard before his shaking hands put it back. These self-battles went on night after night as he struggled to start his book.

On 13 February, a minute before midnight, Ken read back the first typed paragraph, swore, pulled the page from the typewriter and crumpled it. What had the author of that book in *Teach Yourself Writing* advised when faced with writer's block? Ken recalled the advice: just type anything. He heard the DJ on the radio mention it was now Valentine's Day, so Ken decided to write a poem about love. Making words rhyme was just as hard as producing a well-written paragraph. He gave up just before one o'clock, cursed the typewriter and yelled, 'Why aren't the keys laid out as ABCDEFG instead of QWERTY! Bleedin' ridiculous!'

The grandfather clock struck one – and the case door in the clock opened by itself with a creak, startling Ken. It was black inside the clock – no sign of the pendulum or weights. And what was that sweet smell? It reminded the budding writer of lavender.

'Ken,' said an echoing soft female voice from within

the grandfather clock, 'I love you.'

Ken swore loud, jumped up out his chair and looked at the half open door. 'Who's that?'

'Vanessa,' said the velvet voice, 'I'm a ghost. Happy Valentine's Day.'

'I don't believe in ghosts!' said Ken, and he looked about, thinking someone was hoaxing him. There was a clunk, and he noticed the door in the clock had closed. He went straight downstairs and grabbed the bottle of Bell's Whisky. He believed the shock he'd received justified a stiff drink – and another. He fell into his bed at four and had a vivid dream a woman was making love to him. She felt very bony and her tongue was pushed so far down his throat he retched. 'Num-num-num!' she said, close to his ear, kissing and licking his earlobe, and she kept exhaling with pleasure and moaning.

'Who are you?' Ken asked, his hand reaching for the bedside lamp in the pitch darkness but she kept intercepting his hand.

'I love you,' she hissed, 'I love you Ken, you're a real man...oh!'

'Well you know my name so you can't be a prozzie,' Ken reasoned, and the room kept turning left when he closed his eyes. His mysterious lover then started giggling and whispering close to his ear in a very dirty and coarse way which even shocked the former welder, and he'd heard some profanities and vulgar words up in the Scottish ironworks. She made love to him twice, and then he fell asleep. He awoke at eleven that morning and turned to his left, but there was no one there. He got up, still feeling a bit dizzy, and went into the hallway. He saw the empty whisky bottle through the doorway of his study and cringed. He felt so bad; he'd succumbed to temptation and set himself back. When he stumbled into the toilet, he saw in the mirror that he had love bites all over his neck and shoulders – and recalled the erotic dream. He knew he couldn't have given himself those hickies – so who had that woman been? It really shook him. Had someone been in his house and actually slept with him yet he couldn't even remember her? Was this an early sign of some mental illness? Ken said to his reflection, 'Listen bollocks, you have let me down badly. Look at the state of you, you puffy-eyed middle-aged arsehole. You are not to drink – got that?'

At 3pm he went to buy a pack of cigarettes at the off licence, and he just knew he'd buy another bottle of whisky – and he did. When he got home he found his hands shaking as he thought of the battle that lay ahead. He put the bottle away in the usual cupboard, then went and made himself a coffee and studied the racing pages of the newspapers – anything to take his mind off his predicament.

At 10pm he sipped a scotch and lemonade and started to write in his study again, and at 1am the clock struck one – and that door opened in the long case clock. The voice he'd heard last night said: 'I'm sorry for last night, Ken; I shouldn't have made love to you.'

Ken went cold – it hadn't been a dream and those really had been hickeys on him! Hickey from *what* though?

'Show yourself, Vanessa!' he said. He felt brave because of the whisky.

'I can't, you'll be frightened,' said "Vanessa" with a tinge of sadness in her voice. 'People judge me by my appearance.'

'You could be someone pulling my leg for all I know,' said Ken to the clock, 'so show yourself and I won't judge you.'

'If you're frightened when you see me I may kill you,' the voice replied, 'I don't look much but I have a heart of gold.'

'You'll kill me, eh? Not very romantic is it?' remarked Ken, swigging the neat whisky from the bottle.

The thing that emerged from that clock was not at all feminine or even human; it looked like the long skull of a horse with red domed eyes, rows of fangs, slithering snakelike limbs, and a segmented torso resembling a bony spine. Ken backed away so violently he knocked over the desk and the typewriter and bottle of whisky crashed to the ground. The thing shrieked and leaped towards Ken on legs identical in shape to a grasshopper's, but he threw himself at the door, yanked it open, and ran downstairs and out of the building. When he returned with a neighbour, he found the grandfather clock smashed up. They said the creature was the product of the DTs, hallucinated by Ken's fevered mind, and after suffering horrific nightmares about Vanessa he was hospitalised and ended his days on a psychiatric ward. Years later I tracked down Charles Pickering, the man at the Antiques shop who had sold the grandfather clock to Ken, and he seemed to know something about its history but seemed afraid to even speak about it. I pressed him but he refused to say a word. Ken believed the thing was some demonic being till the day he died, but I have a feeling that "Vanessa" was some interdimensional being who had, for some reason, been sexually attracted to Ken Wheeler. Why she had come into our reality via a grandfather clock is unknown. Perhaps some machine was hidden in that clock which could open a portal between this world and the world Vanessa resided in.

Next in this chapter, we come to a chilling example of a possible interdimensional being which is totally nonhuman. This was a terrifying incident which allegedly took place in Birkenhead Park in December 2005 which might throw some paranormal light on some of these perplexing disappearances. On the evening of Christmas Eve, 2005, a thick fog invaded the North West. Hundreds of motorists on the M62 were brought to a standstill after a 26-car pile-up on the motorway between junctions 11 and 12 near Warrington, and Wirral did not escape the chaos caused by the ubiquitous fog. That same evening, a couple in their early thirties, Jane and Steve Havelock were returning with their children - 3-year-old Harry and 5-year-old Grace - from the house of Jane's parents on Egerton Road, and being in a hurry to get home in the freezing fog, the couple took a short cut through Birkenhead Park, as they only lived off Laird Street, which was minutes away. On Ashville Road, as Harry cried and asked his mum if he could have his Christmas presents from his Nan a day early, Grace suddenly cried out and said something had pulled her coat off. Her parka was indeed missing and her mother said, 'Oh Grace, what have you done with your coat?'

Harry started digging his heels in as he pleaded for his presents and then there was a piercing scream from above. Steve and Jane looked up and for a moment they could not believe their eyes. Grace was hanging almost upside down with her hair dangling and coiled around her was the tentacle of something resembling an octopus, and it seemed to be made of a faintly luminous vapour. This thing had two luminous holes for eyes, and one of its tentacles reached for little Harry but his father slapped the thing away, and experienced a stinging electric shock in his hand and wrist. The frantic parents jumped and leaped upwards, trying to grab at their screaming daughter, but the thing drifted away, and as it did, it pulled Grace into its vaporous body. Steve climbed onto a park gatepost and jumped at the tentacled abductor. Each of his hands went into those eye holes, and for a moment he was dangling from the abomination. It let out a screech before its face came apart with a strange ripping sound, and Grace fell from the exposed interior of the bizarre creature's head. Grace's mother caught her but the girl seemed unconscious. Steve fell from the entity, and the thing vanished. He carried his daughter as the family hurried out the fogbound park, and Grace later recovered and said she had seen small human skulls inside that unearthly monstrosity. It took years for the girl to get over the terrifying ordeal, and the family still won't go near the part of the park where the sinister incident took place. I have a feeling Grace was one of the lucky ones who encountered that nameless thing and lived to tell the tale.

We remain in Wirral for the next account of a being that was not of this world. In the many years I have spent investigating the paranormal, I've come across a lot of stories that sound like urban legends, and to cite an example off the top of my head I could mention the Prenton Doll's House Story. A lot of people have assured me that there was once an eerie oversized doll's house – more of a Wendy house that a child could play in – and this house stood somewhere off the main road (possible on Welford Avenue) near the Sainsbury's store on Birkenhead's Woodchurch Road. According to legend, the large playhouse's interior lit up at night, and there was a life-size doll of a little girl always to be seen at the window, and this girl represented the only daughter of the couple living in the real house nearby. The child had been knocked down and killed years before, and the couple never got over the shock of losing her. It was alleged that the doll had the original hair, skin and teeth taken from the corpse of the dead daughter – and what's more, the doll was often seen to wave at passersby and the curious – or so the weird story goes. I happened to mention this story once when I was a guest on BBC Radio Merseyside's *Billy Butler Show* and I received dozens of emails, letters and calls from people assuring me that the story was true. I remain sceptical about this local *Grand Guignol* but perhaps a reader out there knows the truth of the matter.

The following story, which I researched some years ago, also seemed like an urban legend to me initially, but I subsequently found that this did not seem to be the case at all, and there were numerous witnesses to back the eldritch tale up. The incident took place on the Tuesday evening of 22 January 1974. At 7.30pm, Mr and Mrs Jones – a very down to earth and hardworking couple (who hailed from Wavertree but had come to live in Prenton in the late 1960s) left their two children in the care of a 13-year-old babysitter named Susan Woodford at their luxurious detached home on Manor Hill. The Joneses had not been out in six months and were looking forward to a night at a restaurant over in Liverpool with relatives in Wavertree, followed by a drink and catch-up with a few friends at a local pub. They assured Susan they'd be back 'a bit before midnight' and left the girl with lemonade, a box of cakes from Sayers and a copy of *Jackie* magazine. Marianne Jones, aged 5½, and her 4-year-old brother Peter, were allowed to watch an Abbott and Costello film until 8.30pm, and then Susan took them up to their rooms and tucked them in. The babysitter told Peter a bedtime story, and then she moved on to Marianne's room, and the little girl looked worried about something. She said a strange thing to Susan: 'I saw a devil last night.'

'There's no such thing as the devil, Marianne, now have a nice sleep and your mum and dad will soon be back,' said a smiling Susan.

'There *is* such a thing, I saw him, and Peter too,' insisted Marianne, sitting up in the bed. She described what she had seen. 'He had a big fork and he was all in red and he said "Hello little girl, my name is Raffy Mirkuss [the phonetic name given by the child], and if you tell anyone you saw me I'll throw you in the pit.'

Susan rolled her eyes and said, 'Marianne, settle down and stop talking about things like that or you'll upset Peter.'

There was a loud bump downstairs.

'Is that him?' Marianne asked, her large startled eyes looking over the edge of the blankets.

'No, it came from outside, now go asleep Marianne,' Susan told the nervy girl, and then she kissed her forehead and left the room, switching off the light. Susan went downstairs and made sure all the doors and windows were secure, and then she watched *Whatever Happened to the Likely Lads?* on the telly. She sipped Corona cherry lemonade and flipped through the pages of *Jackie* – when she heard a weird voice cry out: 'Susan beware of the devil!'

It came from the kitchen, and as the startled babysitter looked at the doorway to the kitchen, she heard something moving. There had been a song by the British-Jamaican singer Dandy Livingstone called *Suzanne Beware of the Devil* that had been in the charts two years previously, and Susan hoped her ex-boyfriend, Terry, who had loved that song, had somehow got into the house, as she still loved him – but the voice had not sounded like Terry's voice.

And then it came walking into the lounge from the kitchen; it looked like a child or a man of very short stature – around 4 feet tall - in a red devil costume with a ghastly Mephistophelian mask and horns. The eyes seemed to be of a luminous blue, and the 3-pronged black metal fork the intruder brandished looked real – and lethal. 'Dance, Susan, or else!' the devil cried, and made threatening thrusts at her with the fork. Susan screamed and ran to a corner, crying.

'And *you* said there was no devil!' cried the weird masked trespasser. He gave a bow and said: 'I'm not *the* Devil though, I'm Raffy Mirkuss, and I could kill you and no one would ever catch me. I've killed before!'

Susan tried to run around the terrifying interloper and he pushed the points of the fork into her back, but she was so afraid, she didn't feel the pain at the time –

but later needed hospital treatment. She ran up to Marianne's room, opened the window, and screamed for help. A neighbour next door – a retired policeman – had keys to the house that had been left with him and when he let himself in he saw blood on the carpet. The 'devil' had gone. Susan was found in tears in the bathroom with blood streaming from strange wounds in her back: 3 small holes all in a straight line, made by the fork the little "devil" had stabbed her with. The girl was taken to hospital and her wounds were treated but her story was not believed and police thought she'd concocted the weird tale to cover up an injury inflicted by her former boyfriend. That former boyfriend was at home recovering from the flu at the time. I discovered that the entity had been seen at the house from the early 1960s, and the last sighting of it there was in 1993. When I published an abridged version of the Prenton Devil in the *Wirral Globe* in September 2018, I received some curious feedback about the story from a man named David who seems to have encountered a very similar entity at his home on Craigburn Road, Tuebrook. In 1961, David was a 10-year-old who had just moved into a terraced house on Tuebrook's Craigburn Road with his mother and father and two older sisters. It was a beautiful sunny August morning in the school Summer holidays, and at 8.15am David awoke in his bedroom and immediately thought about the album his Uncle Stan had given him to stick his football player cards in. The cards had been given away in the *Wizard* - a comic aimed at boys – and David loved sticking the cards in the album and had also started to collect stamps. On this morning as David lay in bed, about to dress and go downstairs to breakfast, he heard a noise to the left of his wardrobe. He thought his cat, Mr Meekins had got into his room at first, but then the boy was startled to see a head quickly peep out at him for a second before withdrawing back behind the wardrobe. David sat up quickly in his bed, naturally shocked at what he'd just seen. In the brief glimpse he'd had of the intruder, he thought it was a child wearing some sort of red mask.

'Oi! Who's that?' he asked, and he reached out to his old cricket bat, resting across a chair – just in case the trespasser was violent. He then received quite a shock when a head popped out from the side of the wardrobe, because it was a little man, a bit smaller than David, with a red shiny face, horns, and a pair of huge pale blue eyes.

'Is that you, Colin?' asked this weird figure, and he spoke in a very well-to-do voice.

'Mam!' David cried, and he raised the bat, ready to clobber the creepy devil-like bedroom invader.

'Colin, it's me! Put that bat down!' said the horned oddity, and it came out now with his hands raised. All of its skin was as red as its face, and this really unnerved David. He later told me that the shade of red was almost the same as that of a Post Office pillar box.

'Who are you?' David asked, and his right leg came slowly out of the bed and he stood on the floor with one foot, ready to make his escape.

'Colin, have you lost your memory? It's me – Clarence!' said the imp, raising its thick joined eyebrows and smiling as if it expected David to recognise it.

'My name's David, not Colin,' the boy said and jumped out the bed and opened the door of his bedroom. He ran downstairs and seeing his father Albert (who was fixing David's bike) he shouted to him, 'Dad, there's a thing in my room like a devil!'

Perplexed and slightly amused by his excited son's comment, Albert stood up and asked, 'What?'

'He's all red and he's got horns and he was hiding at the side of the wardrobe,' said David, looking up the stairs as he spoke, expecting the weird figure to appear.

'You've had a bleedin' nightmare, lad,' said Albert, and he wiped the black oily mess from his hands on a yellow duster cloth. 'Hey, I fixed the gearchain.'

'Dad!' David's voice rose in tone as he uttered the word. 'I did not dream him – he's up there now! Go and see!'

David's mother came into the hallway and said, 'Come on you two, your breakfasts are on the table!'

'Mam! There's a devil in my room!' David excitedly told her.

His mum just returned a puzzled look and tilted her head about ten degrees.

'He's had a nightmare,' said Albert, throwing the yellow cloth to the floor, 'I'll go and have a look.'

'Be careful dad!' said David as he watched his father walk quickly up the stairs.

The boy's mother watched her husband go up the stairs, then looked at her son and asked, 'There's a *what* in your room?'

Mother and son heard a succession of thumps, and then Albert appeared at the top of the stairs with an expression of horror on his face. When he was halfway down the stairs he said to his wife, 'There's – a – a thing in his room – with horns – all in red and it's going through his drawers and cupboards and throwing things all over the place!'

'Hit him with the cricket bat dad!' David suggested.

'Mind out the way,' Albert shoved his son aside, went into the parlour, and knelt down before the sideboard. He pulled open a door, took out a large biscuit tin, and then his wife hurried to him and said, 'No, Alby, don't!'

'Don't what?' David wanted to know, and he crouched besides his father and watched him prise the lid off the biscuit tin. Underneath ration books, documents and old receipts, Albert's hand rummaged about until he produced a gun. It was a Browning semi-automatic handgun.

'Alby, don't, it's against the law!' David's mother said hysterically.

'Wow, is that a real gun, dad?' asked David, his eyes aglow at the sight of the Browning.

Albert located the firearm's magazine, wrapped up in a piece of brown paper. He shoved it into the Browning and stood up, taking the safety catch off.

'Alby don't be daft!' his wife stood before him.

'Get out me road!' he said, and his gun-wielding hand seemed to be shaking.

'Are you going to shoot him dad?' said a thrilled David, following close on his father's heels as they both went up the stairs.

'Stay there with your mother,' Albert shouted to his son.

David was restrained by the powerful arms of his mother. She almost dragged him back down the stairs as she watched her husband – a former Royal Marine – go to tackle the extraordinary 'housebreaker'. David waited at the bottom of the stairs, expecting to hear the sounds of gunfire he'd heard in films on the television – but instead he heard his father shout, 'Come out!' and then there was a mighty crack. Then David felt his mother's fingers squeeze his upper arm as there were two more loud bangs, followed by a scuffling noise. Albert appeared at the top of the stairs wide-eyed, and his hair, normally combed neatly in a part, was in wild disarray. 'I shot it twice! It's not human - not human at all.'

'Oh my God! They'll hang you, Alby!' cried his wife and she threw her hands to her face.

David ran up the stairs, hand on the rail, taking two steps at a time. On the top step he could smell the cartridge powder from the gunshots. David went gingerly into his bedroom with his father close behind, and he saw a neat hole in the door of the wardrobe.

'I shot it in the eye and the other bullet blew its front teeth out,' said Albert, and seemed to be in a daze.

'Where did it go?' asked David, eyeing the Browning clenched in his father's huge fist.

'It went towards the side of the wardrobe,' replied Albert, 'and then – it wasn't there.'

'Is it a ghost, dad? What is it?' David asked, and he peeped around the wardrobe and saw nothing.

'Put it away now, Alby!' Albert's wife implored him, looking at the pistol in horror.

'The police'll be knocking soon,' Albert said in a resigned tone, 'thanks to the nosy neighbours.'

But no one reported the sound of gunfire and no one ever called. The Browning – smuggled home to England from Germany after the war by Albert - was stashed away. "Clarence" was never seen again at the house – but three years later, David's mother was told by an elderly neighbour that the family who had once lived in her house on Craigburn Road had a young crippled son named Colin, and that child had sadly died from pneumonia aged 9 in the early 1950s. Was this the Colin that the 'devil' entity had mistaken David for? We can rule out someone of small stature or a child donning a devil costume, for how could they gain access to David's bedroom and how on earth could they survive being shot at point-black range in the eye and mouth? Whatever the thing was, it wasn't human and it went back the same way it had first arrived – perhaps in some portal to the left of the wardrobe in a boy's bedroom. In other words, "Clarence" does not seem to have been from this dimension. The case continues to baffle me, but I think the strange diabolical figure was most likely one of the interdimensional beings we have been speculating upon in this chapter.

And finally I must conclude this chapter with a story of a malevolent being which really fits the bill for an interdimensional entity to a tee. Many years ago a very strange story came my way. I'd heard variations of it before and thought it sounded like a typical untraceable friend-of-a-friend tale – a mere urban legend, but in 2009 I happened to mention the story concerned on a local radio programme I appeared on each week, talking about mysteries of North-West England, and I received some very informative feedback – including a relative of one of the people involved in the story. From the feedback I gleaned the following. In 1969, a group of nomadic young people, all in their twenties, squatted at a house on Highfield Road, Rock Ferry. These "hippies" (as they were then called), were four men and five women, mostly from London, and they had been drawn first to Liverpool on a pilgrimage to the hometown of the Beatles (most of the group being fans of the band), and after being evicted from a squat on Penny Lane, they came over to Birkenhead, where they made a derelict house their home on Highfield Road. The leader of the group was said to have been a 25-year-old man named Vincent, and he was a self-proclaimed occultist who studied the works of Aleister Crowley, Carlos Castaneda and Éliphas Lévi, and he also read everything about the teachings, rites and ceremonies of the Hermetic Order of the Golden Dawn – a controversial sect founded in 1887 to study the occult with a view to practicing real magic. Shortly after the hippies had moved into their squat, they were joined by a 17-year-old girl we shall name Lucy – not her real name, because this teenager was the runaway daughter of a well-known aristocratic couple with links to the Royal Family. Vincent had one of the rooms in the squat painted black, and even the windows of the room were painted over. A fire was lit in the grate and cannabis joints were passed around as Vincent played records by The Doors, The Beatles and other contemporary artists backwards, listening for "secret messages" from the Devil. This madness and supernatural mumbo-jumbo culminated one night in an orgy which Vincent arranged as a 'sex magic ceremony' which he called the Amalantrah Working – a ritual from the books of Aleister Crowley to open up a "rent in the fabric of space and time" – a portal in other words – through which liberating demons could enter. Lucy lost her virginity during the 'ceremony' after having sex with Vincent and one of his disciples but nothing paranormal took place as a result of the so-called ritual. Later that evening an old man with a Liverpool accent called at the house and said he had something magical he wished to show to the leader of the group. He was admitted to the house and he shook hands with a bemused Vincent then took a black cylindrical leather case out of a bag. 'This is a Victorian kaleidoscope I've had since I was a child, and there is a spirit of some sort living within it named Lamma. Don't look at her too often or you'll become insane.'

'A spirit you say?' asked a stoned Vincent, smiling at the tube.

'Yes, I don't want anything for it,' said the old man, 'keep it. Perhaps you can learn something from the spirit.'

The old man then left, and the naked debauchees started dancing, singing, and drinking, and all the time Vincent, who had been smoking marijuana, kept looking into the vintage kaleidoscope, which was trained on the light of a candle, when he suddenly exclaimed, 'What on earth is *that*?'

'What's what? Let me see!' said one of Vincent's friends, but he could not prise the tube from his leader, and after about thirty seconds, Vincent turned to his friend and his eyes were staring, mad-looking, and his irises seemed to have a faint blue glow to them. A beam of concentrated light then shone from the tube of the kaleidoscope, projecting a terrifying face upon the wall. The face was made up of what looked like scintillating coloured gemstones and the eyes were oval, neon-green with cog-shaped pupils, and they exerted a powerful hypnotic pull on everyone present. The head was bulbous at the top and tapered to a pointed chin, and from a flat projection it suddenly became three-dimensional. The face of this eldritch being seemed crystalline and as everyone looked on in horrified shock, the mouth of unearthly head opened to reveal a deep tunnel. A booming feminine voice said, 'I am Lamma,' and it was so amplified it made the bones of those present vibrate. Vincent was about to question the entity when it's mouth formed an O shape and it sucked in four of the naked women standing nearby with a powerful vortex. The women screamed and tried to get out of the entity's mouth, but there was a crackling sound within the mouth and the women started to shake violently and seemed to suffer seizures as if they were being electrocuted, The mouth then closed on the stunned and groaning women. Lucy ran naked out of the room and onto the streets. She told an old night watchman what had happened and he covered her with his coat before going into the squat. He found four men dead on the floor of the black-roomed wall, and they all wore expressions of utter terror upon their faces. The bulging eyes of the dead were all fixed on one point on the wall, but there was no sign of "Lamma" – just an odour of tobacco and marijuana. Lucy was reclaimed by her aristocratic family and the four dead men were explained away as tramps who had died from accidental overdoses of heroin – even though Lucy stated that they were only smoking cannabis. There was no investigation into the fate of the four missing girls – regarded as nomadic nobodies by the authorities, and Lucy's well-placed family allegedly had the entire strange case hushed up, but tales of the weird incident continued to circulate for years. I often wonder just what lurked in that Victorian kaleidoscope - and what became of those four young women? In 1918, Aleister Crowley claimed to have contacted an entity known as "Lam" – and this being is described as having no ears, a large bulbous head that tapers to a pointed elfin chin, and two large eyes. Crowley's sketch of the entity shows a being that has a striking similarity to the modern "greys" – the mysterious beings associated with UFO abductions (although the abductions often take place in the absence of any UFOs). Crowley claimed that Lam was from what we would call another dimension, and that Lam could come to this world by a "rent" in time and space. It's intriguing that the being conjured up by the hippies at the house on Highfield Road called itself Lamma – a feminine form of Lam perhaps. This is just one facet of the case which deepens the mystery. So, not all weird creatures are ghosts or demons, but possibly interdimensional beings, interpreted by the zeitgeist of those they visit; today they might be called UFO occupants or demons, and in bygone ages they might have been perceived as devils, angels vampires or any of the unearthly occult creatures that populated the pantheon of monsters stretching back to Ancient Egypt and Greece. I think I might have even mistaken some of them for the many ghosts that are chronicled in this book...

TWO HAUNTED PAINTINGS

To preserve the confidentiality of the people involved in this story, there have been some minor changes in names and places, but the rest is exactly as it was reported to me and the account is a very strange one. The place was a beautiful detached house on Gateacre's Grange Lane, and the time was Monday the 19th of March, 1973. A divorced man, a 59-year-old banker named Nigel Harrington owned the house and lived there with his two daughters, Rachel, aged 17, and Kristine, aged 19. Upon this Monday, a cocktail party was to be held from 8pm so Kristine, who was training to be a chef, could exercise her culinary skills. Her father had been dead against the party at first, citing it as a complete waste of time and money, but his girlfriend Barbara thought the party was an excellent idea and thought she and Nigel should use the occasion to tell guests that they were about to become engaged.

'Is there really *any* need for this, Kristine?' groaned Nigel, looking at his daughter's six friends, chopping a myriad kind of vegetables in a row on two long trestle tables set up in the kitchen.

'Yes there is Daddy,' replied Kristine, studying a Fanny Craddock cookery book, 'It's called *Mise en place*,' and then the teen's big eyes rolled up to the ceiling as she recalled the definition, 'that's a professional chef's term for the highly-organized preparation in readiness for cooking -'

'We're expecting thirty guests, not the multitude at Bethsaida,' her father interrupted, trying to fasten his cufflink. He looked at his younger daughter, Rachel. She was wearing a tall white mushroom-shaped chef's hat. 'What's that on her head?' he muttered with a lopsided smile, and Kristine said: 'A toque blanche of course – don't you know anything? It instils her with culinary confidence.'

Rachel was humming some pop tune, gazing into space with a docile expression as she stirred a huge bubbling pot of beef bourguignon on the cooker with a wooden spoon. Nigel watched in horror as Rachel's equally docile boyfriend Donny poured a prized bottle of Grand vin Rouge de Bandol into the pot before taking a swig.

Nigel could hardly get his words out, and gasped, 'My – my Château Pradeaux – you ignoramus!' to which Donny turned to him, then looked at the label of the vintage wine and said, 'What?'

Nigel snatched the bottle from him and seemed close to tears. 'My wine vault is out of bounds from now on!' he declared, and he then turned to Rachel and said, 'Kindly keep your throwback Neanderthal boyfriend away from my wines!'

Kristine's boyfriend and his friends were continually visiting the kitchen table, which was crammed corner to corner with home-baked pies, tarts, Black Forest trifles and sweet-smelling concoctions of punches, scampi, the mandatory Peach Melba roulades, nutty caramel sundaes, Quiche Lorraine and so on, and every inch of the kitchen's counters were likewise covered with profiteroles and dainty-looking sandwiches. Nigel shooed the teenaged scavengers away, and at 7.50pm the first guests turned up, and then a minibus arrived on Grange Lane laden with

Scottish relatives Nigel hadn't seen for years. They congratulated him on his engagement and headed straight for the drinks. Nigel marched into the kitchen and told Kristine, 'I was supposed to announce the engagement – but it would seem everyone knows already! Did you tell them?'

Kristine simply nodded nonchalantly. 'Daddy, remember what the doctor said about your blood pressure; calm down and enjoy the evening. All of this is for you and Barbara.'

Nigel did calm down once Barbara arrived at eight, but then his ex-wife Carol and her new husband, Mike – a bearded giant of a man who owned a construction company also turned up. He squeezed Nigel's hand when they shook at the door and through gritted teeth he warned, 'Don't start going down memory lane with Carol; she gets emotional in drink; she's my wife now, alright?'

'You're most welcome to her!' Nigel retorted, his face twisted in pain, 'And I am looking *up* the lane to a wonderful future with *my* wife!' he said, then he went back to Barbara and announced the engagement. Nigel then melodramatically asked her to marry him and got down on his bended knee with the ring. Everyone cheered, and the party went on till three, when the last guest left. Donny was so drunk he slept on the sofa in the lounge, and at 3:45am, he knocked on Kristine's bedroom door. She came to the door and was about to pull him into the bedroom when Donny said, 'No, listen; there're two women downstairs scrapping!'

'What?' Kristine asked, and yawned.

Donny looked afraid. He said: 'They're both nude and they're scratching one another eyes out and pulling each other's hair out! And there's something funny about them.'

Kristine could now hear the women screaming as they fought. She went halfway down the stairs and by the light of an overturned lampshade she saw two young naked women she did not recognise, and one had the other in a headlock and was punching her hard in the face. Kristine crept up the stairs and went into her father's room, where she startled him and Barbara as they embraced. Barbara covered her breasts with her negligee and sat up, shocked.

'Kristine! How dare you barge into my – our – bedroom without knocking!' dissented Nigel, and his eyes narrowed to thin slits when Kristine turned on the bedroom light. 'Daddy! There are two women downstairs having a barney!'

'What they do with their private lives is their own concern,' said Nigel, not really understanding what a barney was.

'They're having a full-blown fight!' said Kristine, 'And they're in their birthday suits!'

'Well who are they?' asked Nigel, 'Our Scottish cousins? I thought they'd all left?'

'I've never seen them before in my life, and Donny doesn't know who they are, either,' Kristine told him, and Donny's face appeared over her shoulder. 'They're going to kill one another Mr Harrington,' he said in a sheepish manner.

'You should be a bit more choosy regarding the calibre of guests you invite,' grumbled Nigel, and he got out the bed, put on his pyjama bottoms and a dressing gown, then went downstairs. Nigel rubbed his bleary eyes. He immediately recognised the face of one of the naked women who were wrestling one another; it was "Tina" the girl in a painting of that name that had hung on the wall of the lounge for about ten years. The kitsch painting had been given to him by his mother, and it was a very popular painting that was found in the homes of hundreds of thousands of people. The woman being punched in the face by another woman was definitely the subject of the Tina painting without a doubt – and when Nigel's eyes glanced over at the painting, he saw that the model was missing from the painting on the wall. 'Am I still dreaming?' he gasped to himself, unable to take in the strange scene before him. Nigel did not recognise the other woman, who now had Tina's arm up her back. The two women seemed unaware that they were being watched.

'Stop this!' Nigel shouted – and the two women stopped fighting and looked at Nigel - then vanished into thin air. A moment later the women reappeared in their respective picture frames. This uncanny occurrence was also witnessed by Barbara, Kristine and Donny. Barbara was really shaken by the incident and said that the figures must have been the ghosts of the women depicted in the paintings. The picture of Tina was put away in the loft by Nigel after that night, and the other painting – brought to the party as a gift to Nigel and Barbara by someone – was thrown in the bin. Both pictures had been painted by a mysterious artist named JH Lynch. All paintings by this late artist are said to have an air of weirdness about them. How or why the ghosts of the models of the paintings were fighting that morning remains a mystery. There's a strange postscript to this unearthly story; in early

March 2019, a Gateacre woman named Dawn contacted me by email and said she had heard someone whistling in her living room all hours in the morning, and that she and her husband had determined that the whistling had started after their daughter had put up an old picture she had bought on eBay. That picture was a print of "Tina" – by the artist JH Lynch. The house in question where Dawn lives happens to be the very same house where the apparent ghosts of two artists' models had a catfight that morning in March back in 1973. I told Dawn about the incident at her home and she and her daughter were so scared of seeing the ghost walk, the painting of Tina was thrown out. If you Google "JH Lynch" you will see the paintings he executed and Tina will be among them. More mature readers might even recognise the Tina painting, as it was as popular as that other eerie kitsch painting in the 1970s – the infamous *Crying Boy*...

SQUARE HEAD

One Saturday evening in March 1972, as dusk fell over Kirkdale, a gang of six girls was skipping on Rumney Road, and they were all chanting the nonsensical rhyme: 'One, two three, me Mam caught a flea, she put it in the teapot and made a cup of tea, the flea jumped out, me Mam gave a shout, and in came me Dad with his shirt hanging out!'

The skipping rhyme was interrupted by a girl's scream piercing the air. It came from a nearby alleyway about thirty feet away. The girls legged it to the entry and came upon little Jane Johnson, in tears on top of a backyard wall. She was clinging to the pole of a lamp post to steady herself.

'Ah, what's to do Jane?' Asked a girl named Joanne.

The reply from Jane had a sob between every two words: 'This man with – like a – with a square head – said come down little girl I've got some sweets, and I said no and he said if I didn't come down he'd go to my house and eat my dog, and he even knew his name was Sandy, and I want me Mam!'

'A square head?' A beanpole of a girl named Vicky queried with a toothy grin.

'There's a boy in our school with a square head named Gary Wilson, honest,' said Joanne, wide-eyed and nodding to underline the seriousness of her claim.

'He had big sharp teeth – and they were made of iron!' said little Jane, and her voice went up an octave as she spoke the sentence. Joanne looked up at the child and said, 'Oh my God she's peed herself! Ah, come on Jane, don't be scared!'

And Joanne shinned up the lamp post, getting a good grip on the pole with her new black pumps.

Most of the girls laughed at the talk of a square-headed bogeyman, but 10-year-old Nancy McKinnon didn't – she'd seen Square Head three nights ago, and no one had believed her. She asked little Jane to describe the figure of fear as the tiny girl clung onto Joanne by her neck as the latter slid with a squeak down the lamp post like a fireman coming down a pole. The frightened child said he wore a black jacket with red stripes, and his face was "all horrible and square" – and that matched the description of the man who had chased Nancy down Westminster Road three nights back.

'I saw him, she's not lying – he's a real person!' Nancy told her friends, and one of them cruelly shouted: 'Here he is!' – pretending Square Head was coming and Jane ran off screaming her little lungs out in hysterics.

'You stupid divvy!' Nancy yelled at the joker, and ran after Jane, who suddenly fell, landed on her outstretched palms, then paused for a moment before she began to wail.

Jane's father Frank was furious when he heard about "Square Head" and assumed he was some would-be child molester in a mask. Frank patrolled the alleyways around Kirkdale for a few nights with a cricket bat wrapped in brown paper and a knuckleduster clenched in his right hand, which he kept in his coat pocket. All he met on his belligerent evening 'beat' around the neighbourhood was mischievous kids skitting at him and giggling girls shouting, variations of 'He's just gone down that alleyway Frank! Honest!' One boy even put a cardboard box on his head with two round eyeholes, and Frank chased him the length of Walton Road before he caught the prankster and slapped the backs of his lower legs until a female passerby intervened. Later that year, mostly in the autumn, there were further sightings of the outlandishly dressed bugbear in the red and black boating jacket. He chased a 15-year-old girl and her 11-year-old sister along Orwell Road in Kirkdale one October evening, and the girls said they had heard his metallic teeth snapping at them as he ran at a phenomenal speed behind them. He seemed determined to catch the younger sister, as when the big sister fell over during the terrifying pursuit, Square Head actually ran over her back and left the girl with a bruised shoulder blade as he chased her young sister. The misshapen monstrosity only gave up the chase when his screaming prey attracted the attention of a patrolling police car. Square Head ran off into the gathering gloom to evade the long arm of the law.

I mentioned the bogeyman on a local radio show years ago and listeners contacted me to say that they had either seen him or knew of relatives or friends who had encountered him, and the general consensus was that the bizarre entity dated back to around 1950. The description was always the same; head like an Oxo cube, a massive extendable mouth of metallic saw-like teeth, an ability to outrun cars, and creepy dark-ringed eyes that could glow and immobilise victims with some form of very effective hypnosis. A policeman named Ian called me at the radio station and said he had actually seen the bogeyman on Kirkdale's Barlow Lane one evening in 1957 when he was on his beat. Seeing the cube-shaped head of the figure and striped boating jacket and pinstriped trousers, Ian assumed it was some student clowning about in a weird costume, but then this figure ran off at an incredible speed, reaching Spellow Lane 'faster than Roger Bannister' – and Ian later heard about the frightening and crazy antics of the weird man from a colleague who had a night-time beat that took in Spellow Lane and Goodsion Road. The policeman's itinerary was known as the graveyard beat because part of it took in Anfield Cemetery. This fellow constable told Ian that he had seen the face of "block head" (an alternative nickname for the prowler) close up and it seemed to be three separate faces stuck or sewn together by an upside-down Y-shaped join. The eyes of the freakish man looked pink with bright red pupils which glowed with what seemed to be an electric light. When the constable approached the absurd-looking figure, it turned and ran at an estimated speed of about fifty miles per hour and flew around a corner. Another listener named Ronnie said his brother was giving him driving lessons in his Ford Cortina on Rumney Road in Kirkdale early one Sunday morning in 1971 when he almost knocked down a bizarre-looking man with a cubic head. The man had rushed out into the path of the car, before turning to face Ronnie and his brother, presenting a ghastly face which seemed to be stitched together like a Frankenstein monster. This creepy figure chased the car 500 yards to Fonthill Road then vanished. The sightings with Square Head eventually petered out and just what he was remains a mystery. I feel there is some connection with another figure of mystery we have touched on in this book – the three-legged street performer documented in the chapter entitled "Some Odd Tales". The tripedal performer, like Square Head, also wore a striped boating jacket. Square head's eyes were described as shining like an *electric* light and some said that the three-legged street artist – seen 11 years later in 1983 - seemed mechanical, which begs the questions: are these two "bogeymen" cyborgs? If so, from whence did they come? I've mentioned the fact that this little island Earth is surrounded on all sides by an infinite sea of black space containing billions upon billions of worlds, and many of them *must* be populated by races, and statistically some must be in advance of our own civilization. Perhaps some unbalanced members of the more advanced races come and go to this suburb of the Milky Way galaxy to amuse themselves, perpetrate crimes or even hunt. We would be like the bewildered and terrified baboon family who were recently wiped out by a hunter who landed in Africa to have some "fun" on a trophy hunt before going home. And of course, besides the countless worlds of space, there are infinite vistas of time from which a time traveller could originate. These beings seem to come and go as they please, often leaving us with unfathomable mysteries in their wake which we label as the Bermuda Triangle, the Dyatlov Pass incident, the *Mary Celeste* mystery and so on.

THE MIRACLES OF ALASTAIR

If ever there was a man of mystery it was Alastair – surname unknown. At first I thought he might be Bezzera, the fabled Wizard of the Calderstones or even Merlin in a modern incarnation, but I simply do not know who he was. He *was* undoubtedly eccentric, often producing a pet frog from his coat pocket, and he had a thick unkempt head of hair in a style resembling a Beatle cut with tinselly strands of grey, and he wore a green corduroy jacket, cricket pullover, bow tie, maroon trousers and ankle boots. He would have made a good *Doctor Who* and coincidentally he bore a slight resemblance to the actor Patrick Troughton – who actually played the Second Doctor in the long-running sci-fi serial.

Some thought he was just a very good pub magician, whilst others believed he was a real-life sorcerer. Alastair appeared on the Liverpool scene in the early 1970s, frequenting scores of pubs across the city from the Rose of Mossley Hill to the Majestic on Hall Lane in the Kensington area. At a certain suburban pub in 1973, the long-haired goatee-bearded Alastair appeared in just his y-fronts one evening, attracting bemused smiles and indignant glances from customers, but oblivious to the attitudes of the clientele, Alastair waved to the barmaid, and in his well-spoken and mellifluous voice he said, 'Betty, can you see me?' to which a mystified and somewhat shocked Betty nodded. 'Ah, excellent, thankyou Betty!' replied Alastair, before squeezing his eyes shut and vanishing before the eyes of the barmaid and everyone present. When Alastair came into the drinking establishment – fully dressed - later on, he said he'd 'popped into the pub' earlier during an exercise in astral projection. One of the drinkers – a man named Peter Moss – a research chemist at ICI who regarded himself as the pub's self-appointed scientific expert- tapped Alastair on the shoulder as the latter was about to drink a shandy - and with a smug expression Mr Moss asked, 'How did you do that earlier? Hypnosis?'

'Oh, no, no,' Alastair frowned as he shook his head, 'no mind-manipulation at all; that was my etheric body you saw – ' he tried to explain, but Moss interrupted. 'I was out in Malaysia – saw action out there like, but, anyway – I saw a damned good hypnotist out there who made us think he was an orang-utan!'

'No, as I said, it wasn't hypnosis – it was a simple projection of the astral body,' insisted Alastair, 'and most people can do it – and most people will do it when they are near death. This outer physical body of ours is just a shell you see.'

'Well, I'm a scientist as it happens – a research chemist in fact – and I don't believe in mumbo-jumbo,' said Moss, loud and firm, 'and you know – no disrespect to you or anything, but I've seen your tricks – producing coins from behind people's ears and that – and it's just all sleight of hand.'

'Yes, well some of it is,' said Alastair, trying to diffuse Moss's attack on him with a disarming smile, 'it's just pub magic – entertainment. Can I get you a drink Mister – '

'Moss - Peter Moss. No, I'll buy my own thankyou,' replied the pub bore, looking down his nose at Alastair as the barmaid Betty rolled her eyes; she was well aware of Peter Moss's condescending attitude and his superiority complex.

'I saw him vanish once – in front of me and five other people,' claimed Betty, and she smiled at Alastair as he coyly looked into his glass of shandy.

'Impossible dear,' said the know-all Moss, 'all kidology and suggestion.'

Alastair scratched his head and said: 'Well, if you're a scientist Peter, then you will know that all matter in the universe – whether it's in this bar counter or the human body, is mostly made up of empty space – and in fact there's more empty space in the atom than there is matter. Isn't this so?'

'Well, er, I'd have to look that up in a science book – ' Peter said, unsure of Alastair's assertion.

Alastair nodded and continued: 'By all means, look it up, but here are the facts: the atom – an atom of hydrogen for example – and our bodies are full of them – is ninety-nine point nine nine nine nine nine nine nine nine nine nine nine nine six per cent empty space.'

'It can't be!' said Moss, forcing a laugh that sounded very uneasy. 'That's almost one hundred percent empty space!'

'Correct!' Alastair slapped his hand on the counter of the bar. A dozen drinkers were now intrigued by his claim. He continued his mini pub lecture on atomic structure. 'Now, the diameter of this world we live on is 7,926 miles, right?'

'Right,' said Moss, narrowing his eyes as he wondered what the pub conjuror was getting at.

'So, let me do a quick bit of mental arithmetic,' said Alastair, and he turned his large expressive eyes to the ceiling and muttered numbers and the words, 'divided by,' and 'multiply that' and then he said: 'Okay. If the earth was the size of a hydrogen atom, then the nucleus – which is just one proton - would be just under six hundred feet across – the rest of the atom is empty space and a tiny electron orbiting it at the speed of light.'

'And what's that got to do with your tricks?' Moss wanted to know.

Alastair smiled, pressed his palms together under his chin as if he was in prayer, and replied: 'If we apply the same mathematics to your body, Mr Moss, then it would mean that when we remove the empty space out of your atoms, it would be possible to pass your body's matter through the eye of a needle.'

'That – that's just an exaggeration – poppycock!' protested Moss. 'I've never heard anything as ridiculous; atoms and empty space and eyes of needles!'

'If all the empty space was removed from the atoms that make up every person on this planet – six billion people in all - I could fit them all in a space the size of a grapefruit,' added Alastair, and he sipped his shandy and looked at the clock on the wall.

'Codswallop!' laughed Moss, 'Pure doubletalk. You don't fool me with your pseudoscience quackery.'

'You're entitled to your own opinion Mr Moss,' said Alastair with a shrug, and then to Betty the barmaid he said, 'I've got to go and see a friend in the Gardeners Arms. Probably see you tomorrow, love.'

'Bye Alastair,' said Betty, watching her most unusual

customer walk out the door. She found him a fascinating man.

'Oh look, he's running away now because I'm onto him,' Peter Moss told the barmaid, but Betty ignored him and went to serve a customer at the other end of the bar.

As chance would have it, Peter Moss encountered Alastair again three days later at a pub in Aigburth. Moss came into the parlour and watched as the gregarious Alastair performed a few typical pub magic tricks – producing coins from behind drinkers' ears, and emptying a box of matches on the floor so the matchsticks formed words as they landed. He then discussed the topic of teleportation – the supernatural ability to transfer a person or object instantly from one place to another, and he quoted a passage from Acts (8:36-40) in the New Testament which describes the 30-mile teleportation of St Philip.

'So, we meet again,' said Moss, and as Alastair turned to look at him, Moss said, 'the charlatan of Mossley Hill.'

Alastair looked him straight in the eye, smiled and said, 'Look, Mr Moss, if you think I'm some fake, then that's fine, but please don't ruin the mood in here. I'm entertaining a few friends, some of whom are very stressed out with the cares and worries of life.'

'Teleportation now is it?' Moss pressed on in his criticism of Alastair. 'Pulling rabbits out of hats isn't teleportation.'

'Who mentioned rabbits?' Alastair asked, returning a puzzled look, and the people in the parlour chuckled at Moss, which angered him.

At that moment the door of the parlour swung open

and in barged Mervyn Arnold, a tall, bearded, broad-shouldered 55-year-old businessman. He stormed into the place swearing to himself. 'What an utter arsehole I am!' he seethed under his breath as he approached the counter.

'What's wrong Mervyn?' Alastair asked.

'Memory has always been a weak point of mine,' Mervyn replied, 'and I only clean forgot all about my daughter's bloody engagement party down in London, didn't I? Promised her I'd attend the party and I even circled the date on my calendar but I still forgot all about it. She'll be really upset.'

'Get on the train, mate,' said the pub landlord Billy, 'Tony over there will run you down to Lime Street in his cab.'

Mervyn's eyes seemed so sorrowful as he replied to the landlord. 'Ah, it's too late I'm afraid; the party is due to start at 8pm and it's a quarter to eight now.'

Mervyn cursed his forgetfulness and ordered a double scotch. Alastair came up to him and whispered, 'Mervyn, I believe I can help you but you'll have to give me the address.'

'How can *you* get me someplace two hundred miles away in fifteen minutes?' asked a perplexed Mervyn, 'Unless you've got Concorde waiting outside.'

'Believe in me, okay?' said Alastair, 'That's the first prerequisite. Just accept what I tell you. You've got just the right aura. Now, supply me with the address!'

'Wait a minute,' said Mervyn, narrowing his eyes, 'are you talking about one of your magical pub trick stunts? I'm not in the mood for all that right now!'

'No,' whispered Alastair, 'not a trick – teleportation – you being sent to London in the proverbial twinkling of an eye.'

'You mean like that lost cat you supposedly sent to its owner up in Speke?' Mervyn asked, and Alastair could see anger welling up in his eyes.

Alastair closed his eyes and slowly nodded. 'Yes, I know you think that was all some skilful deception, mere legerdemain – but that cat really was teleported. And I can do the same to you. The atomic-space ratio is virtually the same.'

Mervyn clenched his fist and lifted it, and for a moment everyone thought he was going to strike Alastair, but the so-called pub magician didn't flinch. 'I'm in no bloody mood for your games, Alastair!' Mervyn growled.

Alastair looked up at the pub clock and sombrely intoned, 'It is now ten minutes to eight, Mervyn, and your daughter will be hoping her father will be arriving any moment. If you can just stop those idiotic caveman thoughts from holding up this opportunity, we can get to work – and I can get you to the party.'

Mervyn closed his eyes, gently lowered his fist onto the counter, and in a meek, resigned voice he asked, 'What have I got to do?'

'Well, they say faith can move mountains,' Alastair told him, his hand upon the big man's shoulder, 'but what they should really say is that *hypnotic* faith can move mountains.'

There was a pause, and Mervyn turned to face Alastair and asked, 'You're going to hypnotise me and make me think I'm at the party? That's no bloody good!'

'No, no – don't jump to conclusions,' said Alastair, 'I'm going to boost – to amplify if you like – your faith. It's like when you're learning to ride a bike – there comes that leap of faith and off you go, well teleportation's like that; most people can do it but their disbelief buffer mechanism comes into play and – '

'Look, just get on with it then!' said Mervyn, and now everyone in the parlour was hooked on the strange proceedings – everyone including Peter Moss, Alastair's fierce arch-critic. He was smirking and shaking his head.

'That's a great sign – you wanting to get on with it!' said Alastair excitedly, 'Bravo, Mervyn, just stay in that lovely frame of mind. I'm going to do a little test first, just to work the atoms up a bit.'

'Well get a move on, it's coming up to five to eight!' said Mervyn, looking at his watch.

'One born every minute,' said Peter Moss, looking at Mervyn, and then he turned to the pub landlord and said, 'pint of mild.'

The landlord was too engrossed in the promised build up to a possible teleportation, and without looking at Moss he said, 'Hang on, sir.'

Alastair began to whisper some unintelligible words into Mervyn's right ear, and then he told him, 'Just keep repeating that in your mind. It's a mantra. Think of nothing but those words, and when I tap you on the back you'll feel something very strange.'

Mervyn closed his eyes, silently reciting the mantra, and then after about twenty seconds, Alastair slapped his back – and for a brief moment, Mervyn disappeared completely. And then he returned with his eyes open wide and there was a shocked expression on his face. There was a wave of oohs in the pub at this momentary vanishing act.

'Billy, what's the number of this pub?' Alastair asked the astonished pub landlord. 'Write the telephone number of this pub down please.'

Billy seemed to snap out of a spell, and then he took a pad from under the counter, located a pencil, and scribbled down the telephone number of the pub.

'Put 051 at the front of that number, Billy,' said Alastair, 'because Mervyn will be calling from London.'

'That was bloody amazing!' said Mervyn, turning to Alastair, 'Everything went light grey! I was just in some – some – '

'Void?' asked Alastair with a knowing smile, 'That was absolute elsewhere – the point between A and B. They used to call it Limbo. Now, Mervyn, once you get to the party – and you'll have to give me the address so I can guide you there – can you make sure you telephone me here so I know everything has gone to plan?'

'Yes, of course,' said Mervyn, 'this is bloody marvellous! I'll never need to fly anywhere again.'

'Just keep that positive mood Mervyn,' laughed Alastair, 'now give me the address of your daughter's flat in London please.'

Mervyn told Alastair the address and braced himself for the next step in this unearthly but highly exciting experiment.

'It's all nonsense!' shouted Peter Moss, jingling the coins in his hand as he looked at the landlord again. 'A fool believes everything!'

'Stop that Mr Moss!' Alastair shouted to the persistent cynic, 'You're going to jeopardize this experiment!'

'I'm going to transport *you* now through that doorway behind you!' Mervyn suddenly roared, 'And you better believe it!'

'Oh are you now?' asked Moss with a nervous grin.

The nettlesome defeatist Mr Moss did not even see the punch coming. The fist of Mervyn Arnold slammed into his jaw, and as forecast, the emotionally charged businessman's fist sent Moss through the doorway into the lobby of the pub where he hit a wall with a thump, and the handful of coins Moss had been trying to buy a drink with scattered everywhere. He slid slowly to the floor and came to rest in an unconscious heap.

'Now send me down to London before the police charge me for that!' Mervyn snarled at Alastair, who smiled and replied, 'Oh, I'll send you alright, and I will provide you with the perfect alibi: you were two hundred miles away when someone knocked out that disagreeable fellow Peter Moss. Now, get ready for the translocation – and don't forget to telephone!'

Alastair placed his hands on his subject's square shoulders and began a hypnotic chant for about ten seconds – then Mervyn Arnold vanished into thin air. There were gasps of amazement from the drinkers all around, and Alastair smiled and said, 'Bon voyage, Mervyn.'

A groaning Peter Moss picked himself up from the floor of the hallway, opened the heavy door, and staggered out onto the street. He flagged down a passing police Panda car and told them he'd been assaulted, and when he felt his mouth he realised his front right tooth was missing. He found it shortly afterwards in the pub parlour on the floor. The policeman with him questioned the pub landlord Billy about the identity of the assailant.

'I never saw no one getting a haymaker constable,' said Billy.

'Oh yes you did!' cried Peter Moss, and he felt his jaw because it hurt and clicked and seemed misaligned when he spoke, 'He was with that conman - Alastair – him over there.' He pointed to Alastair, who was sitting in a corner reading a newspaper. 'He knows him, officer, quiz him!' Moss urged the young policeman.

'Is that true sir? You know the gentleman who punched Mr Moss?' the constable asked Alastair.

'I've never seen this man before in my life, constable,' Alastair replied with a shocked expression as he looked Moss up and down.

'His name was Mervyn,' Moss recalled, 'and this lying charlatan here was telling him he could teleport him down to London!'

'The only Mervyn I know is a respectable businessman and he happens to be in London at the moment,' said Alastair, 'attending his daughter's engagement party as I seem to recall.'

'And what's this Mervyn Arnold's address?' the policeman wanted to know.

Alastair shrugged. 'I honestly couldn't tell you, officer. I only see him in here every now and then; he's not a close friend or anything.'

'What do you mean – teleportation?' the policeman asked Peter Moss.

Moss held his jaw as he struggled to explain the word. 'You know – like in *Star Trek* - "Beam me up" – that type of thing.'

The constable's colleague from the Panda car came into the pub. He was much older and asked his fellow constable, 'What's the score?'

The young copper said: 'This man here, Mr Moss, said that the person who punched him was known to this gentleman here,' and he pointed to Alastair, who was grinning behind a large broadsheet newspaper.

Alastair peeped over the top of the newspaper. 'I haven't a clue what's going on, really,' he maintained.

'Oh, it's *you* - the magician,' said the older policeman, and he turned to his younger colleague and remarked, 'He's a harmless crank. Says he can walk across swimming pools and levitate.'

'The alleged assailant has been named as a Mr Mervyn Arnold,' said the young constable, scribbling in a notebook. 'But that Alastair fellah says he's down in London.'

The pub telephone started to ring. The landlord Billy froze and looked at Alastair, who raised his eyebrows, smiled and nodded to the ringing phone, gesturing for him to answer it. Billy lifted the receiver and before he could speak, the policemen, and most of the drinkers, could hear a tinny-sounding excited voice exclaim: 'It worked! I'm in Chelsea. Put Alastair on!'

'Oh that is good news Mr Arnold,' said Billy, and the older policeman reached out with his black gloved hand and took the telephone receiver from the landlord. He spoke into the receiver in a slow precise manner of speaking.

'Hello, is that Mr Arnold?' he asked, then added, 'Mervyn Arnold?'

'Yes, who's that?' Mervyn asked, 'is that you, Alastair? You sound different on the phone.'

'I'm one of the policemen responding to a serious assault at a pub, and you were named as the possible assailant Mr Arnold, but I've been told you're in London; is that correct sir?'

Mervyn felt tongue-tied all of a sudden and stammered, 'Y-Yes, I am, er, yes currently I am – yes, down in London, so your informant must be mistaken officer.'

'You'd better give me the address so we can confirm you really are where you say you are,' said the policeman as his younger associate listened with his ear pressed against the telephone earpiece.

Mervyn was duly visited by two policemen from a station in Chelsea and they confirmed his alibi – that he had been in the capital while someone had assaulted Peter Moss in the Liverpool pub.

Days after this, Alastair walked into the Rose of Mossley Hill public house, and a barman he knew well beckoned him and whispered, 'Don't look around, but there are two men sitting in the corner behind you, and they have been asking questions about you – wanting to know where you live and so on.'

'That sounds a bit ominous,' said Alastair, 'whoever can they be? Thanks for the tip-off.' He ordered a bitter shandy, paid for the drink, then slowly turned – and the two men seated in the corner looked at him as if there was some degree of recognition coming into play. They looked at one another, then one of them got up and walked towards the bar. Like his associate, the stranger had unfashionably short hair and wore a black suit. Alastair put down his drink and was seen to look at the door, as if he was contemplating an exit, but the other stranger rose from his corner seat and walked towards that door. Alastair went into the toilet. A few minutes elapsed and then the two smart but sinister-looking men went into the gents. They came out seconds later and went straight to the bar. One of them said to the barman, 'You – come here.'

'Yes?' asked the nervous barman leaning ovet the bar counter towards the man who was beckoning him with the curled index finger of his black-gloved hand.

'You tipped him off, didn't you?' asked one of the menacing duo.

'Tipped who off? What are you talking about?' the barman replied, and he felt a little intimidated and afraid. He had a feeling the two unknown men had something to do with the shady world of British Intelligence. He was relieved when the two men walked out of the pub, and he never set eyes on them again. Another person the barman never saw again was the enigmatic Alastair, although a few days after this strange incident, a vagrant walked into a pub in the suburbs that had been another haunt of Alastair, and he presented the baffled barmaid Betty with a huge bouquet of roses. 'These are from an old friend of yours,' the tramp said in an Irish accent, 'and he told me to tell you he'll see you again some sunny day.'

Betty then saw through the elaborate make up; the lively eyes gave the game away; the tramp was Alastair in disguise. He put his index finger to his lips, and said, 'Sssh! Bye for now, lovely Betty.'

He walked out of the pub, and the mysterious Alastair vanished into obscurity, leaving an uncanny legend in his wake. Was he just a superior pub magician, or – and many people believe this latter possibility is the most likely one – was Alastair some real-life wizard? It would seem so, and I would hazard a guess and say that someone in the higher echelons of Whitehall – some mandarin in the military intelligence circles – got wind of Alastair's amazing abilities and saw tremendous potential for them in the murky world of international espionage. Today, Alastair probably inhabits that strange twilit world that exists somewhere on the periphery of our civilization – a shady sphere frequented by the likes of Lord Lucan and the cryptic Count of St Germain. I better say no more.

THE ABYSS UNDER
THE BED

On the Friday night of 20 March 1987 – a night of torrential rain - at around 11.20pm, a 21-year-old student named Michelle Keel was dozing off in bed at the six bedroom house on Birkenhead's Park Road East when she was rudely awakened by rainwater dripping through her ceiling onto her head. She had been having a lucid dream in which she'd been lying stretched out on the pavement during a downpour, and now she knew why. She telephoned her landlord Mr Graves to complain about the leak and he told her he'd have a roofer out first thing Saturday morning to fix the problem.

'And where am I going to sleep in the meantime?' Michelle asked, running her hand through her soaked red hair.

'Use your initiative Michelle,' said Graves in an annoyed tone, 'move the bed or sleep in a chair,' Graves suggested, 'it's just for tonight.'

Michelle said she wanted money docked from her rent for the trouble and Graves said: 'Michelle, the line's bad – talk to you soon!' and he hung up. At that moment, Lucy Briggs, Michelle's old friend from school came home and as she was walking along the communal hallway downstairs, Michelle ran out of her flat, leaned over the stair rail and shouted down to her: 'Lucy, I know this might sound cheeky, but can I possibly stay with you tonight?'

'Why, what's up?' Lucy shouted, shaking her umbrella.

'There's rainwater leaking through the ceiling and it's soaked my bed and it's like a waterfall,' said Michelle. 'Only for tonight. The landlord said he'll – '

'Yeah come on down!' Lucy jokily interrupted, quoting Leslie Crowther's catchphrase from the television show *The Price is Right*.

'Oh God bless you, Lucy!' squalled Michelle, and ran back into her room to move the bed and put a bucket under the stream of water.

By one o'clock that morning, the girls were drinking cocoa and eating spaghetti hoops on toast as they sat cross-legged on the bed – a bed that felt luxuriously warm and dry to Michelle. Lucy said she'd just come back from her boyfriend Craig in Liverpool and things weren't looking too good. She'd found Polaroid photographs of a girl who worked with Craig in his wardrobe – and she was topless on the snaps. Craig said his mate Nick had planted them there as a bad joke, but Lucy just knew he was lying, and in a way she was glad, as she'd had enough of his roving eyes whenever anything in a skirt was about. Michelle talked at length about her lukewarm on-off relationship with a lad named Adam and then at 2:30 am, Lucy started reminiscing on her days with Michelle when they attended Gateacre Comprehensive. The girls soon started yawning, and then Lucy said, 'I'm knackered – let's hit the sack.'

'I'll sleep down the bottom end of the bed,' said Michelle, grabbing a pillow, but Lucy smiled and told her: 'Michelle, it's okay, you're not my type – we're not kids sleeping top-tail. But if you start snoring you're going back upstairs; I've got to get up at eight. I'm working in a newsagent's shop and the old biddy who owns it is always moaning about me being late.'

Lucy fell asleep first, and then Michelle dozed off, and had a peculiar dream. She dreamt someone was sucking her big toe – and when she awoke, she felt a cold mouth kissing and licking her left sole, so she yelped and withdrew her foot, which had been hanging out the bed. She heard echoing voices and ripples of reverberating laughter in the bedroom – and the noises seemed to be coming from the floor. Michelle looked over the edge of the bed and saw that there was no floor, just empty black space. She rubbed her eyes and looked again – yes – there was no solid floor, just an abyss of empty pitch-black space – and as she gazed in disbelief, Michelle saw laughing faces appear in the darkness. The faces became more solid as they rose from the blackness. Michelle shook Lucy awake and told her the floor was missing and that there were weird laughing faces on the floor, and Lucy sat up, and when she looked to her right, she saw that Michelle was right – there was no carpet – just blackness, and there were weird heads – mostly of bald men with clownlike features - bobbing up and down in the impossible floor. All of a sudden the room erupted with eerie jeering laughter and echoing shouts. It reminded Lucy of the cacophony she'd hear in the swimming baths when she came out of the water after her ears had popped. There were coarse comments from the entities on the floor. One of the heads with a long broken nose shouted to Michelle: 'You'd never be missed, pissy drawers!'

'We'll have you when that bed falls!' cried the head of a black man with huge bulging eyes and a disproportionately large mouth of mostly missing teeth, and Lucy thought he was addressing her and screamed.

A black silhouetted hand reached up from the empty blackness and gripped the end of the bed, and Michelle screeched as the hand – which felt icy - tried to grab her foot. The girls held on to one another at the top of the bed and surveyed the terrifying scene. They were scared and confused, and Lucy kept thinking she was having a nightmare and pinched her arm, imagining she'd wake up, but this was real – and inexplicable. The bed started to rock and tilt, and the girls clung on to the bed's headpost and at the top of her voice, Michelle cried out: 'Help! Help us!'

The laughter increased as Michelle screamed for help, and the girls heard very offensive swearing from the black void where the floor had been hours ago. Lucy had her left hand on the headpost and her right hand made the sign of the cross because she thought devils were attacking her. She looked down and now there were even more twisted grinning faces looking up from the blackness, and the laughter was deafening. The door to the room burst open and a 23-year-old student named Mark, who lodged in the room next door, looked in at the girls. He'd come to complain about the noise – but his eyes bulged in shock as he saw the sea of jabbering and laughing faces on the floor.

'Mark! Wait there! Don't go!' Lucy shouted to the student, but he backed away in fear from the doorway, bumping his back against the stair rail.

'Come on!' Lucy shouted to Michelle, grabbing her hand and pulling her to her feet. 'We can jump,' said Lucy. Michelle let go of her friend's hand, and she ran diagonally across the bed and leaped five feet through the air and flew through the doorway. She landed and her head butted Mark in the chest as he caught her. Then Lucy took a running jump, and as she did, the bed fell into the blackness. The spine-chilling clamour ceased, the laughing heads vanished, and the floor and its carpet slowly reappeared – minus the old double bed. The girls refused to set foot in that room, and Mark had to go in to get Lucy's belongings. Michelle and Lucy were so spooked by the surreal and harrowing experience, they moved out the house the next day and both went to live together in a flat over in Liverpool. Just what happened that morning remains unexplained to this day; did the girls see some vision of Hell? Was it a glimpse of a neighbouring dimension inhabited by God knows what? If it was all a hallucination, then it must have been a shared one because both girls and Mark, their neighbour saw the same thing. The house Michelle and Lucy lived in did not even have a history of hauntings. I have heard of similar incidents concerning mysteriously dissolving floors before and have catalogued some of them in my books, including a case in Bristol which occurred on 8 December 1873 – and the case in question was documented in many newspapers, including *The Times*. Thomas and Annie Cumpston, were in their room at the Victoria Hotel in Bristol when they were awakened around three in the morning by strange echoing sounds. The floor started to disappear and Mr Cumpston fell into a strange vault of black empty space where the floor should have been, and his wife had to pull him up onto the bed. The newspaper articles tantalize us by stating that "the bed did all sorts of strange things" without specifying what those things were. Mr Cumpston, a man with a military background, was carrying a gun, and fired it into the black indefinable thing which had eaten away the floor, and then he and his wife jumped from the bed onto a window ledge and had to drop down twelve feet into the street and run to a nearby railway station in their search for a policeman. The couple felt the weird black living mass was following them and arrived at the station in a dreadful state. The hotel room was later examined and nothing was found to be disturbed. The floor was checked and found to be intact, and the authorities decided that the couple had probably just had a realistic nightmare. I've heard other similar cases happening in the Everton district in the Edwardian era and even in the 1960s, and all of the incidents start with the darkening of the floor in the wee small hours, followed by strange sounds and echoing voices. I get the feeling that something – some entity – or perhaps entities unknown – "try it on" now and then and attempt to snatch people of this dimension for reasons I cannot fathom. Perhaps something wants to keep people as pets, or wants to torture, abuse or even consume them – the possibilities are the stuff of nightmares. If you should wake in the dead of night and see your bedroom floor dissolve, stay put, but if the bed rocks, perhaps jump onto a window sill. Prayer sometimes works, if you have the faith, that is. Sweet dreams.

THE BED OF VESTA

The strange case of the Bed of Vesta started at a beautiful old three storey house on Mount Pleasant (at the Rodney Street end). The Georgian house still stands today but it is now part of the Liverpool University Campus. The bizarre story starts at lunchtime on Wednesday 11 July 1973. A 35-year-old bachelor named Clive Pepper was in a betting shop on the corner of Myrtle Street and Bedford Street South studying the runners in the handicap race at Newbury. He thinned his baggy eyes and adjusted his Eric Morecambe spectacles as he scrutinised the listings on the newspaper page pinned to the corkboard, and then Clive was startled by the thump of a hand on his left shoulder. Before he could turn, his old friend, 45-year-old Jack Cardiff said, 'A solicitor's looking for you – what have you done, eh?'

'What?' Clive quickly turned his head around to face Jack and his mass of curly hair swung with it. 'What are you talking about?'

'This,' Jack pulled an opened manila envelope with a window in it from his inside jacket pocket and handed it to his friend. 'I thought it was for me; I didn't have me glasses on.'

Clive slowly took the letter from Jack and unfolded it with a wave of dread coursing through his stomach. The letterhead on the A4 piece of paper said Temple & Meredith Solcitors, and the wording stated that Clive's oldest Uncle - Raymond – had died and that there was something to Clive's advantage discussed in

Uncle Raymond's will. 'I think my luck's changed at last, Jack,' said Clive, and a smile broke out on his face.

'As you know, I can't read too well, and I know it said something about someone called Raymond,' said Jack, 'that's all I could make of it. What does it say?'

'My Uncle Raymond's snuffed it,' said Clive, his eyes scanning the wording of the letter again,'and he was worth a few bob. He had shops here and in Chester, and I think he had property as well. He must have left me some money or something.'

'Ah, custy Clive, I'm made up for you,' said Jack, patting the shoulder of his mate's corduroy jacket.

Well, Clive Pepper – and his friend Jack Cardiff - attended the reading of his late uncle's will in the company of three cousins and two aunties he hadn't seen since he was twelve, and each auntie was left a shop, the three cousins were told they'd be getting three thousand pounds each, and then came the part of the will which dealt with Clive. He had been left a three-storey 12-bedroom Georgian town house on Mount Pleasant, worth somewhere in the region of £80,000 – on the condition that Clive was a single man at the time of his uncle's death – and single he was. Clive also received his Uncle Raymond's midnight blue Alfa Romeo Spider, thanks to the bizarre stipulations of the will. The first thing Clive's shocked Auntie Phyllis said was, 'He can't even drive!'

Clive was too shocked to even reply, and instead he clutched Jack's forearm and gazed at him wide-eyed. All Clive had in the world seconds ago was £1.52 and-a-half pence.

'You alright Clive?' asked a concerned Jack.

'He's gambling mad,' said Clive's cousin Sheena,

'he'll fritter the lot away. He never even visited Uncle Raymond in hospital, it's not fair.'

'Are you sure he's supposed to get all that?' Clive's other auntie, Maude asked the executor of the will, Robert Temple, and in a crisp word-perfect "received pronunciation" kind of voice, the solicitor looked over the top of his reading glasses and said: 'Yes madam, I am certain, and I will of course provide you with a facsimile of the will.'

'What are you going to do with all your money, Clive?' asked a beaming Jack Cardiff.

'I – I don't know – I might buy a racehorse,' Clive gasped, looking all flushed.

'See?' said Clive's cousin Sheena, 'racing mad; it'll all be gone by Christmas.'

'You've got more from my brother than me, it's not fair!' said a confrontational Aunt Maude, and she stabbed Clive's chest with her index finger as she promised: 'I'll see my solicitor and contest all this!'

'There's absolutely nothing to contest Mrs Pepper,' said Robert Temple, taking off his glasses, 'this will of your brother's is incontestable. It will be time-consuming, fruitless and quite expensive to contest it because your late brother was certainly of sound mind when he made the will, and he was in the presence of his doctor when he signed the document. It was all done above board and fulfilled the legal requirements to the letter, and may I say that the late Mr Pepper made a very reasonable financial provision for you and your sister and the other relatives.'

'I've got two words to say to you Auntie Maude,' said Clive, looking as if he had suddenly snapped out of a daydream. 'Push off!' he laughed, giving his shocked auntie the offensive two-fingered gesture.

Jack bought a provisional licence and a cheap pair of driving gloves from TJ Hughes' and became a chauffeur to Clive, driving him around in the Alfa Romeo Spider. Clive left his bedsit on Princes Avenue and moved into the magnificent 12-bedroom residence bequeathed to him by Uncle Raymond. Jack was given the basement, as he'd always wanted a basement flat, and Clive racked his mind, wondering whether to sell the house or move into it. 'Don't sell it mate,' advised Jack, 'I mean it's up to you, but I know you Clive; if you sell this place, you'll never be out of the bookies and you'll be buying people drinks left right and centre. Generosity is one of your weaknesses, lad.'

'It's a bit big for just you and me though, isn't it?' Clive asked. 'It's like we've gone from a bedsit to Buckingham Palace.'

'You know what I'd do if I was you?' said Jack, his eyes narrowing and a smug grin forming on his face.

'Go on,' said Clive. His friend was illiterate but he had a brain and had suggested some intriguing money-making plans in the past, despite having no capital to bring them into fruition.

'I'd turn this building into a hotel, or a lodging house,' said Jack, 'an upmarket one. You'd have eleven flats or rooms bringing in money, and if it falls through, sell it and buy a small house for yourself.'

'Could it work though?' asked Clive, his chin between his finger and thumb, 'They've got hotels across the road, and the Adelphi.'

'Alright, a lodging house — accommodation for students etcetera,' Jack proposed, 'they're always looking for rooms in this city with the student population. There's money to be made Clive.'

'That big kitchen and that little box room through there,' Clive looked through the doorway at the two doors down the hallway, 'they could be knocked into one and we could even have a communal dining area.'

'Now you're talking,' said Jack. 'I know a few lads that'd do it, all time served and that. Have a think about it.'

That day, Clive broke out in a sweat when he sold an old grandfather clock that had belonged to his late uncle to an antique dealer for £100. He had a temperature because he knew he was going to put the hundred quid on a horse. He sneaked out of the house under the pretence of going to get cakes and pasties from Sayers – and instead he darted into the nearest betting shop. He put the £100 on a horse running at Bath called Generosity (one of his weaknesses according to Jack) with odds of 9-1. The horse won and netted Clive £1,000. He collected his winnings and fought a tough battle with his devil-may-care gambling brain, resisting the euphoric urge to put the grand on another horse, and when he got outside, he bumped into a local gangster he knew only as Palmer. They said he'd killed someone in the East End and was now hiding up north. Clive had seen Palmer kick a man to within an inch of his death because some harmless jokey remark was made about the East Londoner. Palmer stood there, a small fat bald man with a blotchy face and a big nose. On either side of him stood two six-foot-tall Amazonian women in their twenties, attractive and statuesque. One was blonde and the other a brunette. They both wore their hair in tight buns and wore leather jackets, miniskirts and calf-length black leather boots with platform soles and chunky heels.

'Hiya Palmer,' said Clive, smiling nervously at the gangster and nodding at the women.

'Er, not so fast pepper-pot,' said Palmer, and Clive felt a cold movement in his bowels.

'What?' said Clive, stopping abruptly.

'Don't "what" me, four-eyes,' said Palmer, screwing his face up. He walked up to Clive, followed by his female lackeys. 'Now, a little dicky bird told me you've come into money and property and you've been throwing your cash about in the boozers. Do you mind filling me in with the details?'

'Yes, I won a few bob on the gee-gees that's all, Palmer,' Clive told him, and his throat dried up with fear.

'But what about the property part?' Palmer asked, tilting his head back and looking at Clive down that long snout of his. 'What's all that about?'

'Someone's just got hold of the wrong end of the stick Palmer,' Clive replied, and his right hand felt the bundle of five hundred pound notes in his pocket. The other half of the winnings was in his inside jacket pocket. 'I'm looking after my Uncle Raymond's house round the corner up there,' Clive nodded to the top of Rodney Street. 'He's not well.'

'Oh, is that the Uncle Raymond who snuffed it?' Palmer asked.

Clive was stuck for words as Palmer said, 'Girls.' The two tall women walked casually to Clive and they both pretended to kiss him on each side of his perspiring face as their hands searched his jacket and trouser pockets.

A passing elderly lady halted and looked at the women caressing and apparently touching Clive up, and Palmer said to her, 'Terrible isn't it? In broad daylight as well.'

'There are small children about, it's disgusting,' said the old woman, looking the women and Clive up and down in a condescending manner. 'They should be reported.'

'Get off!' protested Clive.

The dark-haired acolyte of Palmer grabbed Clive's curly hair and shook his head so hard, his glasses came off.

'Oh!' yelped the old woman.

'He likes a bit of rough,' Palmer told the pensioner, 'gets him all going, it does.'

The blonde deliberately stepped on Clive's glasses, crushing them under the sole of her boot. The tall women returned to Palmer with the extracted bundles of money and he took the proceeds and said to Clive, who was picking his crushed spectacles up, 'We'll be round to your lovely new house later Pepper for a nice house-warming party.'

'No thanks! Stay away Palmer!' shouted a ruffled Clive, holding the broken fame of his glasses close to his squinting eyes. He looked up and saw a blurred image of Palmer and his strong-armed girls crossing Rodney Street, heading to what seemed to be a black limousine. Clive had a spare pair of spectacles but they were back at the house, and he had to take great care crossing the road to get home. He felt so humiliated being robbed by two young women who looked no older than twenty-five years of age. He found his spare specs when he got home and went to the basement to tell Jack what had happened. Before he could tell him, Jack pointed to the giant white pentagram on the black wall, uncovered by him after he had stripped down the old wallpaper in preparation for the redecoration of his flat. 'That is bad news that, Clive, said Jack. 'Was your uncle into Devil worship, I wonder?'

Clive didn't seem to be bothered by the inverted image of the five-pointed star on the wall. 'I don't know, but listen to this Jack; I've just had a run-in with Palmer, and he put these two women on me.'

'What? Palmer? Women?' jack gave a faint smirk.

'Yeah, and before you laugh, you should have seen these women – they were like models but about six-feet tall and solid. One slapped my face and the other stepped on my glasses. They took a thousand nicker off me.'

Jack seemed stunned. 'That's bad that, what are you going to do? You can't go to the police over Palmer, he'd just do you in.'

'He's coming round later,' said Clive, and his eye twitched.

'Oh God, no,' said Jack, 'he'll want to turn this place into a club or a friggin' brothel.'

'Do you think there's any way we could sell this house before he comes round?' asked Clive, his eyes brimming with desperation.

Jack shook his head and said, 'No, you're talking daft now. I don't even know anyone who could help us. That bastard's a nutcase. He nearly kicked Tony what's his name to death because he joked about his nose.'

'I was there,' said Clive, having a flashback. He could hear the thump of Palmer's boots as he kicked Tony in the ribs and the vomiting of blood. 'Don't you know any hitmen or anything Jack? I'd pay anything to get him done in!'

'Don't start going down that route, Clive, it's not you. This isn't an episode of *The Untouchables* - it's real life.'

Clive forced the reply through clenched teeth: 'It'll be a bleedin' episode of *General Hospital* when he's finished with us! God, everything was going fine; should have known it was too good to be true.'

'Let's go for a bevy and think it over,' suggested Jack, putting the wallpaper scraper down. Clive reluctantly went for a drink in the Beehive pub further down Mount Pleasant, and here, Jack bumped into an old friend of his named Mickey, a man who had a reputation as a real hard knock. The last time Jack had seen his old mate, he was wrestling with four policemen who proceeded to tear Mickey's shirt off in the altercation. When Mickey went to the toilet, Clive whispered to Jack, 'Ask him if he'd take care of Palmer! Tell him there's a thousand quid in it!'

When Mickey came back from the gents, Jack bought him a pint of black and tan and ushered him to a corner. 'Mickey, a gangster named Palmer is coming round to see me and Clive tonight, and it's not a social call if you get my drift.'

'Ooh, Palmer, bad man,' said Mickey, 'nothing upstairs you see so you can't bargain with him. I tell you what, Jack, if Palmer was after me I'd run from Lands End to John o'Groats. Frig that.'

'So you can't help us, even for a grand?' Clive asked Mickey.

'You'd be better spending your money on a flight to Sydney to get away from that fellah, lad,' was Mickey's reply.

'So that's that,' said Jack in a resigned voice.

'I'm sorry Jack, but I don't even think the Krays would have tackled Palmer,' said Mickey, and he left the pub.

Clive and Jack returned to the house on Mount Pleasant resigned to their fate. All the rooms were covered in dust sheets because the painters had been in earlier, doing the ceilings eggshell white, and the plasterers were due to start work in the morning – and Clive wondered if he's see that morning. The only room that was not covered with dust sheets was Clive's bedroom on the top floor, and he went up there alone and told Jack to continue stripping the walls in his basement flat. He looked at the old four-poster bed his Uncle Raymond had slept in and wondered desperately what to do. He heard a loud knock at the door and a feeling of nausea came over him. Before he could get down the three flights of stairs, Clive heard Jack talking to someone. It didn't sound like Palmer's voice – it sounded like a local accent.

It turned out to be a detective. We shall call this man Detective Brian Norman (not his real name). He was standing with Jack in the hallway, and he wore the stereotypical attire of a detective – fawn-coloured mackintosh, neatly pleated black trousers and black polished shoes. His alert eyes glanced up at Clive as he descended the final flight of steps. 'Mr Pepper I presume?' he asked, and Jack turned and said, 'This is Detective Norman Clive. He was just saying the tax disc on the car expired a few weeks ago.'

'Oh, I'll get a new one in the morning,' said Clive,

and he sensed that was not what this evening call was about.

The detective lit a cigarette, puffed on it and with a skew-whiff grin he said to Clive: 'One of my colleagues saw you having a spot of bother with Eloise and Judy?'

'Sorry?' Clive was puzzled by the remark for a moment, then wondered if the policeman was referring to the two female enforcers of Palmer.

'The two birds with Mr Palmer,' said the detective, and he exhaled the smoke and told Clive and Jack: 'The blonde one – Judy – is a tenth dan in karate. The dark-haired one, Eloise practices Combato – the most lethal self-defence system in the world – kill you with her bare hands. We rarely bargain with anyone who knows Combato – just shoot them.'

'Palmer's coming round any minute,' said Clive.

The detective nodded, 'I know. Been keeping a watch on him. I've got a few of the lads outside in a furniture van, and I'll hide in one of these rooms. Once he starts throwing his weight around we'll have him. He'll probably be armed knowing Palmer, so we'll have him – and the girls - for possession of firearms by persons previously convicted of a crime, assault etcetera, etcetera and all that razzamatazz.'

There was a heavy knocking at the door and Detective Norman flew into the room to the immediate left of the door and hid inside a wardrobe that was covered with a dust sheet.

Clive answered and there stood Palmer, flanked by his attractive but lethal hoodlums. The girls walked in first, and each of them was so laid back they were chewing gum and blowing pink bubbles. Clive stepped aside before the girls marched through him. As Palmer entered the hallway he saw Jack and he asked Clive: 'Who's this?'

Clive smiled and told him. 'This is an old friend of mine, Jack. He's alright Mr Palmer – '

'I don't want anyone around tonight,' said Palmer, 'not while I'm conducting business. Tell him to beat it now.'

'Okay,' said Clive, and he looked at his friend and said, 'you'll have to go, Jack.'

Jack reluctantly left the house and the brunette Eloise opened the door to the room where the detective was hiding in the wardrobe, and Palmer walked in and looked about. 'Very nice, ' he said, pulling the dust cloth off the wardrobe. Clive stood nervously beside him. 'We're decorating these rooms, 'he said, hoping that Palmer would not open the wardrobe, but he placed his hand on the door handle of the wardrobe and tugged, and the door opened. Palmer was standing behind the door as he opened it and Clive could see a tense Detective Norman standing there with a gun in his hand with its barrel pointing upwards.

'That's an antique wardrobe,' said Palmer, feeling the door, 'I'd say Victorian; definitely mahogany. Your uncle had good taste.' Palmer then closed the wardrobe door.

'Oh he did, yeah,' said Clive, inwardly sighing with relief.

Palmer and the girls inspected the other rooms, starting with the basement, and eventually they entered the room Clive was staying in, and here something very strange happened.

'So this is the master bedroom eh?' Palmer said in a

sarcastic tone, and he gripped one of the posts of the four-poster bed – then took a revolver out of a holster inside his jacket. The girls smiled and sat next to one another on the bed, watching their boss. He walked slowly to Clive and pressed the end of the barrel into his forehead. Clive jumped when he heard the hammer of the revolver being cocked.

'Easy now Clive', said Palmer. 'Now, if you go along with my plans I'll make you a deal. I'll turn this place into a club and you can work for me. You can be a barman or something. But if you should go and tell the police, I give you my word that I will blow your brains out. Look at my eyes Clive; can you see how sincere I am? I'm not afraid to kill.'

'Don't shoot me, please,' said Clive, and beads of sweat were already forming on his forehead.

'Well then do as I say and don't make me want to kill you, alright?' said Palmer. His eyes looked insane and devoid of anything human. He slowly lowered the revolver, then slid it back in his holster in his jacket. He turned to the girls and said, 'Right, let's go downstairs.'

The girls did not respond. They were looking into one another's eyes, and their faces were coming closer. When their mouths were about six inches away, each girl blew a bubble of pink gum, and each bubble touched, stuck together, and then the girls moved in to kiss, eating the burst remnants of the bubbles as they did. They kissed each other passionately, and an astounded Palmer said, 'Hey, what the hell are you two playing at?'

They took no notice, and fell sideways onto the bed and continued to kiss and undo one another's hair bun.

Clive ran to the door, pulled it open then ran down the stairs, and as he reached the second flight of steps he almost collided with Detective Norman and five plain-clothed men coming up – and Clive saw all of them were armed.

'He's up in the top room!' cried Clive, stepping aside.

'Get out of here!' shouted Detective Norman without looking back. When the men stormed the room, they found Palmer stripped to the waist, lying between Eloise and Judy on the bed, and the three of them were kissing one another, and when Detective Norman shouted at the threesome and told them they were under arrest, they did not even look his way. The girls and Palmer had to be pulled apart and handcuffed, and only when they were taken out of the bedroom did they seem to wake up to the gravity of the situation.

Sometime later when Palmer and his henchwomen were jailed, Clive slowly realised that a weird face carved into the headboard of his four-poster bed had had some aphrodisiacal effect on Palmer and his girls. The head was that of a horned man with a sinister smiling face. Clive was no Casanova with women and at one point he even wondered if he was asexual, but he met a girl named Karen in the autumn of that year, and as soon as she came into his bedroom, she behaved like a nymphomaniac, and likewise, Clive made love to Karen over and over until he was drained of energy. As an experiment, Clive tacked a piece of cloth over the carved face in the headboard and all feelings of lust in both him and Karen virtually vanished and they would just cuddle and kiss in the bed, but when the cloth was removed and the horned head was on show, the couple went through more positions than the contents of the *Kama Sutra* – and they also began to consider highly perverted acts and games which we would term as obscene even in this sexually enlightened age. When Clive told Jack Cardiff he was now fighting a frightening sexual addiction which was inexorably leading to murder because of the influence of the devilish carved face on the four-poster's headboard, Jack went into his friend's bedroom one afternoon while Clive and Karen were out, and he removed the headboard and tried to burn it in the backyard. He poured petrol upon the headboard and set fire to it and although flames engulfed the wood, it refused to burn, only blackening it slightly. In the end, Jack threw the headboard into an alleyway behind St Andrew's Church, and days later when he went to see if it was still there, it was missing. What became of the headboard is unknown. Years later at a cocktail party, when Clive and Karen were a married couple, they got talking to a man named Martin, who professed to be a Satanist. Clive mentioned the headboard of his late uncle's four poster, and how it seemed to make all those who fell under the gaze of the eyes of the horned man carving extremely oversexed, and the alleged Satanist opened his shirt and took out a gold pendant - and it bore the very same face the couple had seen on that bed in 1973.

'Your uncle must have had a Bed of Vesta made,' said the self-confessed Devil worshipper. 'I'm not allowed to tell you his name,' he said, pointing to the golden horned head on the pendant, 'but he can increase sexual desire in anyone, and sometimes there are unfortunate results which usually end in rape and murder, but when you are versed in the Black Arts, you can control him instead of the other way round.'

Karen backed away from the man and said to Clive, 'I'm going home.'

The Satanist quickly put the pendant back under his shirt and buttoned up, and Clive and Karen left the party and went to a pub miles away. Karen said she felt as if the man who had shown her the pendant had been a rapist, and Clive knew she was a very good judge of character. A few years after this, the man who had shown her the pendant was charged with raping a pregnant woman. He subsequently claimed he was not a Satanist but a self-educated occultist who had stumbled upon an ancient fertility cult and worshipped a deity "older than the Pyramids".

I've asked around in occultist circles, and no one seems to know what a Bed of Vesta is; Vesta was a Roman goddess of the home, hearth and family, but I feel the Vesta depicted in the headboard and the golden pendant is probably to do with the some forgotten deity from an ancient fertility cult of long ago, just as the rapist described.

TIME TRIPPERS

I recall Mother Teresa of Calcutta once saying: 'Yesterday is gone. Tomorrow has not yet come. We have only today. Let us begin.' That's how most of us perceive the order of time: yesterday is dead and gone, the future lies unwritten ahead of us somewhere, and only the present can be experienced – but time doesn't seem to be as straightforward as that when we look at the strange phenomenon of the future being glimpsed in dreams, often in the form of a nightmare. I've talked to many psychics and researchers into dreams and most of them have told me that practically everyone perceives future events in dreams, but not everyone remembers the details of those dreams, and when they are vaguely half-remembered, you experience déjà vu – that mystical feeling that you've seen something before – be it some situation or a meeting with someone – when you haven't been in that situation before and have never met that person before that moment. If you keep a dream diary – a simple notebook will do – and write down a summary of even your most outlandish dreams, you will see that many of the things you describe will come true at some point in the future, although some of the things that are foreseen can be many months or even years away. There seems to be some immaterial, intangible part of our mind that can somehow see beyond this time – and it can apparently look both ways – into the *past* as well as the future, and the ability to look backwards into the past – to events that happened before our own birth or into other people's lives only a few years ago - is known as retrocognition. If time works as Mother Teresa and most people think it does – as some arrow flying from the past to an ever-developing future – how would people be able to catch glimpses of future events that supposedly haven't even happened yet? Well, no one's sure what mechanism the mind uses to look outside the confines of the present, but it hints that our reasoning of time and space is all wrong. Just as some people once believed that the Earth was at the centre of the Universe and that the surface of the planet was obviously flat, we are making false assumptions about time. Einstein predicted that time is not the same everywhere – and what we call "now" is relative to where we are. Starlight shining into your eyes from Sirius, the brightest star in the sky, is over eight years old because Sirius (which is actually a double star) is 8.6 light years away, so the light from the Sirius system takes 8.6 years for to reach us. When we look up at the sun (not recommended) we are seeing it as it was eight minutes ago, because its light takes that long to reach us because the sun is 93 million miles away. Another assumption we make about time is that it moves in one direction all of the time, from the past to the future, but a team of international scientists recently discovered a way to reverse time on the subatomic scale, and this feat was virtually overlooked by the mainstream news. A 9-page account was submitted for peer review on the incredible findings, in which the spin of nuclei in a molecule of chloroform was manipulated by using an immensely strong magnetic field and a suspension of the molecule in acetone. The end result of the experiment was a reversal of the Law of Thermodynamics – temperatures rose instead of falling – and entropy was reversed. This is like a cup of coffee getting warmer instead of cooler as it stands on your table. The laws of entropy will always ensure that the coffee will lose its heat until it gets cold – but when the spin of the atoms in the chloroform molecule were tampered with, the arrow of entropy – and perhaps the arrow of time – reversed. This experiment was just on the subatomic scale, but then so were the early experiments which led to the Hydrogen Bomb.

According to mind-boggling quantum physics, the reality about time is this: the past is still there, and so are countless futures which we move into, depending on what actions we and others take. In one world President Kennedy sneezes as he travels through Dealey Plaza in 1963 and a bullet misses him. He lays flat on the floor of the Lincoln Continental and survives the assassination attempt staged by persons unknown. In our world, the killers achieved their aims. The future where Kennedy survives is as real as the futures we travel through, and there are an infinite amount of these futures existing side by side. We think this is bizarre, but it would be like someone living on a hydrogen atom and thinking that his atom was unique and disbelieving there are almost an infinite amount of identical hydrogen atoms in the universe. We look at ourselves as special, yet we forget that the organisms we originated from – the sperm and an ovum – existed in their trillions as we made it to conception. Without going further into the complex equations and mind-blowing world of quantum physics, let us now look at the purported incidents where the future – and sometimes the past – was inadvertently visited by everyday people. These incidents are known as timeslips, and here are just a few of the ones I've investigated and researched over the years.

One weekend in September 2010, Jon and Grace - a separated couple in their thirties - met up on Bold Street. The plan was to let the couple's 5-year-old daughter Poppy spend the day with her dad, but on this occasions as Grace said goodbye to her little girl, Poppy asked her to stay and innocently suggested that they "should all stay together today". It brought a tear to Grace's eye and she nodded and said, 'Alright, love, if Daddy's okay about it?'

Jon nodded enthusiastically, and seeing as the Bold Street Festival was getting into swing, Jon told Poppy she could have her face painted if she wanted. The child became very excited and let go of her father's hand for a moment – and a split second later, something Jon and Grace could only describe as a ghost swiped their daughter. The thing resembled the blurred outline of a tall woman with blonde hair in a black jacket and short dark skirt who walked between the couple, colliding with Poppy. One minute the child was there, and then came the sound of the girl crying "Oh!" – and she was gone. Some of the people in the immediate vicinity saw this vanishing act. Jon rushed after the invisible entity and he could hear the click of what sounded like high heels and Poppy crying. The unearthly abductor passed between two post office pillar boxes and went down the six stone steps onto Waterloo Place, where cars and motorbikes were parked next to the old Lyceum building. Grace was running behind her husband, numb with shock, and then came the next traumatic jolt: Jon vanished before her eyes and in plain view of many witnesses.

Jon had no interest in the paranormal, and had not heard about Bold Street's infamous reputation for timeslips which date back decades. He found himself in a familiar yet different Liverpool to the one he was accustomed to, where cars and buses were travelling down Church Street (pedestrianised since 1974) – and then he saw a Ford Capri and other backdated vehicles, and the grass-green Leyland 'corpy buses' – and it dawned on him he was somehow back in the 1970s – and there was that blonde marching along, dragging Poppy with her, about fifty yards away. He caught up with the mysterious child abductor and wrenched his daughter from her, and the woman screamed and said Jon was kidnapping her child. People converged on Jon and Poppy, and he picked up his sobbing daughter and ran in the direction of Bold Street. Two policemen closed in on him and a gaggle of bystanders encircled Jon, who really believed he would be marooned possibly forty years in the past, but then he saw his separated wife Grace gradually appear, and the figures from the past faded away, although Jon could feel a hand he could not see grabbing at his right forearm for a few seconds before the grabbing sensation melted away into nothingness. Jon then noticed a strong scent on Poppy's clothes, and he asked Grace if it was perhaps her perfume. Grace said it wasn't and that the scent reminded her of "Opium" – a popular fragrance her mum had worn decades ago. Jon and Grace were so afraid of that female "ghost" making another abduction attempt, they left the area and went to the house they used to share. Jon and Grace were at a loss to explain what

333

had happened, but somehow the traumatic incident brought them back together, and they gave their marriage another try. I mentioned this incident in my weekly *Liverpool Echo* column (which is about paranormal goings on in the city) and a woman named Jane Sullivan got in touch and told me that she had gone ice cold when she read my account of the Bold Street abduction because something almost exactly the same had happened to her in 2017 – and this incident also involved a female child and a blonde woman, only the venue on this occasion was Church Street. Jane was in Liverpool city centre in August 2017 with her 7-year-old daughter Victoria, and at one point the child wanted a donut and something to drink from the mobile refreshments kiosk on the corner of Church Street and Williamson Street, close to the Vodafone store. Jane bought two donuts and two cans of Coke, and when she turned and looked down, Victoria wasn't there. We hear the cliché "every parent's nightmare" whenever a child goes missing, but Jane felt the bottom fall out of her stomach. She looked around and hoped her daughter was just messing about, as in the past she had hid behind Jane for a laugh, but the child was nowhere to be seen – and then she saw her being dragged backwards towards the mobile phone store by a woman with long blonde hair. Jane could not see the face of the abductor of her child, but she was dressed in a blue denim jacket, denim knee-length skirt and flat red shoes. She was about 5ft5 in height, aged about thirty and of medium build. Jane's daughter cried out, 'Mum!' as she saw her mother, but the stranger – who had her arm around the girl's neck, continued to drag Victoria away, and then the strangest thing happened – the blonde and Victoria vanished into thin air. A man in his later sixties was standing nearby and he saw the double disappearance. He turned to a frantic Jane Sullivan and asked, 'Did you see that?'

'She's got my daughter!' Jane told the man, and she walked about near the entrance of the mobile phone shop and looked about, completely frustrated as well as distressed by the weird incident.

'Was that girl your daughter?' the man – who subsequently identified himself as Mike Robinson – asked, and he looked about the crowded thoroughfare and then he noticed something extraordinary, and he pointed it out to Jane – there was a circular area about seven feet in diameter, shimmering behind Jane, almost like a hole which showed a different Church Street. Through this hole, Jane and Mike could see the old store named Solitaire, which stood where Vodafone was in 2017 – and there was that blonde woman wrestling with Victoria, who was crying and punching the woman as she tried to restrain the child. Jane ran through the apparent opening and attacked the blonde, punching her in the side of her face. The punch was delivered with such anger behind it, the woman fell to the ground and two women in their forties stopped walking and one of them said, 'Aye-aye! There's no need for that!'

Jane grabbed her daughter's wrist and angrily told the woman: 'She tried to take my daughter!'

The blonde recovered quickly from the punch and got to her feet, and ran up Church Street. When Jane turned and walked back towards the corner where the donut kiosk had been, she saw that it was no longer there, and through that large hole she also saw Mike standing there, watching her. At this point, Jane noticed a store called Binns that had closed down many years before, but as soon as she stepped through the weird circular 'opening' in mid-air (and Jane described it as looking like a ring of warm hair, the way it was refracting light, very similar to the undulating mirage effect you see on the end of a road on a hot day) Binns vanished. She looked back, and saw that the Solitaire store was not there – and there was no sign of the blonde she had floored with that punch. Victoria burst into tears and her mother went to the mobile shop and collected the donuts and soft drinks she had bought minutes ago. She was confused by what had happened and still in shock. Jane then felt an agonising pain in her right hand, and realised she'd injured it through striking the woman's jaw. Mike went back to the spot where the hole had been, and now there was nothing out the ordinary there. Mike told Jane that when she had walked through that hole she had faded away "like the invisible man". Mike advised Jane to report the attempted child-snatching incident to the police and he eventually continued on his travels and Jane went to a taxi rank on Hanover Street by Lloyds Bank and took Victoria home. Throughout the journey, mother and daughter discussed what had happened, and Victoria said the blonde woman who had try to take her had a perfume identical to the one her late grandmother had worn, and seemed to be referring to the Yves Saint Laurent fragrance Opium. This was very interesting because in the 2010 Bold Street case where a blonde had snatched Jon and Grace's 5-year-old daughter Poppy, Jon had noticed a strong scent on his daughter's clothes which his wife believed to be Opium. I hired an artist to sketch the blonde Jon and Grace had seen in the form of a police identikit picture and showed it to Jane Sullivan and her daughter, but they said the blonde they had encountered had a broader, almost round face and a shorter nose. Jon and Grace said their abductor was tall, had on a black or dark blue jacket, black skirt and black high heels, whereas the abductor Jane and Victoria had encountered was of medium height, and had worn a denim jacket, denim skirt and red flat shoes. Perhaps if she had worn heels, she would have resembled the abductor in the 2017 case. The "Opium" fragrance connection could well mean that the two child abductors were one and the same woman, with heels and without, and of course, the descriptions of criminals by more than one person rarely agree. Who was the woman – or women? Are these people beings from some other era attempting to kidnap specimens just as naturalists and zoologists might collect animals and fishes for zoos and aquaria? Some scientists think nothing of taking healthy animals and "euthanizing" them for inclusion in museum collections, but what if more advanced beings from elsewhere are doing the same to humans – including humans who have not reached maturity? It's a chilling possibility, yet somehow I do not think the mysterious blonde child abductor is collecting children for scientific reasons, and it really does not bare thinking just *what* she wanted them for.

Another interesting account of an apparent slippage in time came my way recently, and it was related to me by an up-and-coming local comedian from West

Derby named Keith. One foggy Saturday afternoon in November 2015, Keith sat in a café on Hanover Street, discussing his idea for a new comedy act with his friend Neil. Keith had created a bizarre character known by the surreal name of Sardine. He wore a pink body stocking, a weird mask with no mouth, and a trilby. The absurdist act would involve Dadaist comedy, illusions, mime, surreal jokes about offbeat subjects ranging from quantum physics and social media to sport and local politicians, and Sardine would even wrestle a planted heckler in the audience (Keith's friend Neil in disguise). It would be a very physical routine with occasional staged outbursts with some very colourful profanities. Keith and Neil worked on the script in the café, each suggesting ideas and sight gags, and either writing them down or rejecting them flat out. Around 3.20pm Keith left the café and walked to the Seel Street flat of a fashion student named Becci to pick up the Sardine outfit he'd paid her to make, and the student had done a very fine job. Keith put the outfit in his rucksack and set off in the worsening fog to meet his girlfriend in a pub called Coopers in Clayton Square. Keith was walking along Hanover Street when he suddenly felt a tingling sensation in his scalp and the nape of his neck. He also felt a strange absence of time, and when I asked him to describe this, Keith said, 'It's hard to explain, but it felt as if time was somewhere else that afternoon. I'm a very punctual person and I'd told my girlfriend I'd be at Coopers at 3.30pm, and when I say I'll be anywhere at a certain time I'll be there – but on this afternoon I had a weird sensation of timelessness – that I should relax because there was no time – it was really odd.'

Keith then noticed the huge chalked words on a large blackboard on a wall on Hanover Street which said, 'Talent Show Auditions – today only' and above it a glowing sign said 'The Crane Theatre'. Keith had never heard of this theatre, and thought the Epstein Theatre had been renamed or perhaps some new theatre had been opened. A lot of change had been going on in this quarter of Liverpool, so Keith just trusted the neon theatre sign. He walked straight into what seemed to be a new theatre and came to a window where a woman with a large head of brown curly hair and silvery blue horn-rimmed glasses said, 'Hello – can I help you?' She was obviously the theatre's receptionist and Keith said, 'I'd like to go for an audition.'

'Oh yes,' said the woman, 'just go straight through that door and go down the corridor until you come to the first door on your right. Just go in there and you'll see a few others who are auditioning. You may have to wait a while because there's been quite a response to the auditions.'

'Thankyou,' said Keith, and then he asked, 'Are there any prizes for these auditions or do they give you a spot on one of their theatre shows?'

'No prize,' said the receptionist, adjusting her glasses, 'but there are talent scouts from the Associated Television Company in there, so it could be the big break you and the others are looking for. Good luck.'

'Thanks,' said Keith, and he had a spring in his step as he went down the long corridor beyond the heavy fire doors. He needed a break to get him out of the club scene, and this would hopefully be the breakthrough he had dreamed about for some time now. Keith saw the first door on his right, and he pushed it open and went into a large room. Here he found himself among a gaggle of aspiring stars that included ventriloquists, a man juggling pots and pans and a knife-throwing act. A docile young man gave Keith a numbered ticket and said: 'You'll be called onstage in about thirty minutes. You'll hear your number, so listen out.'

The youth then left, so Keith changed into his salmon pink Sardine body-stocking outfit – and a silence fell over the room full of hopefuls.

'That's disgusting, you can see his private parts,' said a man in a tuxedo holding a ukulele.

Keith asked a woman in a cowgirl outfit if the place was a new theatre but she snootily ignored him after looking him up and down. Eventually a door opened and a man shouted, 'Number 371! Number 371?'

Keith held his yellow ticket up, and the man who had called his number said, 'What in God's name is that?' looking at the pink body-stocking.

'Oh, you'll see, said Keith, and he carefully slipped on a pink tight-fitting mask, and put on his trilby, and he followed the number-caller onto a stage where the dazzling lights shone down upon him, making the panel of judges in the auditorium very difficult to see.

'Your name is?' said a monotone voice of a judge lost in the glare of the lights.

'Keith,' came the reply; he was already getting into character in his mind, adopting the surreal personality of Sardine.

'Keith, you have fifteen minutes to show us your act, starting from now!' said the more lively voice of another judge.

Before the panel of judges and the ATV talent scouts, Keith performed parts of his new comedy routine. He asked the audience if they played the Grand Theft Auto video game, and he did a strange exaggerated walk around the stage, saying, 'This is how the guy in it walks isn't it?'

No one laughed. And when Sardine started shouting and screaming swear words and joking about a certain sex act, there was an uproar, and the police were called in. The audition was stopped and a policeman charged at Keith from the wings. Keith thought the policeman was some actor messing about at first, but then he saw that this man was rather too realistic when he tried to put a pair of handcuffs on Keith, and when he said 'I am arresting you for the obscenities and filth you have come out with – ' Keith ran off the stage and through corridors, and found himself back on the foggy street. He bumped into Peter, an old school friend who now worked on the hackney cabs, and Peter didn't recognise Keith at first because he still had his Sardine costume on. Then Keith took off the trilby and mask, and after looking back towards the theatre to see if the police were following, he said: 'Take me to Coopers, Peter – and hang on while I go and get Becci! You can drive the two of us home to West Derby.'

'What's up Keith?' asked Peter, 'And why are you dressed like that?'

'Just been to an audition and the judges and everyone turned on me,' Keith explained, and then he asked, 'where's your cab?'

'It's only parked up a side street,' Peter told him, and he nodded to the plastic cup he was holding, and said: 'just been to get some coffee.'

Peter drove his friend the short distance to Clayton Square and waited while Keith went into Coopers and came out with his girlfriend a few minutes later. She told Keith – and so did Peter – that the neon sign of The Crane Theatre was impossible, because that had been the old name of the theatre years ago and it had become the Neptune Theatre in the 1960s. Now the venue had been renamed the Epstein Theatre in honour of the Beatles' manager Brian Epstein.

'Well, they must have changed the name back to the Crane Theatre then,' Keith insisted, 'because I know what I saw.'

Peter turned the hackney cab around and drove to the Epstein Theatre – and he said to Keith, 'What's that then? Scotch mist?'

The glowing sign clearly said Epstein Theatre, and Keith got out the cab and realised that the large blackboard inviting people to auditions had gone, and the place now bore no resemblance to the theatre entrance he had visited. Only then did it dawn on Keith that he had experienced a timeslip. He realised he had somehow gone back in time to the old version of the theatre. He also realised that he had left his clothes and wallet – and his mobile phone - in that bygone theatre and he never saw them again. He wondered what those judges and talent scouts of long ago had made of his surreal profanity-littered act. It would have been shocking to them, and he realised why someone had brought in the police because of the 'obscenities' he had come out with. The blue material of his act would have made Lenny Bruce flinch.

For our next thought-provoking account of a timeslip

we must journey across the Mersey and retrograde some fifty-one years back through the calendar. For legal reasons I've changed a few names in the following extraordinary and intriguing stories, but the rest is alleged to be true. One muggy evening around 7.20pm in the summer of 1964, a 40-year-old constable we shall call Terry (not his real name) based at Birkenhead Police Station on Chester Street, was on his beat on Conway Street when a scruffily-dressed lad of about 13 walked alongside of him. The boy asked, 'Excuse me sir, but I'm thinking of being a policeman but what's the pay like?'

Terry came to a halt, and said, 'Well, for a constable, it's around six hundred and thirty-odd quid, and after nine years it can go up to nine hundred and sixty-odd.'

'When can I join?' asked the lad, all eager with pound signs in his eyes.

'Once you hit sixteen - when your legs have grown a bit longer - you can apply to become a Cadet, sonny, and you'll need an O level,' the policeman told him and he walked along with the boy, who said he had decided to be a detective after watching *Z Cars*, and after Terry and the ambitious youth crossed Vittoria Street onto Park Road North, the boy ran to his home on Aberdeen Street.

'Constable!' cried a female voice in the immediate vicinity. Terry saw a corpulent woman of about fifty years of age trying to run towards him from the corner of Livingstone Street. She held onto her bosom to prevent it from oscillating up and down as she ran. She met him all out of breath and she seized his hands and gasped, 'A man exposed himself to me and a friend about twenty minutes ago.'

'Where was this?' Terry asked, and the woman – whose name was Annie – told him: 'Aspinall Street, down an entry.' She then led Terry to the street, about 150 yards away, and took him to the first alleyway on the left, which ran behind eleven terraced houses of Park Road North. She told the police officer: 'I was taking a short cut down here with our Nelly – she's my sister in law – and *he* was looking at us through this big hole in the wall of a yard, and then he came through it and said "Hello" and then he pulled his trousers down – oh! I'm still in shock!' Annie burst into tears.

'It's alright, Annie, calm down,' said Terry, 'just wait here love in case he's still there. Which wall was it?'

Annie stopped sobbing and said, 'Not sure – one of them ones on the left.'

Terry looked for a hole in a backyard wall, and could find none, and he returned to Annie and asked: 'You sure it was one of those walls, love? I can't see any hole you see.'

'It was definitely here officer, I'm not lying,' said Annie, her shaking hand dabbing her eyes with a hankie. 'I'll go and get our Nelly if you want; she's in the Crown, having a drink to steady her nerves.'

'What did he look like – this flasher?' Terry asked, 'Was he old or young?'

'Oh he was young, no older than twenty-five, officer, and he had a shaved head,' Annie recalled, and what was strange was that he was dressed like a clown.'

'A clown?' Terry muttered, and he immediately linked this bizarre description with the non-existent hole in the wall, and he naturally started to doubt the saneness of this woman.

'On the Seven Sacraments officer,' said Annie in a

solemn voice, 'he had on a sort of white windcheater and it had green and blue and red patterns on it, and the trousers were white, and they had red stripes on, and he had big white pumps on and they had like golden stripes on as well.'

The logical question had to be asked by Terry. 'Annie, listen; don't take this the wrong way love, but had you been drinking when you saw this fellah?'

Annie's mouth formed an O-shape, and then her face reddened, 'Are you saying I'm drunk and that I imagined all this?' she fumed.

'Annie, I'm only asking you a standard question a detective will ask you if this goes further,' said Terry, 'and I mean, *I* think you're as sober as a judge.'

'Come on! Let's go and see our Nelly in the Crown!' Annie said, walking away.

'Hold your horses Annie,' the PC was saying when a voice behind shouted, 'Excuse me constable!' It was a man of about forty in a string vest and pyjama bottoms. He was standing in the backyard doorway of one of the houses. He said his name was Vince and that he worked nights. He'd overheard Terry and Annie and he said he too had seen the flasher. Vince invited Terry and Annie into his backyard and pointed to the wall. 'You've heard of haunted houses haven't you?' said Vince, 'Well this here is a haunted wall.'

'A haunted wall,' said Terry, nodding, his eyebrows rising, 'must be all the sun causing this – or is there a full moon out tonight?'

'I'm serious,' said Vince, 'and I know this will sound barmy but every now and then a hole opens in this wall and you can see all kinds through it; weird-looking people, all dressed funny, and the cars are like

345

something out of Dan Dare, honest.'

Annie stormed off, threatening to make a complaint about Terry, and Vince told the beleaguered policeman no one would believe her story. About a week after this, Terry was on his beat on Park Road North, and Vince came out of his house and almost dragged the startled policeman into his abode. 'Quick! It's there again!' Vince said, pushing Terry down the hallway. He led him into the backyard, and there was a strange shimmering hole in the wall, and Terry looked through it. He saw a young woman with purple and green hair, her face caked in white make up, and a lady next to her covered with tattoos, and she had blue hair and was speaking into what looked like a walkie-talkie – and then the hole closed up and vanished.

'See?' Vince smiled at Terry, who stood there in shock, gazing at the spot on the wall where he'd seen those strange visions – and he wondered if that hole would open again but it remained closed.

'What on earth was that?' the policeman said at last, and he felt the part of the wall that had dissolved before his eyes minutes ago – and it felt solid.

'See? I told you. You thought I was nuts,' said an excited Vince, slapping his hand on the wall, 'but now you know I'm not. I've seen all kinds, I have.'

'Listen, mate,' said Terry, adjusting his helmet, 'don't say a word about this to anyone, alright?'

Vince seemed puzzled by the request. 'Why?'

'Because they'll cart us off to the lunatic asylum, that's why!' Terry replied, and he looked at the wall and said, 'There are certain things we're not supposed to know on this planet; certain things that are not for us to see, that are beyond our ken, and what we saw

346

before was one of them.'

'Do you think it's something to do with the supernatural, like?' Vince asked, and awaited the answer from the policeman.

Terry smiled, because Vince was looking at him as if he should know. In a resigned manner he said to Vince: 'I'm just a copper, mate, and I deal with the everyday situations and problems of this world; I know nowt about the next world or any worlds beyond that.'

Terry walked through Vince's home, through the hallway and out onto the street, and before he continued on his beat he reminded Vince: 'So, mum's the word mate. What's that old saying: ignorance is bliss? Folly to be wise.'

Terry walked away and what he had seen in that backyard vision played on his mind. He felt as if something – some higher being perhaps – or even someone down below – had been playing games with him, and Terry didn't like it one bit. He could face a sawn-off shotgun and tackle killers, but ghosts and the world of the occult scared him.

Forty years later, Terry realised that somehow, back in 1964, he had glimpsed two young ladies of today through what must have been some 'hole' in time. The young ladies of the 21st Century thought nothing about colouring their hair all the shades of the spectrum, and of course, some girls – mostly members of the Goth movement - wore very pale make up. The walkie-talkie he had seen one girl talking into had, of course, been some mobile phone – but how a policeman in 1964 saw two girls of the 21st century will probably remain a mystery to Terry until his dying day.

In my many years of investigating time-slippages I've discovered that certain people are much more likely to step into another time than the average person, and I call these timeslip-prone folk time-trippers. Why a particular person should be more liable to find themselves in another time period is as baffling as the timeslip phenomenon itself but I'll present two cases of this sort to illustrate the effect. The first case concerns a woman named Jackie. In 1997 I interviewed Jackie on the *Billy Butler Show* on BBC Radio Merseyside because she claimed she would often go missing and find herself in another time period – mostly the future. In 1994 Jackie's husband Des reported her missing to the police for the second time that year. Des and Jackie had attended a Mass at the Anglican Cathedral and his wife had gone missing. She reappeared a day later and said she had found herself in the cathedral over twenty years in the future "amongst crowds of heathens" dancing in a frenzy and chanting a weird hymn to a strange glowing symbol on the walls of the holy building. In a desperate effort to get out of the cathedral, Jackie had fought her way through the cultists and found herself wandering through a kaleidoscope of light until she collapsed. Many years later Jackie identified the 'religious' symbol as the iconic Cream Club logo – and of course, in recent years the classic music of the Cream Club has been performed with laser-light shows in the Gothic surroundings of the Anglican Cathedral – so Jackie had somehow gate-crashed one of those gigs back in 1994. In 2000, Jackie was walking down Bold Street with her older sister Heidi when she suddenly found herself alone in a futuristic Liverpool. The ultramodern skyscrapers were a bit disorienting but Jackie realised she was somewhere on Church Street, which was lined with palm trees, and the unrelenting heat reminded her of Florida. Coming towards Jackie from the Whitechapel end of Church Street was the surreal sight of her sister Heidi wearing a pink-tinted glass bubble helmet and a white tracksuit. The brand logo on the white tracksuit was a black triangle with an eye in the middle and the word "Illuminati" written beneath it. Heidi looked a bit younger and she had her rollers in under that daft-looking glass bubble and seemed shocked to see Jackie.

'Mum! Is that you?' said "Heidi" – who turned out to be Jackie's daughter Ava – aged 12 in 2000 – now aged 39. In a state of shock, Jackie asked her grown daughter why she had a space helmet on and Ava said it was a fashion craze to protect the skin and hair from unhealthy ultraviolet radiation. Furthermore, it also stopped rain spoiling her make-up when she was going out. Jackie distinctly saw the Illuminati logo light up on the tracksuit, and as she looked at it, Ava vanished and Jackie found herself on the Church Street of 2000 AD. Minutes later, Jackie's older sister Heidi called her on her mobile and asked where she was. Heidi said Jackie had been there one moment and then she had literally vanished, and a young man who had been walking behind the sisters said to Heidi, 'That lady with you just disappeared into thin air,' and he was understandably shocked. I asked Jackie if she was a nostalgic person who perhaps hankered for times past, as I wondered if such a frame of mind could have something to do with the timeslips but firstly, Jackie said she was not the nostalgic type, and if she *had* been a person who longed for yesteryears, how did she also slip into the future? Just why Jackie is apparently susceptible to occasional involuntary trips into the future and the past remains an intriguing mystery, but she is not alone with her strange talent; an American woman I interviewed also seems to have the same ability. In 2015, Laurie, a 26-year-old woman from Pennsylvania, came to Liverpool to stay with her friend Sarah in Huyton. Both girls had met via an internet forum about The Beatles and both were big fans of the band. Sarah took Laurie to the grave of Stuart Sutcliffe, the so-called Fifth Beatle who had been a member of the band before they hit the big time. Stuart – who was also a gifted abstract impressionist painter – tragically died of a brain haemorrhage in April 1962 and today lies buried in Huyton Parish Church Cemetery. Laurie left a red rose on the former Beatle's grave and she and Sarah often went on the Magical Mystery Tour bus, taking in all the old Beatles homes and places mentioned in the songs like Penny Lane and Strawberry Fields. Sarah soon realised that her American friend was psychic after an incident which took place on the very first night she stayed at her house. Laurie said he had seen glimpses of a family dressed in clothes that seemed to date back to the 1950s or earlier, huddled around a huge vintage looking radio, and the sombre voice on the radio was saying: "I have to tell you now that no such undertaking has been received, and that consequently this country is at war with Germany." This was from the historic speech Prime Minister Neville Chamberlain made to the nation in September 1939, informing listeners that Britain and Germany were now at war. Laurie saw the couple hold hands as they heard war being mentioned and a little red-haired girl said, 'Daddy will you have to go and fight?'

The scene then changed and Laurie was back in 2015. Later that night Sarah also heard what sounded like a monotone voice on a crackling radio mentioning Germany, and it had an eerie echoing quality about it. Laurie said she had a habit of bringing ghosts out of the woodwork wherever she went, and she told Sarah that on many occasions she had stepped into the past. Sarah thought her American friend was joking at first, but Sarah told her how, on six occasions back home in Pennsylvania, she had found herself back in the dark days of the American Civil war at Gettysburg and on one of these occasions she had cradled a dying Confederate soldier in her arms – before finding herself back in her own time, with the blood of the soldier on her coat. Laurie's friend Sarah later heard from an elderly neighbour that the Henderson family had lived in her Huyton house in the war years and they did indeed have a little red-haired girl who sadly died of pneumonia in the 1950s. Was this the girl Laurie had seen in her timeslip at the house?

The most fascinating series of timeslips concerning Laurie occurred weeks later. Laurie and Sarah went to a club near Chinatown, and when they came out around 2.30am, Sarah went down an alleyway to relieve herself, and when she came back, Laurie was missing. Laurie found herself in Nile Street – a street that once existed near the Anglican Cathedral. The Pennsylvanian only knew she'd involuntarily gone back in time when she saw a tram pass the end of the street. A policeman fell off the back of the tram and smashed the back of his head in on the pavement. There were shouts and screams and Laurie tried to help the policeman, who seemed unconscious. Another, younger policeman shouted for a bystander to get a doctor and he made eye-contact with Laurie and seemed to notice her leather jacket, tartan miniskirt, purple leggings and boots. The scene around the American then changed and Laurie found that the street and the people had slowly vanished. She was in Lady Chapel Close, made up of modern red-brick buildings on an estate close to the Anglican Cathedral. I discovered that Laurie had witnessed an accident which had taken place on 5 March, 1883. The man Laurie had seen falling off the tram must have been PC John Quigley, aged 51. Quigley had boarded a tram after seeing that it was dangerously overloaded with passengers. As Quigley stood on the tram's platform about to jot down the details about the overloading in his notebook, the vehicle swung into Nile Street and the policemen fell backwards off the tram and his head was smashed against the pavement as he landed on his back. He was barely conscious and was taken to the Southern Dispensary where he died shortly after his admission.

Days after this, Laurie was shopping on Ranelagh Street while Sarah was at work, and suffered a heavy nosebleed. A policeman approached her by the Midland Pub and pinched her nose and calmed her down – then she noticed it was that same young Victorian policeman she'd seen last time – and now Ranelagh Street was cobbled and horse-drawn carriages and tramcars moved along it. The bleeding stopped and the policeman eyed Laurie's clothes –

black leggings, boots, a pink miniskirt and a faux oxblood leather jacket - and with a bemused look he asked, 'Why are you dressed like that?'

Laurie shrugged and said, 'I dunno - bad taste perhaps?' She thought the policeman's accent did not sound like the modern Liverpudlian accent. She later identified it as a Lancashire brogue. She nervously told him she was from 2015 and he said a strange thing in reply. 'Ah, you're one of them who keeps coming here. You're an American. Is that how they're dressing themselves, eh?'

'My name's Laurie, what's yours?' she asked. She just had to know, and realised she was falling for him.

'George,' he said, after a thoughtful pause, and suddenly Laurie was back in her own time, and she felt heartbroken. She told Sarah what had happened, and said she felt as if there was some link with her and the Victorian policeman – as if she had known him in some previous life. Days later, Sarah came home from work and found a note from Laurie which said, 'Love is the key to getting back there with George. I'll be gone for some time, but don't worry. I'll return. Love, Laurie.'

Laurie went missing for almost a week, and when she turned up at Sarah's home she was dressed in pristine Victorian clothes. She claimed she'd been staying with George in March 1883 and showed Sarah the Victorian currency in her purse. She told Sarah she was in a relationship with the 19th century policeman and planned to have a child with him. Sometimes Laurie goes missing for months at a time, and I believe she is not a hoaxer as she shuns publicity and has shown me some brand new-looking objects from the past. I am still investigating the alleged timeslips at the time of writing and hope to publish my findings in a future book and article.

Some timeslips seem to give a very unsettling outline of the country's socio-political future, and the following two accounts are timeslips of this kind. Quantum physics says we can alter and even prevent these apparently dystopian futures, but of course, if people dismiss these stories as the mere product of hallucinations and downright lying, then they just might come to pass. A case in point comes to mind immediately. In the year 1934 in the March edition of *Opinion: A Journal of Jewish Life and Letters*, a monthly 25-cent American magazine, a number of articles were published by religious and political thinkers of the day on the subject of Adolf Hitler's rise to power, and amongst the writings there was a controversial warning of Nazi genocide concerning the Jews. The article went largely unheeded, for it was 1934, and no one really believed Western Civilization could resort to something we know today as the Holocaust. Heaven knows what's in store for the world in the future, but perhaps some premonitions and timeslips can give us an indication.

On the sunny morning of Saturday 1 March 1975, 13-year-old Tony Drake had his usual weekend breakfast of eggs, bacon, black pudding and two rounds of Mother's Pride bread fried in lard, and afterwards he watched *The Flashing Blade* and *Mr Deeds Goes to Town* on the telly – until he left his Huyton home around half-past noon to the strains of BBC1's *Grandstand* theme. He ran all the way to Jubilee Park to meet up with his best friend Billy Fotheringay, who had a brand new football with him, and Billy was juggling and heading the ball with considerable expertise, until Tony sneaked up behind him, stooped down, and grabbed the back of Billy's knee with a pinch of the finger and thumb, accompanied by Tony's impersonation of a dog's bark. Tony thought Billy would be annoyed but instead his friend said, 'Hey, guess what? I saw a big robot over there before!' And the boy nodded towards the far end of the park.

'What?' asked a bemused Tony as he picked up the ball; he imagined he was a goalkeeper about to kick the football over the half-line. The ball was booted high in the air, but the March winds blew it into a tree – and it never came down. 'Oh, played you divvy!' moaned Billy, and Tony said, 'Well, you're a liar saying you saw a robot.'

'I did, honest to God, over there,' he pointed to the trees bordering the southern side of the park adjacent to Dinas Lane. 'It was like a big man in a metal suit and then he vanished.'

'Criss cross the Bible, never tell a lie, if you do, your mother will die!' warned Tony Drake, and he spat onto the grass to make the oath official, so Billy spat as well and said, 'And me mam won't die because I seen it!'

The two lads went bickering to the tree and Tony, being the tallest, gave Billy a bunk up before needlessly climbing up the tree himself. 'No! Stay down there, I'll throw the ball down,' said Billy, but Tony took no notice, he had a surplus of energy and needed to climb.

'Hey, I say we build a tree-house up here, like a secret den, and live up here!' said an excited Tony, when something strange happened. The blue skies became grey and overcast within seconds, and a thick fog rolled into Jubilee Park. The boys assumed there had been a large fire nearby and thought thick white smoke was heading their way – and then the boys saw it – a weird figure wearing a helmet just like a policeman's one, only this policeman had on some sort of suit of armour and carried a huge rifle. Under the peak of the helmet, the lads could see that the weirdly-attired stranger wore a mask. He came marching out of the fog towards the tree.

'That's it!' said Billy excitedly, 'That's the robot I told you about!'

'Be quiet, he's got a rifle,' whispered Tony, hiding in the branches. His stomach went into freefall at the sight of the huge rifle; it looked as if it could do some damage.

A group of six grey silhouettes emerged from the fog, about thirty yards away, and Tony and Billy saw they were men dressed in very strange clothes. Some wore hoods and one-piece suits – and some of these people had guns pointed at the armoured policeman. One of these figures shouted something at the heavily-armed policeman and in a flash the bizarre-looking lawman dropped to one knee and trained his bulky rifle on the gunman. Five of the figures quickly turned around and tried to run and there was a muffled bang. The man pointing the gun seemed to explode into a red mist, and then there were five rapid bangs which echoed across the park as the five figures also exploded into bits. The boys in the tree were so traumatised by these unearthly deaths, they started to cry. Tony saw twitching legs and arms spurting blood on the grass, and a ripped-apart torso with the head barely attached to it by the ragged red remains of a neck. That head was moving and Tony thought he heard the head cry out, 'Mum!'

Two small flat disc-shaped objects (which seem to have been drones) measuring about six inches in diameter detached from the back of the policeman's armoured suit and hovered silently around the mutilated dead. Some type of spray issued out of the hovering discs, which then returned to the back of the policeman's hi-tech suit. The policeman had now got up from his bended knee position and was heard to say something. Perhaps he was talking into some radio. Billy sobbed and tried to get down from the tree and the policeman swung around and a powerful light from his helmet blinded Tony and Billy, and when they regained their sight, they found the fog – and the policeman - had vanished. The children ran to their homes and told their parents. Most thought the children had made up the story or had seen students playing some prank, and Tony's uncle jokingly said his nephew might have seen a curious futuristic character known as "The Huyton Spaceman" – a helmeted man in a strange white suit of armour who had been seen around Huyton a few years prior (and had been classified as a UFO occupant). On the whole then, no one believed Tony and Billy's story, and years later I traced the lads and interviewed them, and came to the conclusion that they had probably experienced a timeslip that day in 1975, and had seen some future era when armed police – and armed criminals – might sadly be very commonplace. I have the unsettling feeling that time is very near.

We now come to our second possible history lesson of the future, as foretold by the perplexing timeslip.

When people obtain glimpses of future events they are more than often mocked, regarded as prophets, branded as frauds, or deemed to be mentally disturbed. A Bebington night-watchman named Charles Wilson was advised to go and see his doctor when he started to see future events before they happened. In the summer of 1969 the 60-year-old night-watchman was shopping in Birkenhead when he witnessed a horrific crash involving a camper van. Wilson saw the van explode into a fireball, and he actually felt the heat from the mushrooming mass of flames, and then he saw a man run from the blazing vehicle with his clothes on fire. The burning man rushed towards the night watchman, and Wilson took off his coat, ready to beat the flames out. In an agonized voice the man yelled: 'My wife and children are still in the van!' And then he collapsed. Charles Wilson ran to the nearest public telephone box and dialled 999, but when he returned to the crash scene there was no sign of the badly-burnt man or the flaming camper van. Fire engines turned up and Wilson had a lot of explaining to do. A fireman looked him up and down and said: 'Listen mate, you'd better go and see your doctor because you're obviously seeing things! Have you got that you bloody idiot? Go and see your quack because I might do it for you!'

Wilson rushed after the fireman as he walked back to his fire engine. 'But I swear – I saw a camper van burst into flames, officer! I did!' he said, 'I felt the heat, and the man was on fire just - just there!' He pointed to the road, but there was no trace of any burnt body. The Dennis fire engine departed with a roar, and Wilson was left at the roadside, doubting his sanity. He felt scared; what if the fireman was right? What if he *was* seeing things? Wilson went to his doctor's surgery first thing in the morning and told him about the incident.

'You're a night watchman Mr Wilson,' the doctor said, gazing at his patient's green medical record card. 'Are you getting enough sleep during the daytime?'

'Oh yes doctor,' Wilson replied, and nodded, 'I make sure I get at least seven hours – sometimes eight. I've long adapted to that sleeping pattern.'

The doctor continued, 'Only sleep-deprivation can cause all sorts of funny business with the mind. When you miss an hour's sleep here and there it builds up, and you get a sleep deficit, and then your body can't cope. You get fatigue and it puts a strain on some organs and might even contribute to Type 2 diabetes. My main concern here is that there might be some mental strain.'

'Are you going to give me sleeping tablets?' Wilson asked.

'No,' said the doctor, 'I don't think there's any call for that sort of thing. What I would suggest is relaxation. Maybe you should go fishing or go on long walks – anything to calm you down a bit, but I would stress that you need to get your sleep. Now, if there are any more *episodes* I want you to come and see me straight away.'

'Someone said I might be going schizophrenic,' Wilson told his doctor with a worried expression.

The doctor shook his head. 'Schizophrenia very rarely occurs in people around your age. It's often evident before the age of eighteen. But come and see me if you have any other worrying experiences Mr Wilson.'

Wilson tried to relax. He went to the park, did jigsaw puzzles, listened to records of Mantovani, and made a concerted effort to get eight hours of sleep. Wilson experienced no visions during this time. Exactly a year later in August 1970, Wilson went into a shop one day and the shopkeeper said, 'Heard about that terrible crash with the camper van in Birkenhead?'

A stunned Wilson said, 'No.'

The shopkeeper nodded, 'Just heard about it on the radio. Camper van burst into flames and the husband staggered out on fire and said his wife and kids were still in the van. Happened about a quarter of a mile away – real black spot it is. Seven people are dead.'

Wilson stood there in shock, and he could faintly hear the voice of the shopkeeper asking, 'You alright sir?'

Wilson walked out of the shop, and at first he was going to go to the road where he had foreseen the awful crash a year ago, but instead he went home. When he read the newspapers the next day he saw that the crash had been on the very road in Birkenhead where he'd had his terrifying vision – and this crash had involved a camper van. It said in the newspaper article that the man had even run from the van in flames, telling horrified bystanders that his wife and children were still in the van before he slumped to the pavement unconscious. Why had Wilson received a sneak-preview of such a nightmarish crash? He pondered this question – but he had more 'visions' – and some of them were very disturbing. He was drinking with a few friends in the Blue Bell pub on Freeman Street one evening when he happened to find himself unable to move. Whilst in a state of paralysis,

Wilson saw the pub around him melt away into clouds, and in these clouds there appeared two flags – a Union Jack with its cross bent into the shape of a swastika, and a red flag with a white disc which featured a smaller royal blue disc with a ring of yellow stars within it. A lightning bolt zigzagged through this disc and it reminded Wilson of the old flag of the British Union of Fascists he'd seen in the 1930s, back in the days of Sir Oswald Mosley. Wilson could hear his friends in the pub asking him if he was alright but he couldn't see them. He saw armies of men and some women marching the streets of Birkenhead dressed very similarly to the Schutzstaffel – the SS paramilitary organization of Nazi Germany. The vision was so clear he could even see the smiling faces of the marchers and he could hear the rhythmic thudding of their boots as they moved along. The swastika-styled union jacks were being carried by some of the marchers and the buildings and the motor cars in the disturbing vision looked quite futuristic. Britain had not yet even joined the European Economic Community (EEC) yet someone in Wilson's vision was telling him that when Britain left the European Union, a right-wing dictator would come to power. In the disturbing vision, Wilson saw firing squads in parks, executions, and large-scale riots involving the army. Throughout the vision and the deafening clamour of voices, screams and gunfire, Wilson felt as if the sombre voice describing the events was warning him. 'All to come,' said the deep gloating voice, over and over. Before he snapped out of the open-eye dream, the voice told him: 'Concentration camps will be created in Wales to deal with traitors to the state, and their bodies shall make great compost. All to come...all to come.'

Wilson fainted when he regained the ability to move, and when he later described his vision, people said he'd just had a 'funny turn'. It's tempting to muse on the possibility that Wilson had foreseen the political aftermath of Britain's withdrawal from the European Union, but surely we are not headed for a dictatorship - are we?

And finally, to close this thought-challenging chapter on timeslips, I must relate a low-key but nevertheless intriguing account of a timeslip which was reported to me back in 2015.

Like a lot of the goings-on in the field of the supernatural, timeslips have opened my eyes to a basic everyday fact – that things aren't always what they seem. The world looks flat, but we are living on a sphere, and the stars at night seem to twinkle, but they don't, it's just the earth's turbulent atmosphere causing the effect. To a child, time appears to be the same everywhere; if its 4pm in Tuebrook then logically it must be 4pm everywhere else, but time zones mean that when it's 4pm in Liverpool it's 5pm in Paris. We assume time is uniform and runs at the same rate for everyone, but for humans, it runs slower in the mind of a child because so much new information is being processed by the brain; that's why car journeys seem so boring to kids – they seem to take longer for them and that's also why the summers of childhood seem to have lasted much longer than they really did. The human neural timekeeping mechanism in adults is 60 Hertz (sixty cycles per second), but the brain of the housefly operates at 250 Hertz, and so to the fly, we appear to move in slow motion; that's why flies – most of the time, anyway - have amazing evasive reflexes when we try to swat them. Psychological time then, passes at different rates for humans, cats, dogs, insects and so on, and this brings me to another thing we assume about time from an early age: that the future hasn't happened yet. Hannah Green had never really given much thought at all to the nature of time, but she had noticed how time seemed to drag in the doctor's waiting room or at the dentist's, whereas it flew when she was out on the town, partying with friends. In 2015, Hannah and her partner Liam – both in their thirties - moved into a house in Fazakerley. At the time, Hannah was heavily pregnant and looking forward to the birth of her first child. She was unaware at this point of the secret which Liam was withholding from her, regarding their new home. The house they were moving into had been the home of his grandparents until they had passed away in the late 1980s. The house had then been sold and after coming back onto the market Liam had convinced Hannah that they should buy it. He knew Hannah believed in ghosts and thought she might be spooked out if she knew his old grandparents had lived and died at the house, so he said nothing about the place's history. He felt a little guilty about this and promised himself he would tell her the truth after they'd lived in the place for a few years. Liam had even warned his friend Ralph not to say a word about the house being the former home of his grandparents.

The couple started moving into the house in March of that year, and the first item to be moved into the place was an old wing back chair – which had belonged to Liam's late Nan – something Hannah was not aware of. As Liam went to collect the other furniture from a van with his friend Ralph, Hannah sat in the old wing back chair. She was eight months into the pregnancy and Liam told her to rest and not to bring even the lightest stuff from the van. As Hannah sat there in the bare room, she closed her eyes for a moment and sighed – and heard music to her left. She opened her eyes and saw that the entire room was now decorated – in what looked like Seventies decor; orange wallpaper, brass plates, oval mirrors hanging by chains, and an old-fashioned square-looking wall-mounted gas fire with a hissing flame. Facing Hannah was an old man asleep in an armchair. He wore black trousers, a white shirt and a pale blue pullover, and he had a neatly-trimmed white beard and a prominent aquiline nose. Behind him, visible through the doorway of a kitchen, a small curly-haired lady – no bigger than five feet in height - was busy at a cooker, singing *Don't Cry for Me Argentina*. Still in shock at the presence of these strangers and the entire transformation of the living room, Hannah turned slightly in the chair and saw the title of a programme called *Crossroads* on the telly. She also noticed the calendar on the wall said March 1977. Hannah knew she was not dreaming – she was wide awake and she could feel her baby kicking in her.

Hannah's mobile rang, startling the old man out of his sleep, and he looked right at Hannah with a pair of piercing baby blue eyes. He seemed very surprised to see Hannah, and he looked at her bump and his mouth opened as if he was about to say something – but then the whole room reverted back to normal. The man and the woman were gone, along with the orange wallpaper, brass plates – everything – and all that remained was an empty echoing room with newly-plastered walls.

Hannah went outside to tell Liam what had happened and he said he'd been looking for her everywhere with his friend.

'I was in the living room,' she told him.

'No you weren't, ' said Liam, 'me and Ralph looked in there twice! Where did you go?'

Her answer was quite unexpected. 'Liam, before Almighty God, I was sitting in that chair you brought in, and I closed my eyes for a few seconds, and then when I opened them, the whole room had changed. There was orange wallpaper and big brass plaques or plates of some sort on the walls, and there was an old man with a long roman nose and bright blue eyes looking at me, and behind him in the kitchen was this tiny woman with curly hair, and she was singing that song – what was it? *Don't Cry for Me Argentina*. I'm not moving in here, it's bleedin' haunted!'

Liam knew without a doubt that his partner had seen the ghosts of his grandparents, for his grandfather did indeed have a large prominent roman nose and very noticeable pale blue eyes, and his wife – Liam's beloved much-missed Nan, was also a tiny woman with a head of curly hair, and he recalled how she was always singing.

'Ghosts?' said Ralph, looking worried. 'Hey, Lee (as he called Liam), I wonder if they were the ghosts of your Nan and Granddad?'

'Why would Liam's grandparents be haunting – ' Hannah was saying when she realised why her partner had been so eager to move into the house.

365

'What a blabbermouth grass you are,' Liam seethed as he glared at Ralph.

Ralph smiled and said: 'Lee, they were good people your Nanna and Gramps mate, so I wouldn't be arsed if it was me. It's not like Fred and Rose West lived here, is it?'

'Just shut up please, mate,' Liam warned his verbose friend.

Liam begged Hannah to stay, and she said she would on one condition. 'If you respect your grandparents, Liam, you've got to marry me.'

'Go on Lee, I'll be the best man,' chipped in Ralph.

'How have you jumped from being scared of ghosts to marriage?' asked a perplexed and stunned Liam.

'Your grandfather looked at my bump,' said Hannah, 'and I just have the feeling he'd think we were trampy if we lived under his roof without getting married. Just a feeling I got, Liam.'

'Alright then, fair enough love,' said Liam, and a tear welled in his eye. 'Hannah, will you marry me?'

Hannah felt so choked up she couldn't get her words out for a moment, and just nodded, then managed to utter, 'Yeah.'

As the couple hugged, Ralph said, 'Ah, all through me grassing on you Lee.'

The wedding took place nearly six months after the birth of the couple's son, and they went to Spain on their honeymoon. One evening a few days after the return from the Spanish honeymoon, Lee looked at a corner of the newly decorated living room and said, 'My Nan's old piano was there. She was self-taught but she wasn't bad you know? She could play all the modern songs and the old ones like *Roll Out the Barrel*'.

'Come on love,' said Hannah, standing in the doorway in her nightie, 'let's get to bed before you get lost down memory lane.'

'Hey, do you remember Memory Lane cakes? They were boss,' said Liam, joining his wife at the doorway. He switched off the hallway light and started to go up the stairs with Hannah playfully patting his bottom when the newlyweds heard something which stopped them in their tracks – the sound of a piano playing down in the dark living room. Neither of the couple knew of any of the German composer Wagner's works – but they both instantly recognised this tune of his – it was *Here Comes the Bride* - officially known as *The Bridal Chorus* - the tune the organist often plays as the bride enters the church on her wedding day.

Liam and Hannah looked at one another then gave a simultaneous nervous laugh and ran up the stairs. The music faded away, and Liam just knew his Nanna had played that piece of music to let him know how happy she was her grandson was now a married man.

'I'm not scared,' Liam told his wife, 'but can I sleep with you tonight?'

MR METHUSELAH

On the Saturday afternoon 19 January 1974 a 51-year-old window cleaner named Joe Holland called for a month's money due to him from the eccentric Professor Donaldson. Joe knocked on the doors of the workshop in an alleyway off Back Renshaw Street – a street unknown to most locals, with the exception of that breed of taxi driver with a comprehensive street-map of the city etched into his brain.

'Professor?' Joe shouted, and cupped his hand on the grimy pane of glass embedded with fine criss-crossed wires. There were three of these small square windows set into the wide maroon wooden door with flaking paint, and Joe could see something white moving about behind that door; it was the Professor in his white lab coat. There was a faint cry of: 'Wait there Joe, trying to find the key!'

It was Professor Donaldson's voice. At last Joe had caught up with him.

'Okay Mr Donaldson, take your time!' Joe replied, and he looked left and right up the deserted back street and stamped his boots in the cold.

There was a metallic click and a rattling noise, followed by the grating sound of a bolt being forced out of its staple.

When the door opened inwards, Joe received quite a shock. Professor Donaldson answered with a huge head of red hair and a thick beard. 'It's not a wig, pull!' he urged Joe, who smiled and said, 'Nah I believe you, how did you manage that? You were bald as a coot.'

'I found the cure! The cure for ageing!' was the reply and the Professor pulled Joe in and explained. 'Joe, in the Bible Adam was 930 years old when he passed away. Now, we are all supposed to live that long, but we all succumb to a progeria virus in the womb which causes accelerated ageing – so we only reach one-twelfth of our intended lifespan! I found a way to kill the virus and then you just need a three-month course of antibiotics! I'm 70, so I'll live till 2764 AD!'

'Nice one Proff. Er, you owe me four quid,' said Joe, sheepishly, and he looked at a blank page in his notebook to avoid eye contact with his customer. Joe hated asking for money. It made him feel like a leech.

The Professor laughed at Joe's words. 'Joe, you're so funny, but so typical of homo sapiens. I have the secret to eternal life here and you're concerned with four pounds.'

'I know,' said Joe, already feeling like a money grabber, 'but it's okay if you're a bit short Professor, I can wait a week or two.'

Professor Donaldson swept back his thick long overhanging fringe over his head and said: 'Joe, I will pay you with the greatest gift a human being could possibly want! I have something which the alchemists of old strived to find for centuries. It literally is the Secret of the Ages – the Philosopher's Stone – the Fountain of Youth – the Elixir of Life!'

'Four nicker will do me fine, honest Professor,' said Joe, 'I'm just a simple man.'

'What's your second name, Joe?' Donaldson asked with a smirk.

'Holland,' said Joe, 'why?'

'Joe Holland, you are about to become the Second

369

Adam! I give thee eternal life!' the Professor declared, and his troublesome fringe flopped down off his head, covering his face, and he blew the hair out of his eyes for a moment with a puff and grabbed the hand of the window cleaner. Before Joe could even pull his hand away, Donaldson pushed the needle of a golden metal syringe into his wrist, and a shocked Joe could feel the contents coursing into his vein.

'Hey! What d'ya do that for?' cried Joe lifting his wrist to his wide spectacled eyes. 'What was in that?'

'A cure for ageing,' the Professor casually replied, ' And in about one-and-a-half hours the virus that's been slowly killing you with failing eyesight, a profusion of hair sprouting out your nose and ears and a thickening of the arteries will start to die, and your body will become it's real age. You will look and feel as if you're sixteen again.'

'Is it safe? Could it kill me?' Joe asked, looking at the tiny red puncture dot in his wrist.

'You know what *could* have poisoned you, Joe?' the Professor asked.

'Huh?' Joe was stumped by the eccentric's rhetorical question.

'That stuff could have poisoned you,' Donaldson reached out and placed his index finger on the top of Joe's head, and then he wiped his finger downwards, creating a slippery track through the layer of black shoe polish Joe had put on his head to disguise his baldness.

'What are you doing?' Joe asked, stepping backwards, and then he saw the black tip of the Professor's index finger.

'It's a common remedy for hair loss, Joe;' the

Professor told him, 'some people even rub carbon paper on their head to hide a bald spot, but shoe polish contains toxins and it's carcinogenic – and it goes right into your bloodstream through those tiny pores and hair follicles on your head.'

'It's not boot polish, just dye off my cap,' fibbed Joe, 'the rain soaked through.'

'Joe, it's quite alright,' said Donaldson, 'your hair will grow back soon – and it will return to whatever colour it was when you were young. It can be traumatic when a man loses his hair, but he doesn't receive any sympathy - he's told to accept it. Thick hair is full confidence. Your hair will be back with a vengeance!'

'When?' Joe wanted to know. He started to calm down, and he wiped the smear of boot polish from his forehead. 'When will it grow back?'

'Give it a few days,' said Professor Donaldson with several slow nods, and he went to a medicine chest, opened the door, and started to root about in it. 'Your scalp will become very itchy, and then the new young hair will come through, You will also see spots in front of your eyes and hear a pounding drum sound in your ears – all signs that your vision and hearing are improving.'

'Will I really be young again? Are you sure it works?' Joe asked, thinking of all sorts of possibilities involving sports and sex.

'Yes you *will* be young again, but as I said you'll need to take antibiotics for three months straight to keep the leftovers from the virus at bay. Now, here's a bottle of Ampicillin, and that's all I have;' said the Professor, 'you'll need another few bottles to last two months or you'll age again. Gargle with salt water, give yourself a red raw throat and tell your doctor you have sore tonsils and he'll prescribe Ampicillin. If you can't get hold of any, just come back here and I'll see if I can get hold of some from a pharmacist cousin of mine. If that fails, you may have to pay someone to break into a chemist and get hold of them. Ask friends and relatives if they have any knocking about too.'

Joe went home, and sure enough he noticed floaters in his eyes and a thrumming sound in his ears kept him awake at night. He awoke with an itchy head and something he hadn't suffered from in years – jock itch; he felt as if a colony of ants were crawling all over his testicles. He went to the bathroom mirror and there was a sharp intake of breath because there were thousands of fine black hairs coating his scalp. 'He was right. Donaldson, you're a genius,' Joe said to his reflection. The hair thickened and more spouted as the days went by. He ran his hand through the healthy-looking black hair and because his eyesight improved, his spectacles made things look blurred, so he took them off. Then he began to get agonising pains in his mouth, and he was shocked when the tip of his searching tongue detected a tooth coming through in the gap where one had been yanked out years ago.

Joe was the talk of his local pub. His comb-over was replaced by a head of curly black hair, his eyesight returned, and his sciatica had vanished. They all thought he had on a wig, and the barmaid tried to yank his hair off and Joe yelled 'This is how I'm supposed to look! I'm gonna live 900 years! I'm Mr Methuselah!' His looks and sex-drive returned, and he embarked on a passionate affair with the barmaid. And then he asked a librarian out who was young enough to be his daughter, and the day after he had bedded her he went out on a prowl of the clubs looking for more 'conquests' as he termed them. The neighbours' tongues wagged; it was down to monkey gland treatment, some said, and others thought the answer lay in nothing more than a silly mid-life crisis and a realistic wig, coupled with a little pinch of exaggeration. Someone said they had seen Joe dribble the length of the full-scale football pitch down at the Simpson playing fields off Hillfoot Avenue and he'd shown the skill and stamina of a professional footballer.

Then the Ampicillin ran out, and the doctor refused to prescribe him with the antibiotics, saying Joe had never been fitter. Joe broke into a chemist to obtain the pills, but got caught. He tried again and they jailed him – and in the open-air prison up in Kendal he lost his hair, his eyesight worsened, and his sciatica returned. The prison doctors laughed at his far-fetched story of ageing being a disease. Joe visited the Professor's workshop when he came out – and found it deserted. He later learned Donaldson had been knocked down and killed by an elderly motorist who had run over him after he had suffered a stroke.

THE SHAPESHIFTER

On Tuesday 16 December 1980 a football-sized chunk of ice of unknown origin fell out of the sky over West Kirby and smashed through the roof of 90-year-old Mary Nickson's home, showering the elderly lady with fragments of glass-hard ice and plaster. Minutes later, five miles away, an ice block of similar size smashed to earth on Birkenhead's Upper Flaybrick Road in front of two 13-year-old girls, Valerie and Rose. The bang was deafening as the "cryometeor" - as astronomers call such blocks of ice from space - struck the wall of Flaybrick Cemetery, and Rose screamed in pain because a particle of ice stung her cheek. Valerie had a cruel sense of humour and she giggled at the way the fragments of sharp ice had hit Rose in the face, and laughingly told her friend the skin on her face was not broken, just a bit red. On the floor among the white fragments of the smashed chunk of ice were two weird creatures, about three inches in length and each resembled a dark green species of Smooth Newt, only the heads of the creatures seemed to have a humanlike face. One of the creatures was wriggling about with its tale encased in the ice, but the other one looked as if it was dead. It lay there inert as the girls crouched to see what these creatures were.

'Eww, what is it?' Valerie picked the dead-looking slimy skinned "amphibian" up by its tail and tried to look at it close up – when it suddenly seized her middle finger and bit it hard. Valerie screamed and threw the thing over the cemetery wall. 'Bastard!' she cried, and looked at the red fang marks on her longest finger. 'That really hurt!'

'Valerie, look!' Rose pointed to the other creature on the floor. It had freed its tail from the ice and now it was changing to a pinkish colour. It quickly turned into a tiny man which reminded Rose of "Morph" – the little plasticine character featured on Tony Hart's *Take Hart* show. Rose backed away, scared of the sudden metamorphosis. The little pink man said, 'Hello,' in a barely audible voice, and Valerie stood up and kicked the tiny humanoid from the road into the kerbstone, where it seemed stunned. 'Val! Why did you do that?' asked a shocked Rose.

'They bite, that's why!' Valerie replied, and she looked about and picked up a stone. She tried to hit the little figure with it, but missed. 'Leave him alone!' cried Rose, and crouched to look at the miniature pink figure. It had its hands together, as if praying, and its tiny two black shiny eyes were staring up at Valerie. Rose thought she heard it say: 'Don't hurt me,' and then a black dropping fell out of the little figure. Rose thought the thing had defecated with fear.

The thick sole of Valerie's shoe stomped down on it. Black and green fluid squirted from the tiny squished body, and Rose swore at Valerie and ran in tears to her home on Upton Road. Valerie kicked the flattened corpse of the unknown creature down a grid and spat at it.

Rose didn't talk to Valerie for a week, and then when they became friends again, the girls went to look for the creepy creature Valerie had thrown over the wall of

Flaybrick Cemetery after it had bitten her finger but they could not find the thing.

'Valerie, why are you so cruel?' Rose asked her friend as they walked to Valerie's home on Lansdowne Road.

'I told you – because it bit me – I'm not cruel!' Valerie snapped back, overreacting at Rose's question.

'You told me you were going to use an electric drill on your hamster once, and then you said the hamster went missing,' Rose recalled.

'Stop bringing up all these horrible things Rose or I'll start knocking round with Kerry Brown!' yelled Valerie. People passing by looked at the girls because of the outburst.

'*Did* you kill your hamster?' Rose asked, looking if she could cry at any moment.

'I've had enough of this!' Valerie announced and started walking faster. She then ran off shouting, 'Best friends aren't supposed to bring up the past all the time!'

The years went by and eventually the memory of the strange creatures faded. Rose married when she was nineteen and moved to Liverpool with her husband, but Valerie took a wrong turning in life and resorted to crime, drugs and occasionally prostitution. In 1993, she was aged 26, and already had a criminal record for theft and possession of what we would now term as Class A drugs. On the Wednesday evening of 30 April 1993, at around 11pm, Valerie was walking aimlessly along Boundary Road with nowhere to go because she had just had a blazing row with her parents over alleged heroin use. As Valerie passed the gates of Flaybrick Cemetery's Memorial Gardens, she saw a man's face peering through the railings. He shouted,

'Hey, do you want to make a quick fifty quid?'

Valerie halted. The man had obviously assumed she was a prostitute, and Valerie needed the money because she was extremely broke. Her plan was to demand the money up front from the man then run off. She had no intention of performing any sexual acts upon this potential customer; she just wasn't in the mood after the row with her parents. She walked over to the cemetery and had to climb the railings because - for once - the gates were locked. The man was peeping over a bush at her and by the light of the full moon she saw he was only young, nervous looking and of small stature. It was probably the first time he had propositioned a woman of the night and in all probability he was still a virgin. When Valerie walked around the bush, the youth changed before the girl's eyes into something grotesque and snakelike. The creature shot forward and before Valerie could scream it coiled its enormous long icy body around her. The thing was like an anaconda with two legs and two arms, and the head was broad, but tapered to a point like the outline of a birch leaf. The jaw line of the monster went up past the thing's ears as if the jaw was double-jointed so it could open further than normal to consume large prey.

'Help!' Valerie screamed but a bony, scaly hand was clamped down on her mouth and she felt a slithering forked tongue stroke her face. She heard slow, heavy breathing down her ear. The entity shook rhythmically as if it was laughing, then tightened its coiled body until Valerie was ready to pass out from the pain and an inability to breathe. 'Val! Why did you do that?' said the unearthly creature, mimicking what Rose had said that wintry day in 1980. 'They bite, that's why!' the shapeshifting being said, impersonating Valerie perfectly. She realised what the thing was now – some relation – a brother perhaps, of that little creature she had crushed under her shoe. This was payback. 'I'm sorry,' Valerie gasped, and fainted. They found her face down in the cemetery at 8am, suffering from exposure and loss of blood – a Class II Haemorrhage. She had a perforated left ear and a small hole under ler left breast where blood had been siphoned out. A specialist at the hospital said she had hallucinated the "shapeshifter" assault through some drug overdose, but Valerie still refuses to go anywhere near Flaybrick Cemetery. Was it all in Valerie's mind? Her friend from years ago, Rose, confirmed the story about the little creatures in the smashed ice block. The main question is: could that shapeshifting being be still at large in Flaybrick Cemetery today? There's a gruesome possibility too; that thing might burrow into graves and copy the likeness of a dead person to go about its sinister work under many guises.

TROIKA

The cocktail party at the palatial home of the Tates on Queen's Drive, Wavertree was in full swing that evening in 1964, when 7-year-old Marianne Tate came sleepwalking down the stairs. The guests smiled at the pretty little raven-haired girl in her nightie with her arms reaching out, thinking she was just play-acting but her divorced father Patrick hurried towards the stairs and whispered, 'No, please don't wake her – it can be fatal.'

'What? You're joking.' Patrick's bank manager Jeremy Stevens smirked at the scene as everyone formed a semi-circle at the bottom of the steps.

'I am *not* joking at all, Jeremy,' said the worried father, and he moved guests out the way as Marianne crossed the hallway and headed for the lounge. She went to a young advertising executive named Ian who was seated on a sofa with a Martini, and she placed her hand on his head and announced: 'Death to you!'

Marianne then opened her huge eyes, and those eyes rolled back into her head and she fainted.

'What was all that about?' Ian asked, adjusting his glasses and watching Patrick Tate pick his daughter up off the floor. Patrick took Marianne upstairs, followed closely by his partner Alexandra.

This had all happened before. Marianne walked in her sleep whenever a party was being held at the house and she would touch guests and usually say: 'Death to you,' and then in days the guests she had touched would be dead. On this occasion, the advertising exec Ian died in a car crash.

On the advice of his partner Alexandra, Patrick Tate went to a priest to tell him about his little sleepwalking prophet of doom, but the priest just returned a deep-frozen smile and said a psychiatrist was needed. This suggestion really upset Patrick and he decided to stop attending church. He told Alexandra: 'I'm afraid to involve a psychiatrist in this matter – they might end up giving Marianne pills and sedatives or even put her away.'

'It won't come to that, darling,' Alexandra assured him with a hug, 'we'll sort this thing out, somehow.'

'We'll have to stop holding cocktail parties here and perhaps employ a good nanny,' Patrick suggested. 'I'm so bloody disappointed by that confounded priest! I thought they were there for spiritual guidance and advice.'

That afternoon, three sharply-dressed young men in bowler hats and finely-tailored suits turned up at the Tates' home. They were Richard Lion from West Derby, Barry Sullivan from Sydney, Australia, and John Shepard from San Francisco – and they called themselves Troika – Russian for 'set of three'. The three lads, all aged 22 and all musicians, had met in a pub one evening and had formed a trio, but then they discovered they shared a common interest in the supernatural and the downright strange, and when Richard Lion rented a flat in Rainford Gardens, a drumstick's throw from the Cavern Club, John and Barry moved in and it became Troika's office. Richard told Mr Tate he'd heard about his daughter's 'condition' from a woman who preferred to remain anonymous and he offered to help for free. Mr Tate was naturally cautious about the three eccentrics but sensed they were genuinely offering him help and had the best intentions, and so they were admitted to the house.

Richard asked Mr Tate a battery of questions concerning his daughter; how long had she been sleepwalking? Had there been any poltergeist activity at the house? Had anyone held a séance or dabbled with the Ouija board recently? John Shepard noticed no pictures of Mrs Tate knocking about and Patrick said he was divorced, and that the child stayed with her mother at weekends. Troika then spoke to one another in Esperanto for a minute – this was their code to prevent outsiders from listening in.

Richard Lion whispered to Barry and John: 'Do eble ni bezonas iomete da hipnoto kaj kaptiloj?'

'I'm sorry to interrupt you Mr Lion,' said a slightly ruffled Patrick Tate, 'but I'd prefer guests in my home to speak in the English tongue.'

'I do apologise Mr Tate,' said Richard, 'but it's merely a safeguard measure to discuss highly sensitive information between ourselves without fear of being overheard.'

'Well, have you formulated any ideas to rid my daughter of her accursed condition?' Patrick asked Richard Lion, who nodded then replied: 'We need to talk to your daughter – it is of paramount importance.'

'In my presence,' asserted Patrick.

'Yes, by all means Mr Tate,' said Richard, 'in fact it will be most conducive to the hypnotic session if Marianne has someone close to her – '

'Hypnosis?' Patrick leaned forward in his chair with a look of disbelief, 'You mean you want to *hypnotise* my child?'

'Well, this *is* a problem stemming from her unconscious,' said John Shepard, the American member of the unusual trio.

'But isn't hypnosis dangerous?' Patrick asked, 'Especially where children are concerned.'

'No, I guarantee your daughter won't experience any ill effects Mr Tate,' Shepard assured the worried father. 'I'll just put her into a light trance, to plumb the depths so to speak, and try and find out what's behind all this.'

'I just hope you know what you're doing,' sighed Patrick, 'are you even qualified in hypnotism?'

'I do know exactly what I am doing sir,' said Shepard, 'just trust me, and yes, I was taught hypnosis by my father - he's a doctor.'

'I just want my child to be normal again,' said Patrick, his voice sounding broken.

'As indeed I'm sure we all do Mr Tate,' intoned Lion.

'I do hope this will work,' said Patrick, 'I have been told that hypnosis is a load of mumbo-jumbo.'

'It's not mumbo-jumbo Mr Tate,' said Shepard, 'just a few months ago there was a mass hypnosis experiment in Denmark where a hypnotist was allowed to hypnotise hundreds of thousands of listeners to a Danish radio station to cure them of smoking.'

'And did it work?' Patrick wanted to know.

Shepard nodded enthusiastically. 'Yes, I believe quite a large percentage kicked the habit but I think it's against the law to hypnotise people in Britain via the radio or TV.'

Marianne was brought from the back garden, where she had been playing, to the lounge, and here the blinds were drawn and the child was told to sit in her father's chair.

'Now Marianne, this man here is Mr Shepard, and he is going to try and hypnotise you,' Patrick said, nodding to John Shepard, who was sitting in a dining chair that had been positioned six feet in front of the comfy armchair Marianne was seated in.

'Hypnotise me?' Marianne asked, and returned a puzzled look on her angelic face.

'Yes dear, you won't feel a thing and it won't hurt or anything. You'll be fine because your daddy's right here watching you,' said Patrick, and he patted his daughter's head then sat on the chesterfield. Richard Lion and Barry Sullivan watched the proceedings intently from the other side of the lounge, keeping out of the line of sight of the child so as not to distract her. Barry had his pencil poised over his open writing pad to take notes.

John smiled at Marianne and then he told the little girl to hold her right hand up, and then he told her how it was feeling heavy, and as it became heavier she would fall into a lovely light sleep. 'But you'll still hear my voice Marianne,' said Shepard, 'and you will tell me anything I ask you. You have no secrets and you can tell me and your daddy anything because you're a good girl.'

The girl closed her eyes and bowed her head. John spouted more of his hypnosis routine in a monotone voice for a few minutes to get the child into a state of full relaxation. And then the questions began. John Shepard asked: 'Marianne, why do you tell people they are going to die?'

'She tells them because I tell her to,' said a weird male adult voice with an almost musical quality to it. The voice came from Marianne.

John looked over at Barry, who was writing the conversation down between him and the girl. It was what they suspected: possession.

'Who is that?' Patrick Tate asked, and seemed shocked and naturally concerned about his little daughter.

'Please stay calm Mr Tate,' said Shepard, and then he looked at Marianne and asked, 'And who are you?'

'A very old one,' said the weird voice, and now the child's lips were not even moving as this entity spoke. 'You know what I am Mr Shepard, don't you?' said the voice.

'What we would call a demon I'd guess,' said Shepard.

'You guessed right there, and you'll never get rid of me,' said the voice. 'The Pope himself couldn't drive me out of this girl.'

Shepard addressed the demon in Latin. 'Quod nomen tibi est,' he asked, which means, 'What is your name?'

'Non possum dicere,' said the entity within Marianne, which is "I can not tell,' in English.

'Barry?' John said to the Australian member of the trio, Barry Sullivan, 'what do you think?'

'He's definitely one of the Ancient Ones,' said Barry, 'not a demon at all. That Latin sounded stilted. The Devil usually talks fluently in Latin. This fellah's a plastic demon, looking for attention and wanting power to scare people. He can see some events before they happen - people dying in accidents - and he pretends he's causing their deaths.'

'Wrong!' said the voice in Marianne, 'You're all going to die for saying that, and I shall take the child first!'

'No!' Patrick rose from the chair, and placed his shaking hand to his face, 'don't do that please! She's my child!'

Barry and Richard came over to Patrick and attempted to reassure him that the thing talking through his daughter was an entity known as one of the Ancient Ones – spirits from a previous civilization which existed on Earth millions of years ago, long before the rise of the early humans.

Richard gently took hold of Patrick's forearm and sat him back on the chesterfield. He told him: 'Mr Tate, the entity using your daughter as a mouthpiece is just a weak spirit from a race that wiped themselves out through corruption millions of years ago, long before the Egyptians and the Atlanteans walked the earth. They lived on a continent that doesn't even exist now – it was wiped out when an asteroid hit this world.'

'Liars! All lies!' said the melodic voice, 'you'll all see! You're all going to die.'

'But if that's so, why is this thing using my daughter?' Patrick asked Richard. He seemed confused and very afraid for his daughter.

Richard explained his belief. 'Someone close to Marianne has been carrying out some ritual, and this Ancient One has come through to this world because of that ritual and settled in the most vulnerable host present – a child. We'll get shut of him now – '

'Ha! No you won't you idiot!' said the voice, 'I'll get rid of you all!'

'Barry knows a very powerful ritual,' Richard continued, 'and when we get rid of the entity, we'll have to discover who is dabbling with the occult in your circles Mr Tate or it could happen again.'

'I don't *know* anyone who's dabbling with the occult,' said Patrick, 'and what if this thing *is* a devil? You might be wrong, young man!'

'Barry, get rid of it,' said Shepard, and the Australian walked towards Marianne and halted about three feet from her. He closed his eyes and held his head back as he said, 'I call on Barnumbirr, creator spirit, to cast this old dark spirit from Marianne!' said Barry, and then he began to hum a tune for a minute or so, and then he began to talk in a language no one present knew – and then the young Australian took a stone out of his pocket; it was a sacred aboriginal talisman known as a *churinga*, inscribed with magical symbols, given to him by his wise grandfather, a Bushman who virtually lived in the Stone Age, and a man who knew the ways of the Aborigines and their magic. The room was suddenly filled with the a strange rhythmic sound – a low-pitched revving – the sacred sound of the bullroarer, and then they heard the sound of a gum-leaf and a distant orchestra of didgeridoos – and that gloating melodic voice which had spoken through the 7 year old began to scream and cry, 'Stop! I don't want to go back! Stop!'

Barry continued his strange prayer, and ended it with the name of the deity he had enlisted to help him - Barnumbirr.

Then came silence.

'Have you gone?' John Shepard asked, and no reply came.

'Well done, Barry,' Richard said to Barry Sullivan, who looked at the cherished talisman and put it back in his pocket.

'Marianne, at the count of three you will wake up and you will be calm and glad to see your daddy,' said Shepard, 'One, two, three!'

Marianne opened her eyes, then looked at her father and got off the chair and threw herself at him. Patrick laughed and cried as he held his beloved daughter.

Troika delved further into this strange case and discovered that Mr Tate's wife had moved in with a man who secretly professed to be a Satanist, and during a ritual and an orgy held by this man, Marianne had been staying with her mother and had been possessed. Richard Lion gave Patrick Tate a special miniature talisman – a tiny ruby engraved with a certain ancient symbol with a very good track record for warding off evil spirits. The ruby was set in a little ring which Marianne was told to wear all the time. Patrick insisted on giving Troika £100 for their services, and that money paid the rent on the office for about six months. Marianne Tate never again sleptwalk down the stairs during any parties held at the house on Queen's Drive, and her mother ditched the man who had been dabbling with Satanism and moved in with a stockbroker. Troika continued to investigate the intriguing and often dangerous sphere of the supernatural, and allegedly encountered vampires, witches, murderous cultists and even timeslips. I hope to feature more of their adventures in my books in the near future.

TWO VENGEFUL
FEMALE GHOSTS

Here are two eerie tales of female ghosts who got revenge. The first one is identified, but the second one remains a mystery to me, but perhaps there is someone out there who knows her story.

One Wednesday afternoon in March 1969, in the third-floor CCTV control room at a certain well-known department store in Liverpool, a 60-year-old Birkenhead man we shall call Jock Stephenson (not his real name), was unblinkingly watching eight monitors as he fed his mouth a stick of spearmint gum. In his mild Glaswegian brogue he said to Phil, the young man sitting with his back to him: 'Look at number 6; she's back.'

Phil looked at the monitor displaying the input from camera 6 downstairs. It showed a typical monochrome scene of women milling about in the knitwear department. 'Which one is she?' Phil asked.

'The one to the left with too much make-up on. She's around my age and dresses too young,' said Jock, 'mutton dressed as lamb.'

'Oh I see her,' said Phil, operating the controls to zoom in on her. 'An old hand, eh?'

'Yeah, her name's Heidi – she's loaded as well,' said Jock, 'but all her fingers are the same length. Said she's turned into a klepto since her husband died, but she's just a tealeaf. Just watch her – she's a case, man.'

Heidi left the knitwear department and went to the

perfume counter, so Jock radioed one of the store's detectives, a 35-year-old woman named Pam, and told her to go and shadow her. Pam, like Phil, had only been working at the store for a month, so Jock had to describe Heidi and guide Pam to her. Pam saw Heidi point to an expensive perfume on the shelf, and when the woman behind the counter went to get it, Heidi picked up two boxed bottles from a display on the counter and pocketed them. She made eye contact with Pam, winked at her and whispered, 'They have more than us, love.'

She walked quickly away from the counter and Pam followed her out of the building and seized her arm. 'Heidi, I'm a store detective and you've just stolen two bottles of perfume. You'd better come back into the store with me.'

'Oh no,' Heidi said, and then she smiled at Pam and said, 'if I put them back could you let me go love? I feel ill and I don't think I could face a court in the state I'm in.'

'I'm sorry Heidi,' said Pam, 'but I'm just doing my job.'

Jock laughed when he saw Pam escorting Heidi back into the store. Phil asked what type of punishment she'd receive. Jock gloatingly answered: 'Well, this is no first offence, laddie, so she'll probably be fined about £75-£100 and be ordered to pay – I don't know – thirty guineas costs. Serves the fool right. The country's shoplifting bill was £120m last year.'

Jock talked about Heidi for hours and how he loved "catching the bitch" red-handed, and Phil got the impression the Scotsman was obsessed with the woman.

The very next day, Jock made a serious error of judgement. He watched a 'long-haired lout' (as he called him) walk out the store with a shirt and two male store detectives apprehended the man – who happened to be a solicitor named Thornbury. 'I bought the shirt in Burtons! How dare you!' protested Thornbury, but the detectives manhandled him, pushing him through bemused crowds as one detective joked, 'Come on Raffles! You don't like it when you get caught thieving do you, eh?'

Thornbury was taken down to the department store's basement interrogation room. The store's senior security officer said, 'Mr Thornbury, our CCTV officer Jock Stephenson saw you take that shirt! Where's the receipt if you bought it in Burtons?'

Thornbury rummaged in his pockets for a minute or so, then located the receipt in his wallet. 'Here!' he roared, slapping it down on the table, 'And you have detained me against my will for quarter of an hour, and I have suffered the indignity of being searched! I have a cast iron case for slander against this store and I bloody well intend to sue! One of those lackeys of yours called me Raffles in front of dozens of witnesses and said I didn't like it when I was caught thieving! I am a solicitor too, by the way!'

Jock Stephenson was instantly sacked. The department store had to pay out over a thousand pounds to Thornbury for slander, assault and false imprisonment. Jock was hired by another department store over in Birkenhead a year later on half the normal salary because of the incident that led to his dismissal in the Liverpool store. A week into the job, he saw Heidi up to her tricks again at the Birkenhead department store, and alerted the in-store detectives but they could never find her. Then one day Heidi looked straight into the CCTV cameras on the ceiling of the store and pulled tongues at Jock Stephenson. He seethed – but then something gruesome and inexplicable took place. The woman put her hands on each side of her head – and held her head above her body. Her detached head grinned and winked at Stephenson, and he was so shocked at what he saw, he suffered a coronary spasm. He staggered to a colleague in the next room getting coffee and told him what he'd seen, before collapsing. Jock Stephenson woke in hospital and was told by a heart specialist he'd suffered a minor heart attack and was being kept in for observation. At 2am, Stephenson awoke in the darkened ward and saw Heidi sitting at the end of his bed, grinning. She nodded and her head fell off her neck and landed in her hands. Jock screamed for help and headless Heidi thrust her severed head into Jock's face and that head said to him, 'Giz a kiss!' and then the ghost vanished before the night nurse arrived. When Jock was discharged a week later, a store detective told him Heidi had died a month back in a horrific car crash in Cheshire - in which she had been decapitated. Her twitching body had been found sitting in the front passenger seat with its head resting on the corpse's lap. Jock never returned to store surveillance and ended his days as a caretaker.

Here's another case of a female ghost that exacted a strange supernatural revenge on a man.

On the afternoon of Friday 29 November 1985, 37-year-old estate agent Tony Stanford March left his office off Dale Street with his young secretary Trisha and got into his Austin Maestro. It was 5.30pm and if he could get home a little earlier than normal he could have some fun with Trisha before his wife returned around 8pm. He waited at the lights on Cook Street and when they finally changed he found an elderly woman standing in his way. She stood motionless in the road in his headlights. He beeped his horn, wound down his window and yelled: 'Come on! What are you waiting for? A written invitation? You silly old twat!' Trisha giggled at the outburst. She knew Tony was randy and wanting to get home as soon as possible so he could get his 'oats' – as he often called sex.

The old woman Tony swore at came over to the vehicle and looked in at the estate agent. She had large cold ice blue eyes. 'What did you just call me?' she asked, and Tony sped off, curving into North John Street. At his Aigburth home, Tony took Trisha straight up to the bedroom. He started to kiss the secretary and soon the next-door neighbour was knocking on the wall and yelling for the couple to keep the noise down as they made passionate love. At 6.30pm Tony dozed off, but was awakened by Trisha screaming. 'What is it?' he asked.

Trisha shouted, 'She's here!' She pointed to the outline of a woman at the end of the bed.

Tony thought his wife had come home early for a horrified moment, but when he looked, he saw it was that old woman – the one he'd verbally abused on Cook Street, standing at the foot of the bed. 'What the bleedin' hell are you doing -' he was asking – when the woman vanished. Trisha became hysterical, and refused to stay in the house. Tony had to drive her home. Everywhere he went, he saw that old woman with her woolly head of white hair and her long dirty mackintosh. He saw her in supermarkets, she sat near him and his wife in a darkened cinema, and even appeared in his dreams. Then Tony's wife saw her in the back garden, looking through the kitchen window. The ghostly old lady then started to sit on the couple's bed all hours in the morning, nearly driving Mrs Stanford March to have a nervous breakdown. On one occasion Tony had a vivid dream he was drowning and when he awoke at four in the morning he discovered that the ghost of the old woman was pinching his nose hard, preventing him from breathing properly. He swore and threw a book at the ghost but she simply vanished.

Then one morning at around 3am, Trisha let out a scream in her bedroom which awakened her neighbours. Her body was found the next day; she had died from a massive heart attack. Tony was sure the ghost had paid "his bit on the side" (as he often referred to Trisha) a visit. Eventually the ghost stopped stalking Tony but she is still occasionally seen on Cook Street. Who she is – or was – I do not know. I mentioned the ghost once on BBC Radio Merseyside when I was a guest on a Halloween programme and several listeners called in and said the old woman's ghost was often seen hanging round the Watson Prickard clothes store - which once stood close to the spot on North John Street where Tony first encountered the old woman and swore at her.

Printed in Great Britain
by Amazon